HOW TO RESTORE YOUR CHEVY TRUCK 1947–1955

Deve Krehbiel

Car Tech®

CarTech®, Inc.
6118 Main St.
North Branch, MN 55056
Phone: 651-277-1200 or 800-551-4754
Fax: 651-277-1203
www.cartechbooks.com

© 2020 by Deve Krehbiel

All rights reserved. No part of this publication may be reproduced or utilized in any form or by any means, electronic or mechanical, including photocopying, recording, or by any information storage and retrieval system, without prior permission from the Publisher. All text, photographs, and artwork are the property of the Author unless otherwise noted or credited.

The information in this work is true and complete to the best of our knowledge. However, all information is presented without any guarantee on the part of the Author or Publisher, who also disclaim any liability incurred in connection with the use of the information and any implied warranties of merchantability or fitness for a particular purpose. Readers are responsible for taking suitable and appropriate safety measures when performing any of the operations or activities described in this work.

All trademarks, trade names, model names and numbers, and other product designations referred to herein are the property of their respective owners and are used solely for identification purposes. This work is a publication of CarTech, Inc., and has not been licensed, approved, sponsored, or endorsed by any other person or entity. The Publisher is not associated with any product, service, or vendor mentioned in this book, and does not endorse the products or services of any vendor mentioned in this book.

Edit by Wes Eisenschenk
Layout by Hailey Samples

ISBN 978-1-61325-888-0
Item No. SA460P

Library of Congress Cataloging-in-Publication Data
Names: Krehbiel, Deve, 1958- author.
Title: How to restore your Chevy truck : 1947-1955 / Deve Krehbiel.
Description: Forest Lake, MN : CarTech, 2020.
Identifiers: LCCN 2019027724 | ISBN 9781613255025 (paperback)
Subjects: LCSH: Chevrolet trucks–Conservation and restoration.
Classification: LCC TL230.5.C45 K74 2020 | DDC 629.28/73–dc23
LC record available at https://lccn.loc.gov/2019027724

Written, edited, designed and printed in the U.S.A.

10 9 8 7 6 5 4 3 2 1

CarTech books may be purchased at a discounted rate in bulk for resale, events, corporate gifts, or educational purposes. Special editions may also be created to specification.
For details, contact Special Sales at 6118 Main Street, North Branch, MN 55056 or by email at sales@cartechbooks.com.

CONTENTS

Dedication 4
Acknowledgments 4
About the Author 5
Preface 5
Introduction 6

Chapter 1: The Frame-up Restoration Philosophy 10
Choosing the Pickup 10
The Skills Required 12
Preplanning for a
    Positive Result 13
Plan of Attack 13
Final Thoughts 15

Chapter 2: Taking It All Apart 16
Frame Subassembly
    Removal 24

Chapter 3: Frame Repair and Restoration 25
Sandblasting 26
Frame Repair 26
After the Frame Repairs ... 31

Chapter 4: Putting a Rolling Chassis Back Together 32
Tools and Incidentals 32
Leaf Springs 32
Rear End 32
Painting Tools and
    Equipment 35
Front End 37
Brake System 38
Brake Lines 40
Wheels 42
Bumpers 42

Chapter 5: The Engine 47
Engine Improvements 48
Cooling System and
    Related Issues 50

Chapter 6: Transmission and Drivetrain 52
BorgWarner R10
    Overdrive 52
Driveshaft 53
Flywheel and Clutch
    Assembly 54

Chapter 7: Preparation, Paint, and Color Sanding/Finishing 56
Prep for a
    Perfect Paint Job 56
Body Filler 58
Understand the
    Paint Products 59
After the Sheet Metal Is
    Reworked 59

Chapter 8: The Cab 63
Let's Get to Work! 64
Seat Belts 66
A Unique Drawer
    System 73
Cab Paint 75
Cab Glass 80
Sound Dampening 82
Gas Tank 83
Seat Pedestal 84
Electric Wipers 84
Parking Brake 84
Miscellaneous Items 85
Steering Wheel 90

Chapter 9: Fenders, Hood, Doors, Etc. 91
Inner Fenders 91
Fenders 92
Hood 94
Doors 96
Reassembly 106

Chapter 10: Heater System Restoration 110
Disassembly 111
Motor 113
Ranco Heater
    Control Valve 117

Chapter 11: Front Clip, Hood, and Door Installation 122
Front Assembly 122
Hood Installation 126
Door Fitment 129
Running Boards 130

Chapter 12: The Bed, Rear Fenders, and Aprons 131
Custom Bed
    Configuration 131
Rear Fenders, Aprons, and
    Taillight Assemblies 140
Bed Side Rails 141

Chapter 13: Electrical 142
Electric Wiper System 142
Overdrive Electricals 148
Electric Fuel Pump 149
Wiring Harness
    Electricals 149
Front End Electrical 151
Inner Fender
    Terminals 155
Wiring Harnesses 161
Testing Your Work 166
Radio Installation 167
The Critical Information
    System 170
Small Things Worth
    Mentioning 171

Chapter 14: Final Thoughts 172
Prepping for the Road 172
About the First Drive 174
What Would I
    Do Different? 174

Deve's TechNet
    Resources 175
Source Guide 176

DEDICATION

Besides having the best wife ever that allows me to do this, I want to dedicate this one to all of those out there who have a project vehicle and the desire and the drive to restore it but for some life reasons haven't completed it over a long period of time. I can totally relate! Just put one hour a day aside for your project and watch what happens over the period of about a year. Hang in there!

ACKNOWLEDGMENTS

I may write what you see, I may even do all the physical labor, but the component that makes this endeavor a guaranteed success is the people who are giving of their time and knowledge to make this document as exacting and precise as possible.

The way it works is, I ask at least three professionals the same question. If all three agree and it makes sense, it goes in the document. If two agree, I get a fourth person's perspective, always keeping the odds well in the favor of precision. This is done at every step using Chevy documentation, outside sources, and the expertise of restorers, metal workers, etc. from all over the world. Some of these people are notable because of their giving attitude and the fact that they were always just a phone call away. The hub for all this activity is forums.devestechnet.com, where we discuss these trucks and their nuances!

The late John Erb was known around these parts as the expert on this vintage, and I was honored to have spent many hours in salvage yards all over Kansas helping him salvage parts for our vendors. This was an amazing learning experience that I will never forget. Another great man, Gene Swartzendruber, taught me how to weld, how to view things in the light of a mechanical engineer, and how to work with metal. His influence can be seen all over our shop. Pat Duffy introduced me to bodywork and paint, and his expertise and patience made that very difficult chore less stressful. I am so grateful for the influence of these great men.

There are many knowledgeable people who have mentored me in one way or another. They include Dave Folsom, Nathan Hall, Allen Jones, Jeff Pohlar, Jeff Nelson, Tom Caperton, Brad Allen, Tim Lederman, John and Peggy Milliman of the Stovebolt Forum, Jim Carter, Jeff McCoy, and the list goes on and on; you *know* who you are. Thank you from the very bottom of my heart! If you are not mentioned here, you are certainly not forgotten, I am just getting old! Check the sources section at the back of this book for even more wonderful resources, thus wonderful people!

Disclaimer: I, as well as most of our contributors, am retired and give information freely for the sole purpose of helping others. If you attempt any of this, you should follow accepted safety procedures and clearly understand the dangers of machinery, equipment, etc., and how to mitigate the dangers by being cognizant and diligent while operating machinery. Please just use your common sense! And don't forget to have fun!

ABOUT THE AUTHOR

I started my journey with these trucks about 42 years ago, and through much trial and error and through many restoration projects I learned many of the nuances of this vintage. The key to really knowing this vintage is to do nothing else! Every restoration I have done to date is a 1947–1955 Chevy truck! I learned a lot of what I know the hard way, but I really must credit many friends along the way. I hope you enjoy reading the book as much as I did writing it!

I took lots of pictures of this process that did not get into the book, so if you have questions at any step, be sure to check out devestechnet.com/Home/MorePix. Also, new stuff is being added all the time pertaining to everything about these trucks at devestechnet.com.

PREFACE

I love these old trucks. They are solid, well built, and have character. It was this series, the Advance Design, that rebuilt America after World War II and had a serious impact on where we are today as an industrialized nation. They are elegant in their simplicity and sturdy in their design. I could go on and on about how wonderful they are, but if you purchased this book, you know that already! I have had many of these trucks over the years and have learned the nuances, tricks, and tradeoffs. I hope you get something out of this effort. We will not be creating a completely stock specimen, rather we are going to take some poetic license in this restoration.

Part of the reason we are not going to restore this truck to its perfectly original glory is because it would not be useful or even safe under today's road conditions. A great many people would not be as enamored with the end result if we didn't add safety features or if we were limited to the 50-mph top speed the stock pickup was capable of originally. For these reasons and more, I will take my 40 years of experience with them to create the very best pickup I know how with sensible upgrades that are not over the top.

Let's define "over the top." To me, that is stuffing a V-8 between frame rails that weren't designed for such a monster, boxing in frame rails, moving the steering gearbox, or adding motor mounts to our precious vintage frame. No can do! Neither can we add a more modern automatic transmission that requires us to hack into or completely remove the main (riveted) crossmember. Hacking the front of the frame to install independent front suspension is also a no. It's a vintage truck, and for me, a great deal of its original character is that 6-cylinder Stovebolt riding on a solid axle front end. It takes talent to do all those things right, but there are other places we can prove how talented we are on this particular build.

INTRODUCTION

There is a little-known phenomenon that can totally change a person's life. It has to do with what we are all capable of. Most people think we learn at the same speed/rate we were accustomed to in K–12 and college (or in my case, the military). It is ingrained in all of us. That is a total misconception and one that holds us back from doing extraordinary things.

I stumbled on this amazing revelation during my career in electronics. The PhDs that were working with me on building new technology were taught everything they knew in the normal manner: formal and very advanced schooling. But what if a person is exposed to this experience and has no formal schooling? Will they reach the same conclusions on how to solve problems or will the fact that they did not go to formal school actually *help* them think outside the box? I can't count the times I saved the PhDs from certain doom by suggesting (very diplomatically) that they do something different.

This is a very important prelude to this book and one that I hope helps you understand what is possible. To get the very same superior results in vehicle restoration as the major players without spending years learning at the normal rate, bypass the concept of normal and change gears entirely. I wrote books in my last job that made electronic technicians with little to no experience perform maintenance on very complex systems as if they were the engineers who designed them, so why not apply that to vehicle restoration? This concept has proven to be a smashing success, and I hope my suggestions throughout this book give you the confidence of someone who has done this all their lives. Sure, there is absolutely some nervousness to get over due to unfamiliarity, but no, that is not a reason to give in to the norm.

I tested my theory on automotive painting. This is by far the hardest thing to master in vehicle restoration. Though practice is essential, you have the ability within yourself without ever picking up a paint gun to paint a vehicle to an astounding level of perfection. I had no idea how hard it was. Read as: I had no idea how easy or hard it was. I just didn't know. So, what is the big secret? Part of it is determination to succeed no matter what. Part of it is not allowing preconceived notions to mess with your mind. Once you have the correct attitude, take the time to learn by watching someone else.

With the advent of the internet and search engines such as Google, we have everything we need to learn new skills. Watch paint videos from several people. Watch from at least 10 different sources. Why? Because of the point of this whole tirade! One of the guys (or more) in the videos might have gone to formal school to learn this trade. Another video might be from a self-taught individual who didn't know he was doing it all wrong but provided superior results from learning things differently. Now that you are armed with the best information from the best teachers in the world—the guys who had the guts to show you what they learned the hard way—you can pick up a paint gun armed with all the information (and then some) that the professionals use (or not) every day.

This endeavor and the result of this philosophy are evident in every chapter of this book. I am not a "professional," and I am proud of the work I did. This truck came out absolutely phenomenal! I wanted to share with you the secret in this introduction so you can have the exact same result. If I can do this, *you* can do this. I have 4 titanium rods, 2 plates, and 13 screws in my lower back, and I am 61 years old. This book and everything in it is dedicated to *you*. Don't be pigeonholed by strict adherence to mediocre education that could very well *not* have all the nuances and answers taught in the way *you* learn best; instead, get your information from many sources and then use the most important thing God gave you: your own common sense!

History of the Advance Design

Just after World War II, General Motors went from building tanks and other armaments back to consumer vehicles. The automaker knew the public was tired from four long years of war and wanted to put the past behind it. Chevrolet's radically

INTRODUCTION

Deve's 1950 Chevy truck is shown near a Piper J3C-65 that was manufactured by the Piper Aircraft Company of Lock Haven, Pennsylvania, in 1946. Special thanks to Carl Weaver.

different light-duty pickups represent a sea change in pickup design and appearance. General Motors was the first domestic car manufacturer to release these new post-war trucks; they were introduced to Chevrolet dealer showrooms on June 28, 1947, and were available later that year.

The reason for the excitement was because the new design featured a larger windshield, bigger side and rear window glass, higher and wider cab doors, a fresh-air heating/defrosting system, and larger seating capacity with a roomier cab (8 inches wider and 7 inches longer than earlier models) to name a few of the highlights. The lineup for pickups included three sizes: half- (3104), three-quarter- (3604), and one-ton (3804) models with cargo boxes that were 78, 87, and 137 inches, respectively. All three boxes were 50 inches wide with $16^{1}/_{4}$-inch side walls and 14-inch end walls. The wheelbases were 116, $125^{1}/_{4}$, and 137 inches.

Compared to previous models, the cargo box was shifted forward for better load distribution in relation to the rear axle, and it provided better support by the frame rails. The new models had Chevrolet's signature bed design of wooden floors with steel skid strips that continued through most of the 1960s.

The engine was a 90-hp 216.5-ci overhead valve 6-cylinder with 174 ft-lbs of torque. The trucks could be ordered with a 3-on-the-tree 3-speed transmission or a floor-shifted 4-speed. Back in those days, this was modern technology at its finest. And each year they made changes to improve on it.

1947

On June 28, 1947, General Motors introduced the new Advance

INTRODUCTION

This photo is of my uncle Art changing a tire at the farm near Elyria, Kansas. The story was, in the winter they would share the 8-volt tractor battery to get the truck started for school. I learned at an early age what an abomination a 6-volt system can be without a lot of care.

Design (AD) truck. The gas tank mounted under the bed and was filled through a hole in passenger's side of the bed. A 3-speed transmission (non-synchromesh) was floor shifted on all models (3- and 4-speed alike). The doors had one-piece glass with no vent window, and the door handles were turn-down type. The windshield was two-piece. The hood side emblem said CHEVROLET and THRIFTMASTER. A headliner center bow was screwed to the roof of the cab.

New features included cab "corner windows" and a fresh-air heater/defroster. A hand-operated emergency brake handle was located on the right-hand side of the floor shifter. And a radio was available as an in-dash option for the first time.

1948

This year, the shifter for the transmission was moved to the column (creating 3 on the tree), and the synchromesh transmission was introduced. The emergency brake moved to the far-left side of the steering column and was changed to a foot-operated mechanism. The 1947 and 1948 models had red needles on the gauges.

1949

Hood side emblems now had CHEVROLET along with the series designation (3100, 3600, etc.). The THRIFTMASTER hood side emblems were discontinued. The gas tank moved to inside the cab behind the seat. In midyear 1949, cab windlace rubber changed from black to gray/tan and now slid into a track. The headliner center bow was changed to a floating type and was not screwed to the roof of the cab as before.

1950

For 1950, lever-action shocks were replaced with modern tubular shocks. This was the last year for the driver-side vent. The handle for the side cowl vent was flat steel, not maroon plastic as it was previously. The wiper knob was chrome-plated steel.

1951

The one-piece door glass gave way to two-piece glass with vent windows. During 1951, Chevy changed the bed from a nine-board pattern to an eight-board pattern. The front bumper was standard, and the rear bumper was an option. Only a top cowl vent was offered; the driver-side vent was discontinued. This was the only year with vent windows *and* pull-down exterior door handles. It was also the final year for chrome inside window handle knobs and a chrome wiper knob.

1952

In 1952, the exterior door handles became a push-button type. The speedometer changed from a max of 80 mph to 90 mph. Halfway through the year, General Motors stopped using 3100, 3600, and 3800 emblems on the side of the hood, whereas Chevrolet kept them all year. This year, no rear bumper was offered. The horizontal strips below and above the radio speaker grille and glove box door changed to painted steel (they had been stainless steel). Hubcaps changed from chrome to gray painted steel with black block letters, but the stamping and the shape remained the same as prior years. Bumpers were no longer chrome; they were now gray painted steel.

1953

This was the last year for the 216-ci engine. The hood front emblem was now stainless steel, and the hood side emblems lost the CHEVROLET but kept the series numbers (3100, 3600, etc.) This was the first year that a side-mounted spare was offered as an option. A rear bumper was reintroduced. It was the last year for wood blocks under the bed. The wiper knob was maroon plastic, as it was in 1952. For the first year, a blue and silver ID door plate was used (prior years were black and silver).

1954

A high-pressure 235-ci 112-hp engine was introduced for pickups, and a 261-ci engine was introduced for larger trucks. Hubcaps were the same shape as previous models but now had only the Bowtie emblem. The old horizontal grille gave way to a new bull-nose grille. This was

INTRODUCTION

Chevrolet Pickup Truck Notes

Keep the following in mind when restoring:
- 1947–1950 trucks had standard chrome bumpers on the front and the rear.
- 1947–1949 trucks had a large fuse block on the firewall.
- 1947–1950 trucks had a driver-side vent.
- 1947–1949 trucks had lever-action shocks.
- 1947 to midyear 1949, a cab-opening windlace seal attached to the cab with a metal retainer. Midyear 1949, General Motors installed a track with a new style of windlace that slid into the track.
- With 1955 and earlier trucks, the raised letters on the tailgate were not a contrasting color but were body color. Bed planks were hard yellow pine and were painted black.
- Prior to 1955, dark green was the standard paint color; other colors were available as a no-cost option.
- During 1947–1948, the Chevrolet painted grille bars and "back splash" bars were body color. In addition, the leading edge of each painted outer bar had a horizontal stripe matching the cab stripe. On the 1949–1951 Chevrolet with a painted grille, the back splash bar was white. In 1952–1953, this changed to light gray to match the hubcaps and the bumpers. On chrome grilles, only the outer bar was plated. The back splash bar was the same as the painted grille. ∎

the first year for parking lights, which were introduced with a new grille. The two-piece windshield was replaced with modern one-piece curved glass. The dash instruments and steering wheel changed to a modern design. The bed was redesigned, and the top rails were now flat, not sloped like previous models. The taillights were now round. The rear bumper now had a notch in the center for a license plate. The Hydramatic transmission was available in trucks for the first time. Two-tone cabs were also available as an option for the first time but only with a white top and only on more deluxe cabs. Full wheel covers were now available as an option too.

1955

This was the first year for an open driveshaft on pickups and panel trucks. It was the final year for the 6-volt electrical system.

GMC Crossover

General Motors, the parent company of Chevrolet, also made the GMC series of trucks during these same model years. A great deal of this book will apply to the GMCs; however, some of it won't. The engines were different as were the grille and many other small parts. My apologies to GMC owners who feel left out. My experiences are solely with the Chevrolet version of these trucks. ∎

More historical data for the AD era can be found at devestechnet.com/Home/History. The official GM Restoration Package for your truck is available at gmheritagecenter.com/gm-heritage-archive/vehicle-information-kits.html.

Identification Note

A common question asked by new enthusiasts is "How do I identify my truck?" It is not as complicated as it is for later-year models. Simply, there are no uniform stampings anywhere on the truck with a few exceptions. You won't find any way to verify a numbers-matching truck. The ID plate on the driver-side door will tell you a great deal. The casting number and serial number on the engine will provide important information concerning the engine and what it was made for. Since the vendors sell new ID plates and most of the engines of this vintage have been replaced, there is really no way to prove providence beyond a doubt.

CHAPTER 1

THE FRAME-UP RESTORATION PHILOSOPHY

The plan is to take an Advance Design (AD) half-ton truck and restore it. Easy enough, right? Except we need to stop and think about how far we want to take it. Are we interested in an old truck that is just prettied up a little and made operational, or do we want a pristine truck that is better than when it came out of the dealer's showroom and uses all the superior features of all the AD years?

I will assume that you want it to come out better than new. To do this, no amount of time or effort will be spared to get a pristine result. But let's think a moment about the hows and whys that come with this type of endeavor. There are two disciplines to adhere to: preservation and restoration. These two things go hand in hand, as you will see as we go through the process. What does this mean exactly?

After spending a lot of time in salvage yards picking parts, I can tell you that cadmium (cad)-plated hardware (nuts and bolts mainly) have a life span. In the name of preservation, stainless steel hardware will last forever because it is not a plating. For my restoration, I used polished stainless steel for all the bright work and stainless steel everywhere else. I also used superior paints and coatings for this same reason.

Choosing the Pickup

If you are in the market for one of these trucks to restore, there are a few considerations that may be of help in your search. Even though Chevrolet learned lessons that made these trucks better as the years went by, I still prefer the 1950 model. This is because all of the cabs of the AD era were pretty much the same with a couple important exceptions.
- The 1947 model cabs only have

This is Mike Fahrbach's 1951 3/4-ton that he named Virgil. The 3/4-ton trucks with the original engine/transmission combination could easily pull 2- to 3-inch tree stumps right out of the ground. Low-end torque was exceptional. Virgil sports a full-flow 261 with a Tremec T5 transmission.

THE FRAME-UP RESTORATION PHILOSOPHY

three mounting locations to the frame. For late 1948 through 1955, they went to four cushioned mounting locations for the cab, which made the ride more stable.

- For 1947 through 1950 only, the cab had a driver-side vent to the outside for pulling in fresh air. For 1951 and beyond, that vent was removed and new door window vents were relied on for venting. I prefer the driver-side vent and four cab mounts.

The 1950 AD frame is my choice because it has modern tube shock mounts for the first time. The beauty of the AD era is the ability to interchange most of the parts. For example, I do not like the doors that come with the 1950 truck (I like vented windows and push-button outside door latches, which were not available until 1952), so I am going with 1952–1955 doors. In my opinion, you cannot have enough venting into the cab. Vent windows, a driver-side vent, and an upper cowl vent allow for a nice breeze in a truck with no air-conditioning.

Another reason to like the 1949–1950 model is the more robust, more useful, and tougher underbed spare tire carrier system. In addition, the half-ton with rear corner windows (referred to as a five-window cab) seem to be the most desirable from the public's perspective. Personally, if you own any AD truck, you are on top of the game. But for this restoration, I am going with a 1950 Chevy half-ton with rear quarter windows.

This is my first 1950 pickup restoration, and I really like that driver-side outside air vent.

When searching for your project vehicle, it can be a good idea to purchase a parts vehicle. The 1950 truck (white) became our restoration project vehicle. The 1955 model (brown) was too far gone to restore but was used for parts for this restoration, such as the doors.

This is hard work and something that you must have the right mindset to do. If you are there, just the accomplishment is very rewarding.

CHAPTER 1

Disclaimer

I am going to do everything for this restoration myself. I know this seems crazy, but I have more time than money, so I am going to be the laborer for this project with the fewest exceptions possible. It's a learning journey to say the least, but I will prove it can be a one-man job! Engine machine shop work is outsourced, but other than that, it will be a one-man show. Even the engine rebuild is done right here in the shop. ■

I paid $600 for the white 1950 AD truck several years ago. The truck had massive amounts of body filler hiding a great deal of damage. It was almost a hopeless case in the way of rust and damage, which made it a great candidate for this project.

The victim for this project was in much worse shape than it looked. Once torn down, my mentors said right away to junk the cab and get another one. It was unanimous among my friends that it was too far gone. There was no floor after the seat pedestal, most of the toe board was gone, and all of the structure below floor level was rusted out completely. The frame had some serious issues, and everyone thought I was crazy for even trying to salvage the truck. But honestly, we don't have an overabundance of five-window cabs in better shape, so I felt we needed to salvage it if possible. Part of this is being a good steward in saving our heritage regardless of the climb to get there.

The Skills Required

So, we have the material for the job, now how do we do it? The nice part about the AD era is it is very straightforward. Each subassembly is carefully thought out but simple in design without computers, unnecessary wiring, etc. First, carefully disassemble the entire truck, placing all nuts and bolts in labeled bags attached to the parts they come with. With the entire truck in pieces, assess the frame, the engine and the drivetrain, the cab, and each individual part for serviceability. That's the easy part.

Next, it will be obvious that it is important to learn how to weld with a MIG welder. There will be no getting around it because there will be a *lot* of rust damage from 60-plus years of wear and tear. The rust may be hiding under the paint or what's left of it.

It will also be a good idea to learn how to sandblast. It is important to get down to the bare metal on all parts for the project; no exceptions. This will help you find what others covered up or didn't catch.

After welding and sandblasting, it is time to move on to becoming a

MIG welding is relatively easy to learn and a very handy skill to have. Be sure to get a good gas-type 110/220-volt unit so you have the capability to weld thicker materials.

It's a messy job, but someone has to do it. Sandblasting using #1 silica sand is hazardous to your health and best done outside while wearing an appropriate respirator.

THE FRAME-UP RESTORATION PHILOSOPHY

painter. There is a lot to painting if you are going to do it right. Finally, there is the engine and drivetrain parts. We are going to learn how to rebuild engines, service transmissions and drivetrain parts, and do tasteful upgrades to make this restoration the best it can be.

Engine Differences

The 1954–1957 235 or 261 engines are also fine for a 1950 model restoration. The differences are minor except for the 261. In 1958, General Motors introduced full-flow oil filtering with that year's 261. Find more on this engine at devestechnet.com/Home/TheVenerable261. ∎

Preplanning for a Positive Result

Let's ask ourselves a few questions prior to getting our hands dirty:

Q: Is this going to be a show truck (trailer queen) or are we going to actually drive it?

A: We are going to drive it. We want to enjoy the vehicle the way it was intended. This does not mean skimping on quality. It will be a show truck to begin with.

Q: Will the truck have a stock single master cylinder with drum brakes?

A: No, for safety reasons on today's modern roads, adequate stopping power and stopping distance is needed. While good drum brakes are fine for this, a more-modern dual master cylinder is safer, so we will take this opportunity to install front disc brakes. All will be bolt-in replacements with no modifications to the vintage parts.

Q: Are you happy with a maximum speed of 50 mph?

A: No. A 1962 261 6-cylinder engine will be installed since it's a bolt-in replacement for the original 216 engine. While we are at it, we will add a 1962 vintage BorgWarner R10 Overdrive with 3-speed and a more modern open driveline with a 1955 first series rear end, which are all bolt-in replacements.

As you can see, I am not a purist making a stock specimen suited for a museum or a hot rodder who will chop and hack through to make something that looks vintage but isn't. I am middle of the road and will only make tasteful upgrades. The 6-cylinder stays, the 3-speed stays, and the suspension stays. All the things that make this pickup charming will stay.

There is a reason the charming attributes will stay as they are: preservation. Every upgrade will be a bolt-on upgrade that can be removed should a new owner come along who wants a perfectly stock truck. At this particular time, there are fewer and fewer people interested in perfectly stock, so some exceptions are made, but in the end, we are going for tasteful.

Addressing all of this and more with the work done by someone else would make the cost astronomical. It's much less costly to learn to do all these things. It is not as daunting as you may think. The way I look at it is, if I can do it, anyone can. Another cool aspect of learning all this is, you will have the tools to do it again!

Plan of Attack

You know what they say about best laid plans, but in this case, solid preparation work is essential and will cost you much less in the long run. To do a hurried job and have something half-baked in the end will cost the very same as doing it carefully in a slow, meticulous fashion. Let's take a moment to discuss a plan for this project.

Engine

The AD era (with the exceptions of 1954 and 1955) had the 216 90-hp babbit bearing motor in it. That engine was the last in Chevy history to not have replaceable insert bearings. These older motors required a professional engine rebuilder who understood how to pour a lead derivative called babbit into bearing caps that were formed for this purpose. Then, a machining process called align boring was necessary to make the babbit uniform. Due to a less-exacting machining process than we have now, the crank bearings required shims.

Since insert bearings came out in 1953, how old do you suppose those professional babbiters are by now? Rest in peace. So, while you are going to all this trouble, locate a 1958–1962 235 or 261 motor for your project. These are the best years and are easy to rebuild. The benefits of this are even more: they are a direct bolt-in replacement with a few minor exceptions we will talk about in chapter 5.

Drivetrain

If you have a 140 hp in the newer 235 or 148 hp with the newer 261, there is a problem. The older AD

CHAPTER 1

trucks through 1954 had a torque tube rear end. This means the driveline is enclosed, hard to maintain, and not compatible with more modern transmissions. But there is a glimmer of hope. Turns out General Motors went to the open driveline in 1955 (still an AD half year). So, it happens that designers kept the same rear end from 1955 through 1959, and it's another direct bolt-in replacement (with a minor exception presented).

The transmission is a nuance all in itself. You can keep your enclosed driveline and transmission and change the 4.11:1 rear end gears to 3.55:1 and get about 60 mph out of it. That is definitely a way to go. But if I am going to all this trouble, I have my eye on 75 mph or more. My choice was the BorgWarner R10 Overdrive unit coupled with the SM319 3-speed transmission because it is another direct bolt-in replacement, it gives me essentially six speeds to choose from, and it enables a smooth 75 mph and will push to 80. This is a vintage engine with vintage parts, so that is more than I can ask for.

Then, there is the shifter. I am a floor shifter kind of guy. I like to have one hand on the tall shift knob and one resting on the windowsill. You couldn't do that with a 3 on the tree until now! I built a shift mechanism for the floor and now I have a truck reminiscent of my granddad's and without any of the sheep zooming past!

Brake System

I do not recommend keeping the stock brake system. First, you have a single master cylinder, which means there is no backup if one gives out. Second, at best these trucks stopped in a more vintage and longer stop time. If you are planning on driving on today's roads, take the time to replace at least the single master cylinder.

There is a direct bolt-in replacement available from a few vendors. They have created the brackets and parts to make it possible. There is a lot of re-creating brake lines, adding both residual and proportioning valves, etc., but it's worth the trouble to know you have a method to get the truck stopped if one cylinder goes out. I took this one step further and added front disc brakes with a kit that bolted right up.

Frame and Suspension

The frame needs to be blasted down to the bare metal and very carefully inspected for major rust damage. There are parts of this era

Another Conversion Option

Another good engine option is the Tremec T-5. I have friends who made this conversion and they are very pleased with it. It is a vintage late-1980s 5-speed with Overdrive, and the best part is, it's not electric in any way. This makes it a less-complicated setup than was available in 1962 with the BorgWarner R10. I used the BorgWarner R10 for this project, but I recommend the T-5 these days because of the rarity of the BorgWarner R10. However, if you can find one, it is a very solid choice.

This is a whole new shifter mechanism I made specifically for the Saginaw SM318 or SM319 with Overdrive 3-speed transmission. It was a very difficult undertaking due to the lack of space under the cab floor, but it works very well in the end. It comes up out of the floor in the exact spot the stock 4-speed did, which allows me to use the original 4-speed transmission cover.

THE FRAME-UP RESTORATION PHILOSOPHY

frame that is very susceptible to complete rust through, which must be repaired. Any loose or missing rivets also need to be dealt with.

The leaf springs from a 60-plus-year-old vehicle will not be acceptable for a frame-up restoration. They will be replaced with brand-new ones with the same look. In doing so, we will use an open drive rear end from a 1955 first series so we can bolt it right in.

Since it is a 1950 frame, we have modern tube shock absorbers. If that was not the case, tube shock perches are available for welding to an older frame. I advise to add those for the better ride and easier parts availability.

Cab

There will be rust through somewhere. I have never seen one without some rust through, usually at the front fender wells or rear cab corners. If there is no rust through visible on your project at first glance, you may very well see it after sandblasting. You just do not know what you have until you blast it.

We will do metal repair wherever needed. That is a given, but I have my welder out, so I am going a few steps further. For example, you know that dual master cylinder? Well, it's under the cab floor, and the round hole isn't sufficient for refilling a rectangular dual master cylinder. I will make the hole bigger and put a nice vendor-supplied stainless steel door in the floor. And you know how you must lift the seat to get to all that space underneath? I will install two locking drawers with ball bearing slow sliders, so I can get to the jack, a fire extinguisher, and other miscellaneous items.

The welder is right there! How hard can it be? If you keep that attitude throughout and take your time, you will be very pleased with the results.

I am also adding Zeus quarter-turn fasteners to the center transmission cover. I do not like sheet metal screws. To me, they are a cheaper way out and, even if original, problematic. They rust faster, they poke anything in the vicinity, and they work themselves loose.

Bed

Our project used red oak painted with several coats of specialized black, which gives it a very hard surface but looks very nice. Stainless steel bed strips were used because stainless steel doesn't rust and it will outlive its regular steel counterpart. In fact, stainless steel hardware is used everywhere. I gave the folks at Mar-K Manufacturing in Oklahoma City a call and had them make me the new metal bed parts. I prefer the flat rails of the 1954 and later bed sides, so they made them to fit the 1950 frame. It is harder and more time consuming to try and make a dented old bed straight again, and the new beds are the same gauge metal as the originals. I will cut and shape the oak too.

Electrical

Electric wipers were used because everyone knows what happens when you are sitting at a stop sign and accelerate during a rainstorm. We are going with 12 volts for many good reasons, the main ones being: it allows us to go with modern accessories, we can get roadside assistance, and we can add air-conditioning maybe. Many other reasons will become obvious as we progress.

Final Thoughts

I suggest you make your own plan of attack and carefully look over your expectations versus your expenses and your labor versus someone else's. Really outline everything on your wish list. A frame-up restoration starts at the frame and goes up! On the sources page, I have included where I purchased each subassembly listed, which will help you a great deal, the way those same resources helped me.

Now I must also state the obvious: this is going to cost you a lot of money. And when you are done and decide to sell, do not expect to get anywhere near the money you have in it. Two things come into play here. First, the public has no idea how hard this is or how much it costs to have these things done. Second, if you are too meticulous for your own good, it could be said you are throwing away money.

I don't care what the cost is because this is a one-of-a-kind vehicle that will never be the same as any other. We do this for the enjoyment and satisfaction, not for the money. Also, the average frame-up restoration takes about three years for a single person to do it right. It can take much longer, depending on the time you can devote to it. This is genuinely a labor of love. I would say if you get away with less than $25,000 you are doing better than I did for the project. You can almost purchase a new truck for what it will cost you, so be aware.

CHAPTER 2

TAKING IT ALL APART

A few things to mention before you get excited about tearing down the truck. If it's in drivable condition, take it for a drive and write down all that is wrong with it. Those parts can be mixed into the parts stream when the time comes. Take it to a car wash or get out the pressure washer and clean. Then, clean some more. Get as much grime out of the way as you can. Be sure to have a camera handy and take pictures as you go. This will prove to be a very smart move. Make notes and carefully track expenses as you go too.

There are a few guidelines that I loosely follow. I will not go into tremendous detail here because it is all very straightforward. Here is what I do:

1. Get many large and small resealable bags and a permanent marker. Mark the bag with its contents.
2. Store all subsystems together and include all their hardware in bags taped to the subsystem they belong with. Even if you do not use the old rusted bolts, keep them with the assembly.
3. Remove the bed, fenders, inner fenders, bumpers, bumper brackets, any tin skirts, running boards, etc., leaving the cab for last. At this point, in theory, you can still drive it.
4. Make sure you park the vehicle where it can stay for a long time. Drain the radiator, remove it and all of its associated parts, and put a bag over the carb inlet. Take the radiator to a radiator shop to have it checked and repaired properly. There is no need to have an unchecked radiator lying around. Now you can remove the engine and transmission and the steering gearbox. This will require a steering wheel removal tool. Remove three bolts at the frame and a few on the inside column brace. It comes out from outside. Disconnect the pitman arm by pulling the cotter pin and loosening the very large screws on the ends to release the ball. Do not force anything (within reason).

The teardown can reveal a lot of things that require time. The removal of years of undercoating, rust, and dirt is the messy part. In the upper right is that driver-side cowl vent I like so much.

 **Copper Lines**

When removing gauges and heater control valves, understand that they used copper lines filled with a special gas to make the water temperature gauge and the heater control valve work. Do not pinch or damage these copper lines. They are very fragile and very useless if compromised!

TAKING IT ALL APART

5. Remove the cab internals: the seat, the headliner, the heater, and all controls, gauges, and wiring. Take your time and don't get ruffled. The heater can be hard to remove due to the location of the screws, etc. Remove the glass. This is just a matter of cutting the rubber away from the glass edge, carefully popping out each piece, and saving the intact glass for a template for new glass. Take all the flat glass pieces to your local glass cutter and have them make new ones. Be sure to tell them that measurements are critical. If you need rear corner glass, many vendors sell them. Remove the gas tank. Start by draining it from below. If it is stock, there will be a drain cock to use to drain it. I replace that short rubber hose just for safety, so I cut the old one and drain the gas into a sufficient container. Remove the straps holding the tank and the tubing holding the spout to the cab, then take the gas tank to a gas tank cleaner. Sometimes radiator shops do that service. We need to clean the tank thoroughly and inspect for any rust pinholes. If it is painted, sandblast it first. We need to see if any old brazing jobs or any rust pinholes are present. If the tank is iffy, we need to replace it.

6. With it now lightweight due to removing everything in the cab, remove the two shackle assemblies that hold the rear cab to the frame and remove the two large bolts in front. Don't forget to put everything in labeled bags. Now the cab can come off. It is a good time to stop and think about how you are going to move this cab from process to process (sandblasting, cleaning, painting,

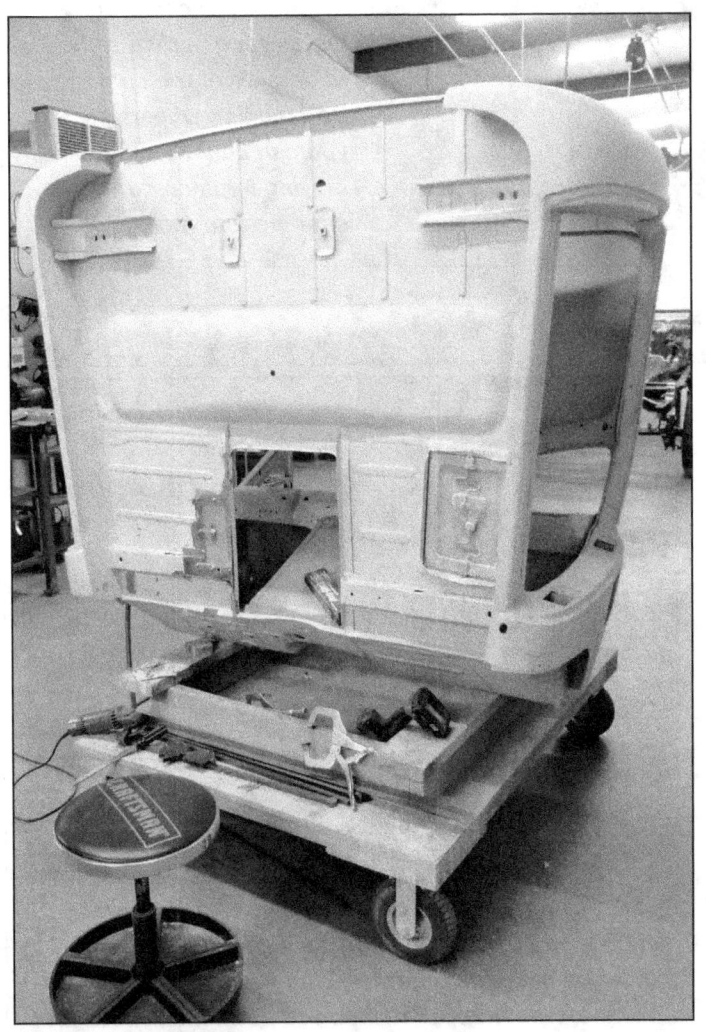

The wooden cab cart has a platform with a pedestal that fits the underside of an Advance Design cab.

The cab cart works great for outside work and is very stable, even when doing distasteful work such as sandblasting!

I suggest making the cab cart with a hitch so you can pull it around in places where a 6-inch wheel makes it difficult. Then tow it with a lawn tractor, a side-by-side, or a four-wheeler. I did not find it necessary to fasten down the cab.

CHAPTER 2

etc.). A cab cart made of wood does the trick and is worth the time and effort for sure.

7 Remove the old torque tube (enclosed driveshaft) rear end connection at the transmission only, then remove the transmission, the bellhousing and flywheel, and the engine. An engine cart will make your life easier when moving around your shop. The plans for this engine cart and much more pertinent information can be found in my book *Chevrolet Inline-6 Engine: How to Rebuild*.

You still have a rolling chassis if you tie the end of the torque tube up, but now we must decide how to get down to the frame. I made a frame rotisserie for that purpose. It pays to take the time to do this because it will be used for sandblasting, frame repairs, priming, and painting. It will be on that rotisserie for a long time.

Building a Cab Cart

The overall size is 60 inches wide by 48 inches long. On top of the main platform, stand four 2x6 boards up on edge and make a center frame that is 43 inches in the front and 46 inches in the rear with 38¼-inch sides. Stack five 2x6 boards on top of each other to raise the cab to a nice height for getting paint all around the bottom of it. The front ones are 48 inches long, the rear ones are 50 inches long. Wheels are 9 inches with the front two being swivels. I suggest getting locking wheels. This will make the cab more stable during sanding. I also added rubber to the top of the stack so it wouldn't be hard on paint when painting the bottom of the cab.

Measure the underside of the cab to make sure your stacked risers fit nicely on the cab mounting surface and fit in the underside of the cab. Add locking wheels so you can count on the cab staying in place during sanding and moving.

Making a Frame Rotisserie

Shown is the finished frame rotisserie. It is perfect for working on pickup frames. I couldn't be happier with the result. Painting a frame is very hard, but this makes it so much easier.

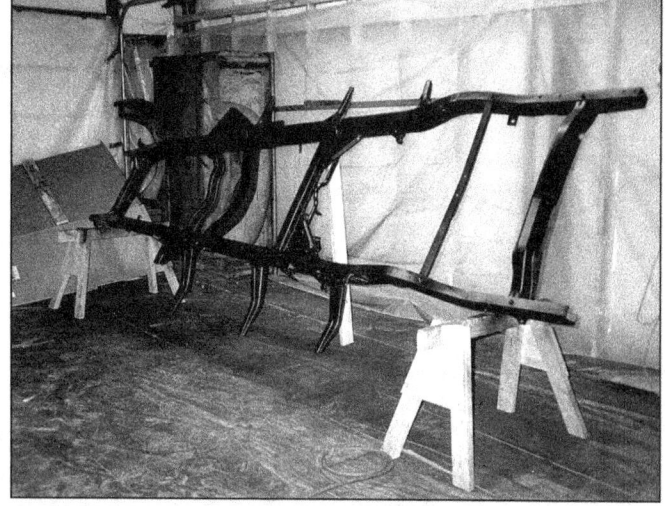

I have been doing this for many years and started working the hard way. I once used wooden sawhorses to hold up the pickup frame. A long 2x4 is holding it at an angle. What happens when you accidentally kick that 2x4 when you are trailing a paint gun and an air hose?

Making a Frame Rotisserie (Continued)

This is a relatively easy conversion. It starts with two Torin engine stands I purchased at Northern Tool (part number 144850). The cost as of January 2015 was $109. The engine stand is unsuitable for my purposes because the neck is angled backward. That neck needs to be straight. Other than that, the procedure is pretty straightforward.

This style of engine stand is crucial because it has the proper legs for the span needed. This model of engine stand has legs that protrude completely parallel to the stand, which means two of them can be tied together with very long angle iron.

Rotisserie Materials List	
2	Torin engine stands (part number 144850)
2	1/8x3-inch angle iron, 15 feet each
2	1-inch-diameter ACME screws, 18 inches each (or cut one 36-inch screw in half)
4	1-inch ACME screw nuts
4	Very large, very heavy 1-inch fender washers
Misc.	3/16-inch scrap for making brackets and braces (a 24x12-inch piece will suffice)
12 feet	1 1/2-inch square tubing with at least 1/8-inch walls
4	3-inch swivel casters
2	7/16x6-inch Grade-8 bolts with nuts and washers
2	7/16x4-inch Grade-8 bolts with nuts and washers
1	2-inch square tubing by 21 inches with 3/16-inch walls
2	1 3/8-inch steel spacers with 1/2-inch through hole
Note: The source for the hardware, including the 1-inch ACME screw and nuts, was McMaster-Carr.	

The best way to approach a project like this is to decide how it should work, look, and feel before starting. This is where solution criteria comes into play. I have this policy of making the solution criteria set in stone no matter how hard it is to accomplish. For the frame rotisserie, the solution criteria is:
- We want this so that one person can easily manipulate the rotational axis movement and roll it around the shop.
- It must not cause problems in getting the paint exactly where we want it, even at the mounting points.
- It must rotate through the entire 360 degrees.
- It must have raising and lowering ability so that a person can choose the height they want to work at, and then lower the entire frame effortlessly onto the leaf springs at the end.
- Raising/lowering must be easy for one person.

Getting Started

Begin by putting together the two new engine stands per the instructions from the manufacturer. The only place to deviate is when it comes time to install the wheels. All wheels must be the swivel type. It simply will not function correctly with non-swivel casters. I purchased four replacement 3-inch swivel wheels from Harbor Freight. Also, no need to install the neck piece yet.

Once your base has four swivel casters on it and it rolls smoothly, look at the neck. Out of the box, the neck is not perfectly straight up and down. Instead, it's tilting backward, which made sense for its intended use, but modifications are needed for our purposes. Cut the neck off its mounting bracket flush. Use your tool of choice to cut the bottom so that it's straight. Do not shorten the neck at all. Once the neck has a straight profile at the bottom, cut 2 inches off the bottom of it. We will use that 2 3/8-inch square by 2-inch piece as the mounting support for the telescoping part at the base.

NOTE: If you are interested in saving time, do these same procedures on both stands at the same time.

Clean the neck bases and weld the 2-inch piece back on, making sure it is straight and true. Do not weld on the inside, just the outside. The metal is too thin, so we need to strengthen things up a bit. Once you have the receiver installed on the neck, place a 2-inch square by 21-inch piece inside of it. They used a non-standard 2 3/8-inch dimension, so now we have slop to contend with. We want that mast to be 100-percent straight and level on all four axis. What I did was make some 2 1/4 by 2-inch strips out of 1/16-inch material (close is good enough) and installed them in place to reduce stress on the weld. Once you have it shimmed and in place straight, weld it really good to the base.

Now it is time to make four brackets for the ACME screws. Make them out of heavy stock because there is a lot of stress on this area during use. Bend four pieces of 3/16-inch or thicker material that is 2x4 inches in size. Put a 3/4-inch, 90-degree bend in the 2-inch side. Take it to the drill press and drill a 1 1/16-inch hole so that the center of the hole is exactly 2 inches from the side of the neck that is centered on the bracket.

Making a Frame Rotisserie (Continued)

The brackets for the ACME screw must be very stout. It will be pushing against half the weight of the frame.

This image shows the completed screw assembly.

These two heavy-duty fender washers were welded to the ACME screw, so they float over the bracket, capturing the ACME screw and keeping it from moving.

Weld the brackets on the base with the 3/4-inch angle facing down. Be sure it is level and do not mount the neck to the base just yet. Now weld the other bracket to the outside mast with the angle pointing upward, being sure to keep everything nice and level. Place the neck over the 2-inch mast and make sure the holes line up on the brackets fairly well. You will notice a lot of slop between the 2-inch and the 2 3/8-inch neck. To aid in making this smoother and less sloppy, I cut some 1/16x2-inch wide strips about 10 inches long, spot welded them in place, then greased them. With the right number of shims, it will move very nicely. Be sure to clamp them tightly before welding so they don't push away. Once you can easily raise and lower by hand, install the ACME screw.

The 18-inch ACME screw system is pretty straightforward. First, weld a very large washer on one end. Make sure it's very thick and very wide. Weld it very flat because it will be turning in a stationary position and always rubbing on the bracket. Insert the ACME screw into the lower bracket with the washer on the very bottom. Push the washer hard up against the bracket.

To ensure we have no binding problems, place two small 1/8-inch pieces of flat plate stock on either side of the ACME screw on the other side of the bracket, then lay your washer over it. These 1/8-inch pieces act as shims so that you don't weld the second washer in too tight. In other words, the washers need a 1/8-inch clearance between them and the bracket. Weld the second washer to the ACME screw. Again, it works best when everything is straight and true and there is some slop between the two washers for movement. The ACME screw will now spin inside the bracket without going anywhere.

There is a welded nut on the top bracket, and the top of the ACME screw has a welded nut for grabbing it with the impact wrench.

This brings the neck assembly to its highest point. This system lifts from the normal wheel height of the frame up to about chest height.

Next, put the neck assembly over the mast and put the ACME screw through the hole in the mast bracket. Let the whole thing rest as low as it can get. Thread on a 1-inch ACME nut until it sits flush and hard against the top bracket. Weld the ACME nut to the bracket. Now all we need is a way to turn the screw. I thread the remaining ACME nut flush to the very top of the ACME screw and welded it on from the top only.

TAKING IT ALL APART

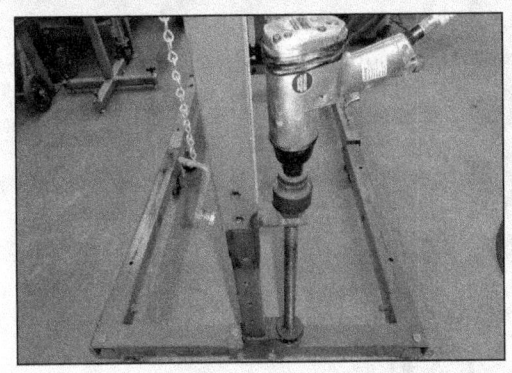

A 1⁵/₈-inch impact socket will raise and lower each end separately.

After the modification, the frame can be raised and lowered with an impact ratchet.

By attaching from underneath in this manner, the only paint touch-up we will need to do is right at the leaf-spring mounts.

Now it's just a matter of finding a 1⁵/₈-inch impact socket for your impact driver and you are set! I also drilled holes about every 5 inches all the way through to bolt the frame securely in position. I did this in case I needed more stability as I went up with the frame. Turns out I didn't use them, but that option is still there. If you got this far, you should have a nice swivel base with a neck mounted tightly to it, and you can raise and lower both of your carts. Great job! You are about halfway there!

Making the Rear Frame Mount

Both front and rear mounts will need the same size of mounting plate, so make two of them. Cut 3/16-inch plate steel to 5¹/₂x10 inches. Hold the plate up to the cart's mounting plate and mark the holes. The bolts can go anywhere as long as there is at least 1³/₄ inches between the top and bottom bolt sets for the cross piece to fit.

Once that is done, cut a piece of 1¹/₂-inch square tubing exactly 46¹/₂ inches long. Find the center of the tubing, center it on the mounting plate, and weld it in place. Be sure to weld it straight and even by putting a level on it.

Next, we are going downward on both sides with a 1¹/₂ x 5¹/₂-inch piece. Use a square to ensure everything is straight. At this point, braces are needed for stabilizing the design. Cut a 4x4-inch piece of 3/16-inch plate and then cut it in half diagonally. Place these braces on each side in the corner and weld them in. The distances are important. Next, cut a 18-inch piece of 1¹/₂ inch for each side and weld to the bottom of the downward piece. Put another 4-inch brace in the corner.

Use at least 3/16-inch plate steel for the mounting plate across the top for stability.

This works great for mounting. Remember that the frame itself is what gives this system its rigidity.

HOW TO RESTORE YOUR CHEVY TRUCK: 1947–1955

Making a Frame Rotisserie (Continued)

The next thing to do for the rear frame cart is to make the mounting plates. Cut four pieces of 3/16-inch plate steel to 2x5½ inches. Drill a 7/16-inch hole about 1/2 inch from the top and round the corners. Weld the plates in straight and true, then take a piece of 2-inch square tubing and reshape those pieces so there is a nice 2-inch gap between each set of brackets. This is where your rear leaf spring perches will be bolted to. Use the 4-inch Grade-8 bolts for this purpose. The geometry of this mount is such that it makes for really easy rotation.

The rear cart is almost done. Let's work on the center rotator pivot on both. It was sort of handy that this big center pivot was part of an engine stand so we didn't have to make it ourselves. On the very top of this round assembly is a hole for pinning it in place. The round inside part has holes every so often, so when you turn it, you can lock it down at most any angle. The problem is, this hole is a bit too big for the pin, so there is a great deal of sloppiness that you don't want when you are sanding or putting any pressure on the frame.

My solution was to cut a piece of solid 3/8-inch steel rod 5½-inch long, weld a 1/2-inch nut on one end of it, and bend the other end 1½ inches down to 90 degrees. I then slid the nut into the pivot under the top hole, dropped a 1/2x1-inch bolt through the hole, and tightened it. End of problem. I put this unique tool on the end of a chain and hung it on the side of the mast with a magnetic hook. I did the same with that cheapo pin that came with the engine stand, so if I don't need it super secure, I can just pin it in place.

Make sure the cross-handlebar is in place when a frame is on these carts. The only thing keeping that center pivot from pulling out is that handle! It's also a good idea to add grease to that pivot every now and then. It is a must to grease the ACME screw, especially at the base where the washers are. Now that we are done with the rear cart, let's finish this project!

Making the Front Frame Mount

Proceed the same way as you did with the rear mount by finding the center of a 31¾-inch piece of 1½-inch square tubing. Weld this crosspiece in the center of the mounting plate. This time, we only need to weld arms to this cross piece. Cut and weld 7x1½-inch square tubing arms in place. Cut two 2-inch diagonals out of a 2x2-inch piece of 3/16-inch material. Weld them in to give that arm assembly some support.

Now drill a 7/16-inch hole about 1/2-inch from the end all the way through the 1½-inch tubing. Put a bolt through

Having a method to lock down the rotation of the frame is important. This bolt/lock combination solves the problem.

The handle with a nut welded to it fits inside to lock everything down.

I made this tool for keeping the frame from free spinning. It works very nicely.

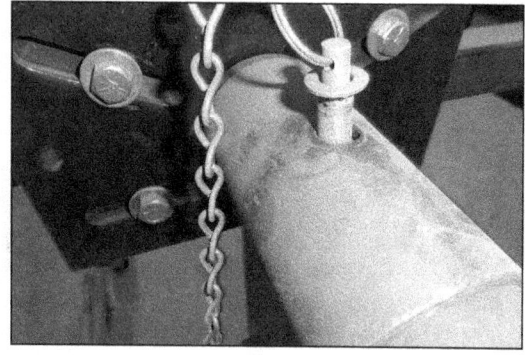

When you want it to sit in its flat position, use the pin that came with the stand.

TAKING IT ALL APART

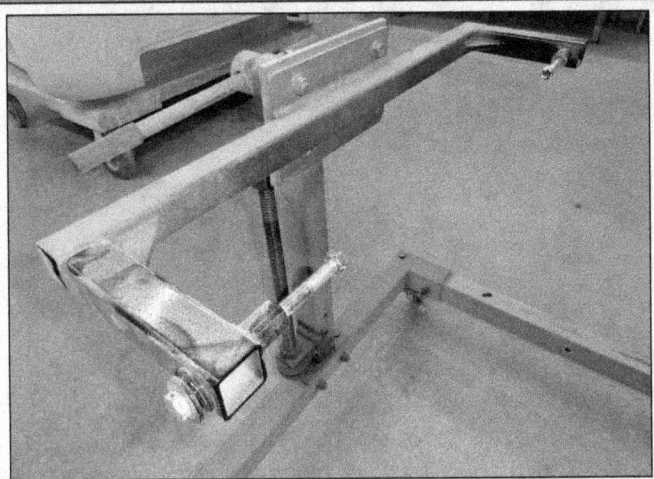

The front frame mount is similar to the back. There are just a few differences.

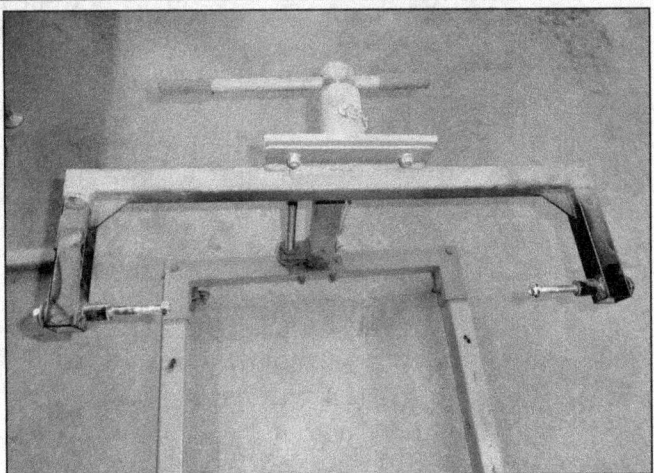

This front frame mount will grab the leaf spring perch from the outside for greater stability.

the hole and be sure it's long enough to tighten the 1$\frac{3}{8}$-inch spacer needed to support the frame. Tighten it down with a washer and nut and weld the base of the spacer to the tubing. This is exactly the space needed to support the front leaf spring support at the front of the frame. Now put the long bolt through the frame's leaf spring hole, tighten it, and you are done.

The final assembly step is to attach the 3-inch by 15-foot angle-iron rails to the carts. The individual carts do not cooperate with each other without this rail. It is a heavy solution that adds weight in the right place and really makes this system stable. To connect them properly, put the frame on the carts and secure it by clamping the rails firmly in place.

Drill two holes through everything on top and on the side for 3/8-inch bolts, nuts, and washers. Fasten securely. When I am done with the rotisserie, I always tuck those long rails under a bench somewhere out of the way.

The idea is to push these carts up to the front and rear of the frames at the height it is sitting, adjust the cart, temporarily support the end of the frame you are working on, bolt this thing up, do the same on the other end, and raise it so that the running board brackets clear the floor when you are rotating it, and everyone is happy. Once the frame is ready for the leaf spring assembly, reverse the process. This cart is great for all repairs, preparations, sandblasting, and finish painting. It has been a real success in my shop for sure!

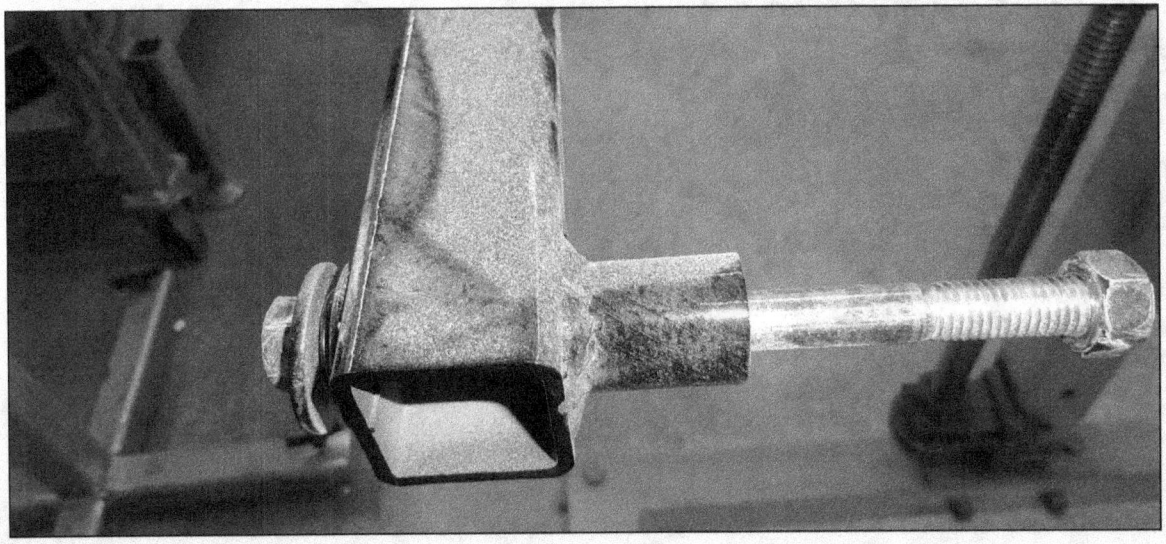

By keeping the spacer relatively thin, we are not impacting the paint more than we have to. When finished, the touch-up will be concealed by the leaf spring mounts.

CHAPTER 2

Frame Subassembly Removal

With the frame on your new rotisserie, the suspension parts can be unbolted, bagged, and stored for later. Removal of the torque tube rear end, the front-end parts, etc. is straightforward. I recommend taking plenty of pictures to guide you in a few years when you put it back and have forgotten how.

Be sure to remove all subassemblies, nuts and bolts, and everything that is attachable. I didn't make any exceptions; everything that can come apart is taken apart. Note: This does not apply to the engine or mechanicals yet.

Sandblasting

Before getting much further, we need to completely refurbish all the small parts of the truck. From parking brake parts to bumper brackets, there is a lot of miscellaneous stuff that needs sandblasting. The cabinet sandblaster is one of the most used tools in my shop.

I purchased the Skat Blast 940 blast cabinet from TP Tools. It is not big enough to do the larger items, which forces you to go outside with them. Honestly, I would prefer one about twice the size. The vac system that comes with it is important, so don't try to save money there. You will ruin your shop vac quickly. Ask me how I know. Be sure to order a carbide tip for it and a few extra pairs of gloves. You can get the replacement glass made at any local glass company. It is just automotive safety glass.

In addition, you will also need a really strong air compressor. It should be a two-stage, 80-gallon unit to put out the necessary cubic feet per minute (CFM) for sandblasting.

My system is two single-stage 60-gallon units plumbed together. This gives me 120-gallon capacity and two pumps, which does the job fine. You will use this compressor for just about everything, so get a good one while you are at it.

I started with the left air compressor and added the one on the right by plumbing them together when the red one wasn't enough. This seems to work very well. Both are single-stage compressors.

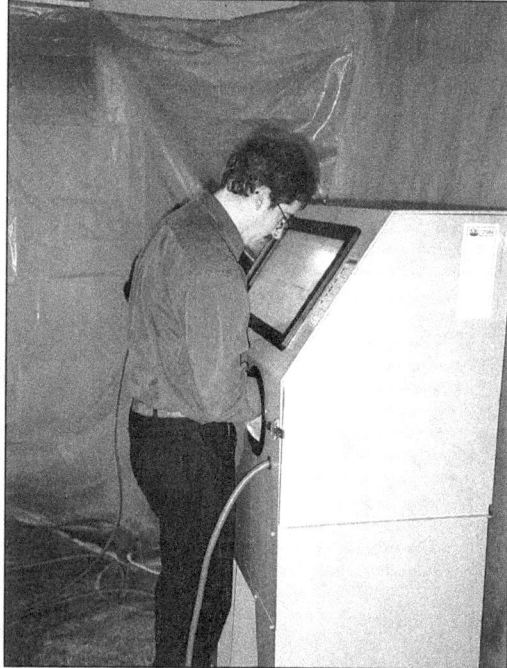

You will be spending many hours standing at the blast cabinet while cleaning all your metal parts. It is the best way to remove all paint, rust, and dirt from your parts.

CHAPTER 3

FRAME REPAIR AND RESTORATION

The first order of business after the frame is stripped completely is to assess its condition. This simply cannot be properly done without sandblasting. There are a few ways to accomplish this. You can take it to a professional blaster and pay to have it done or you can use that money to purchase a pressurized blaster to do yourself.

On the left is the result of doing the sandblasting myself here at the shop. On the right is what I got back from the sandblasting shop I used. It is not advised to apply any coatings to something that very likely will have flash rust on it in the very least.

This photo was taken before the rotisserie. There is sand everywhere! My ancestors came off an open combine during wheat harvest, so dirt and grime everywhere is just in my nature!

Two realities converted my opinion on this:

Reality Number One: I am over-the-top picky and meticulous. The blasting shop I tried was not. They did not get in close to the crevices or as far into some of the channels as I would have liked. Not that all of them are that way. In my case, I had to do it again myself.

Reality Number Two: The cost was $600 for the frame and a few larger sheet metal parts. I paid about $200 for my pressurized blaster, and now I have it for the many other things I find myself doing.

 **Sandblasting Exceptions**

Sandblasting is not a panacea. Things that do not sandblast well include undercoating, any rubberized or plastic derivative, and grease. You must get rid of those things the hard way with a scraper and some elbow grease. Also, use common sense when it comes to things made of metal. Pot metal, stainless steel, plastics, etc. are *not* good candidates for blasting. ■

HOW TO RESTORE YOUR CHEVY TRUCK: 1947–1955

CHAPTER 3

You will need a long air hose and a water trap on the pressurized blaster. Be sure to use #1 silica sand or finer so your lines do not clog up. Also, do some research on the harmful effects of #1 silica sand and wear the proper protection. The truth is, there are no fine particles that are not harmful to you if ingested.

Sandblasting

The pressurized blaster is an important tool that can be frustrating and confusing. It pressurizes the sand, so it can come out at high velocity, but there can be no large pieces of sand, moisture, or anything that can clog the system. Once you get the hang of it, a frame takes about a full day to strip. It is slow, laborious work, and the safety helmet makes it hard to breathe. I personally do not like this task, but I look around and there is nobody standing beside me, so let's git-r-dun!

The sand is reusable if you scoop it up and run it through a screen, so I keep buckets handy to refill the 40-gallon tank. The cost is not that high; 80 pounds of #1 silica sand cost about $6. I will go through about 15 bags for this process, including recycling. Even with a backstop, quite a bit of sand is lost. The #1 silica is very fine and it will not warp sheet metal, so I use it for everything.

Frame Repair

With the sandblasting finished, it's time to inspect what we have and make repairs.

Patch Welding

This frame had a large chunk of metal missing at the center crossmember inside the channel. I used a Makita grinder and thin metal cutting disc to square up the rust hole. Then, I made a patch the same size as the hole and welded it in with a butt weld. Butt welding means having no overlaps so the welds will fill in the outline of the metal. This is a good way to go if you want to hide the weld completely. Once the excess weld is ground off, there is no evidence the patch ever existed.

Replacing Rivets

Welding patches is easy once you get the hang of it, but a task that was daunting was replacing the loose and missing rivets. The factory used the cold rivet process to rivet frames, which meant a lot of hydraulic pressure was needed to set them. We use a hot rivet process instead.

Re-riveting a Vintage GM Frame

This procedure was done on a bare frame. It would be very difficult to do this on a complete truck due to the fire hazard. Please observe all safety precautions and use common sense.

First off, the good news. It's not all that hard! The hardest part was getting good information on where to begin. Different procedures and different opinions abound. Where the opinions vary is a lot of the old timers used the boiler rivet method where you heat the whole rivet red hot, insert it in the hole, and with a bucker (person) on one end holding a very heavy bucking bar, the other one hammers the rivet

My metal working mentor, Gene Swartzendruber, is shown here teaching me the finer points of the riveting process. I am so grateful to him in so many ways.

Re-riveting a Vintage GM Frame (Continued)

home. They insist this is the only way to get the proper heat throughout the rivet.

After researching this, I contend that by the time you have put the tongs on the hot rivet, pushed it in the hole, and put the bar against it solidly, you have cooled the head sufficiently to the point where you might as well have just heated the rivet in the hole. The problem of heat shunting out due to the surrounding metal and bucking bar being cold is a real problem. Maybe that's why our friends at Chevrolet used hydraulic riveters and set them completely cold.

So, after a very large amount of research and asking seemingly stupid questions on various forums, this is what actually works!

What You Need

- At least a 4x air chisel/hammer. I used one with a 0.401 hole to accept the readily available rivet setter. If you need to purchase one, get an Ingersol or Chicago Pneumatic. They make chisels for these units that very nicely cut sheet metal, so there are other applications (excuses) for having this around the shop.
- An 11/16-inch rivet setter with the 0.401 shank. This is what does the shaping of the squashed rivet to make it look like factory. They are around $30 each. The one you need for most of the rivets on this frame is the 11/16-inch round head version made for a 3/8-inch rivet. I got mine from Byler Rivet (part number SM50 430-12).
- An oxyacetylene (OA) torch with a #4 medium rosebud (heating) tip. My research told me to get a Victor Setup, not a Victor Style setup. The Victor Performer Edge Medium Duty Kit cost $230 on Amazon and the regulators and everything are excellent quality.
- If you are new to this, you will also need bottles. Your local welding supply can provide them at reasonable cost. Don't play with fire! Get good OA torch equipment because of the fire hazard and possible leakage from inferior tooling.
- You also need 1⅛-inch-long, 3/8-inch shank diameter, round head, steel rivets. I got my rivets from Jay-Cee Rivets (part number S0375R01125). I purchased 100 for about $15 (smallest quantity they sell). For those who are wondering why 1⅛-inch long, I chose to get 100 of the same size and then cut them down to the appropriate length after I got them. The longest application is when you are riveting the front leaf spring mounts together with the rear engine crossmember. The rule for the length you need is 1½ times the shank size sticking out of the hole. So, you have a 3/8-inch rivet, you want the thickness of what you are riveting plus 3/8 inch plus 3/16 inch (half of the 3/8 inch) or, to make a long story short, 9/16 inch sticking out of the hole. This works flawlessly and provides a very factory looking rivet.
- Bucking bars can be made in your shop. Ask a local welder for scraps of 1/2-inch-thick steel. The dimensions can vary, but I used 1½ x 8 inches for most of the job and a 2x10 inch for the rest. Read the rest of this

A 4x air hammer and conical riveting head is shown here.

This acetylene torch setup is needed for heating the rivets.

Re-riveting a Vintage GM Frame (Continued)

procedure before starting so you understand the concept first. You will be clamping this bar in place to hold the rivet, so you will need to drill a 9/16-inch concave into the steel where the rivet will be placed. Put the bar against the hole, mark the hole, then drill the hole. Make the hole *only* deep enough to complete a full circle with the tip of the drill bit. You just need a very slight but complete concavity. Anything more will change the appearance of the rivet head when finished. Another contributor pointed out that the entire rivet head is about 11/16 inch and if you shape that hole a little bigger and a little deeper you won't have as much of a problem with the C-clamps failing. Don't make the hole too deep or the rivet won't tighten down. Also, the reason I chose 1/2-inch steel is because of some of the tight places, but if you can get thicker steel with more mass it will be easier on the clamps.

- Very beefy, very stout large C-clamps are needed for this. The biggest problem you are going to have is keeping that bar in place when hammering, so go overboard and get a few good Bessey welding clamps if you can afford it. Locking plier types will not do, and cheap woodworking clamps won't do. The Bessey 4800S or 7200S are good but very expensive. If they are too pricey, find really good C-clamps and hope for the best.
- A way to cut your rivets, such as a DeWalt Porta-Band with the Swag Offroad Table. I drilled a 3/8-inch hole in a stick that was approximately the thickness of the shortest rivet, then I used washers to adjust the depth.
- A clean hole is very important to the end result. Make sure there is no paint, rust, or crud inside or near the hole. Also, the hole must be perfectly round.

I use homemade bucking bars.

You will need to cut the rivets to size. I accomplished this by finding an appropriate width stick and drilled a hole in it to accept the rivet then ran them through the band saw.

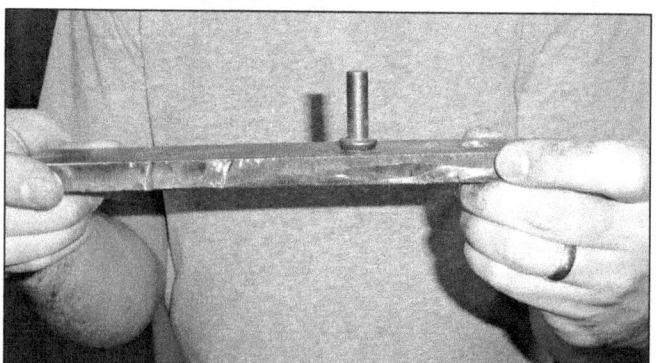

The length of the rivet is important for proper mushroom effect.

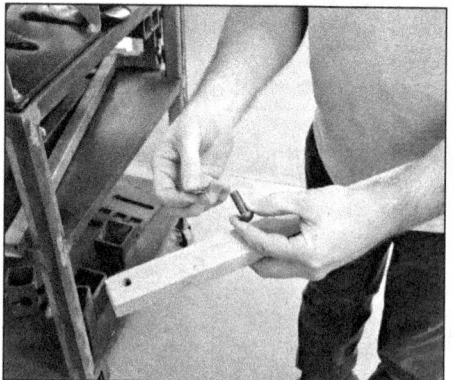

You can use washers with that stick to make a longer rivet. Put the washers on the rivet first, then push the rivet through the hole and cut off the excess.

FRAME REPAIR AND RESTORATION

Replacing the Rivets

Make sure you have a nice fit by placing the rivet in the hole to check that it's not binding or too loose. A 1/32 inch or so looseness is fine. In my case, someone torched the old rivets out and ruined the holes, so I had to go in and weld them shut and redrill them. Don't expect the rivets to be very tight in the hole. The procedure will squash them very nicely to the proper size. For these vintage frames, the 3/8-inch rivet is the most popular.

Place the rivet, cut to the appropriate length as previously mentioned, into the hole. You can grab it with a pair of locking pliers so it will stay there. It should sit with the head in the most inaccessible place pointing outward, so the hammer has the best chance at a straight shot. You can't come at this at an angle at all!

Place the custom bucking bar over the head of the rivet and very securely clamp it in place. The clamps shown are not good enough for this job, but they were all I had. Later, after fighting the problem of them falling off, I went to the heavier-duty clamps. I can't express enough the importance of a good clamp. The hammer hits with such force that what you think is tight enough, probably isn't.

Ensure you have the secured rivet sticking straight out of the hole and not at an angle. Once it is straight and very secure, insert the rivet setter into the air hammer, connect it to a normal (90- to 125-psi) air supply, and pretend you are going to use it to ensure there are no obstacles in your way. You want a totally unobstructed means to hammer the rivet home, and the rivet setter must be totally straight to get a nice rivet head.

Have Help

While one person can do this, it is nice to have two people. The reason being, one person heats the rivet and pulls the torch away, turns it off, etc., while the other hammers the rivet. The heat doesn't last long enough to heat the rivet, then mess around with turning off the torch, setting it down, and picking up the gun and rivet. If you had some sort of torch stand that you could just quickly set it on, maybe one person could do it. Get a friend to help you. It's just safer that way. ■

The head of the rivet needs to be in the location you cannot get to with the air hammer. There are only two possible locations.

If the clamps hold, we are ready to do the job. This was a problem.

While Gene heated the rivet cherry red and focused only on the rivet, I was waiting with the air hammer for him to pull the torch away.

Re-riveting a Vintage GM Frame (Continued)

Once you are sure you can push the rivet straight, fire up the acetylene torch and heat the rivet shank evenly. Go around the diameter a few times and at the base of the rivet with the idea of getting the shaft as hot at the base as possible. I was lucky because my friend Gene was also the town blacksmith and engineer and knew how hot to get the rivets before they melted. They should be glowing red hot and not just a little. If they start to turn white, back off. You need all the heat that rivet can stand.

Apply heat as close to the rivet head and base as possible as well as the entire shaft for best results. By the way, you can't be reading this and doing the procedure at the same time! You simply don't have time! It takes about 10 to 15 seconds to heat the rivet.

Speed is of the essence here. If you are a slow person, get someone else to do this. My friend Gene heated up the rivet while I stood right beside the work with both hands on the rivet gun. The very second he took the torch away, I hammered the rivet down. Be sure to have the rivet gun ready, place the rivet setter very squarely on the top of the red-hot rivet, and pull the trigger while pushing down. Push hard and straight until the rivet setting tool is almost completely against the frame. This takes about 2 seconds. Everything happens really fast!

Admire your work. My first attempt was perfect, and the rivet looked amazing. My second attempt wasn't so pretty, so I had to grind off the rivet head and start all over. This turned out to be very revealing. There is some controversy about this procedure shunting all the heat into the bucking bar, thus making for a less secure rivet. I assure you this isn't the case. On close examination of the cross section, the hole was completely filled, and it took a very large punch and a very big hammer to knock the rivet out of the hole. Due to the properties of steel, heating a rivet, squashing it in the hole, then letting it cool makes for an extra tight fit since steel expands when hot and contracts when cool.

At this point, all that's left is cleaning around the rivet. If there was paint there before, there isn't much left now due to the heat. I used 80-grit sandpaper to prepare the area for primer and new paint. If you aren't going for show quality, a wire brush will do. Whatever paint is left will be suspect, so I used a sharp scraper to remove what was there. What is so cool about re-riveting this way is no one will ever know, and you will feel confident that you did it right! I hope this helps someone and takes away a lot of the mystery. ∎

Once the shaft of the rivet is super red hot, it is time to drive it home.

If you did this right, the rivet looks just like any of the others on the truck and every bit as tight as it did it at the factory. This new rivet cannot be distinguished from any of the other rivets in the truck. In fact, if you really look at your frame rivets, you can see they were in a hurry at the factory.

FRAME REPAIR AND RESTORATION

After the Frame Repairs

With all the frame repairs made, it is time to continue with our philosophy of preservation in restoration and make this frame look like new. This is not as easy as just throwing primer and paint over everything. Over the years, these frames were dented, bent, and abused. On the rotisserie, the damage from large rocks and other debris denting things is clearly seen. We will hammer out what we can, then use sparse amounts of very high-quality filler to make the frame look as perfect as the cab sheet metal will. We do not discriminate between other parts and the frame. Everything gets the same attention to detail.

After performing a lot of work smoothing the metal; filling the minor pits; welding cracks and erroneously placed holes; fixing a myriad of dents, bumps, and wear on the frame, apply the first shot of primer. We do not use etching primer these days; instead, the new preferred way is to use epoxy primer to seal in the filler and protect the metal.

My preference is DPLF40 epoxy primer. It's a PPG mainstay, and I am very happy with it. Just don't forget the very important induction time. See chapter 7 for a full explanation of my painting process.

Now it's time to decide what is next. We will do this very same work to the rear end, front end, and all associated parts.

The way these frames are stamped means they were never as straight as this in the first place. We must be careful not to have filler around bolt holes, where it could chip off later.

The end result is solid, very smooth, and very nice looking. Frames are very hard to paint, so it is a great thing to have this rotisserie.

Sanding Primers

You have seven days to coat DPLF40 epoxy primer with whatever you feel is next because DPLF40 is not a sanding primer. If you are not ready to paint and want to stop that seven-day clock indefinitely, hit the work with K36 high-build urethane primer (another PPG product compatible with this process) the day after you put on the DPLF40. Now, when you are ready, you can sand it smooth to ready it for the sealer and urethane top coat. ∎

That was a long process, but the gratification comes at the end of each step. I couldn't be happier with the way this turned out! For the frame, I used PPG's Single Stage Urethane Topcoat in Gloss Black.

CHAPTER 4

PUTTING A ROLLING CHASSIS BACK TOGETHER

Once the framework is repaired, you may want to move the project around, so let's concentrate on getting it rolling again. To do that, we want to address as much of the drivetrain as possible. There is no better time to make sure all the mechanicals are in perfect order. Once you have sheet metal surrounding the chassis, it gets harder to work with. We will see to it that brakes, engine, transmission, driveline, suspension, wheels, etc. are all dealt with the best we can while everything is easily accessible.

I have a ritual of painting the differential cover the body color of the truck. You will see subtle accents of body color on other parts as well.

Tools and Incidentals

You may or may not need these items; it just depends on how far you go with the rebuild process. I used a three-jaw slide hammer for pulling seals, a telescoping magnet to retrieve parts that fell down into the bottom of things, an impact wrench to get things apart, and brake cleaner for cleaning.

Vendor Research

Research your potential vendors carefully. Ask around and make sure the shops you do business with are reputable and understand the value of time. Now that we are putting things back together, it is an important step toward success to have your vendors vetted and lined up. I will do my best to suggest vendors as we go; however, certain aspects of this will require you to find a local shop. ■

Leaf Springs

In my area, Wichita Spring and Axle Co. does leaf spring work for a living. The company will test old springs, tell you they are not adequate for a frame-up restoration, and make new ones for you. I like this better anyway because all of the springs will be bent the same, so the truck doesn't sit funny when it's all over. New leaf springs are dirty and won't hold paint. Clean them with a pressure washer and wipe them down very carefully with lacquer thinner prior to painting them.

Rear End

Any GM half-ton rear end between 1955 and 1959 are the same with a 3.90:1 gearset. The Bendix drum brakes with the brake line tab is in the correct location. This is the easiest way to go to an open driveline with no penalties. I took mine apart for cleaning and put in new seals and bearings. I have an aversion to doing things twice, so now is the time to address all mechanical

PUTTING A ROLLING CHASSIS BACK TOGETHER

Torque Tube Rear End

It is very important to remember that the 1947–1954 trucks had a torque tube rear end. The spring perch for mounting the springs to the rear end were not in the center of the springs. You *must* have the spring and axle company put the mounting nub and bolt in the very center of the rear springs if you are going to an open driveline. Tell them to use the 1955 template. If you opt for using your original 1950 ones, it is possible to make about a 4 1/2-inch plate with a hole on one end, and a nub about 3 inches farther up the plate as an adapter. The 1955–1959 rear end is a direct bolt-in with that exception. Everything else fits the truck like it belongs there.

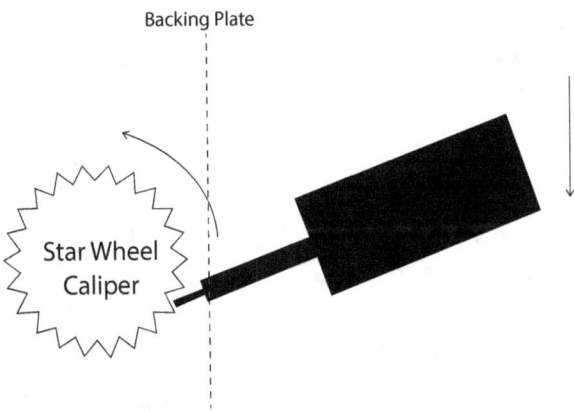

Loosen Brake Shoes
(for Drum Removal)

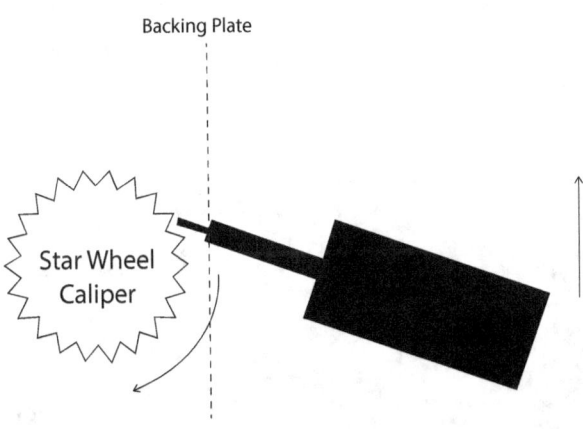

Tighten Brake Shoes

Illustration to show the direction of adjustment for Bendix style brake system (1955–1959 Chevrolet 3100)

I get confused as to which direction to flip the brake spanner, so I made this diagram.

issues; not when your pristine truck is all put together!

With the drums removed so we can get to the axles, it is time to pull the axles out for further inspection. Start by removing the lock bolt from the pin that holds the large block in place. Use a 1/2-inch wrench and remove the special bolt that acts as a pin. Inspect the pin to ensure it is serviceable and set aside.

Remove the large pin that holds the center block in place. It should just fall out if the assembly is rotated properly. Set the pin aside. At this point, you can pull out the steel block that separates the axles. It should just fall out as well.

Push the axles inward until you hear a *tink*, which is the sound of the C-clips falling out of the axles inside the differential. Push in both axles and then use a telescoping magnet tool to probe around for these clips. Pull out the axles carefully, being sure to keep the shafts centered so as to not disturb the very delicate seal at the backing plate.

After the large block is moved out of the way, push the axles as far in as they will go. The C-clips will fall right out.

CHAPTER 4

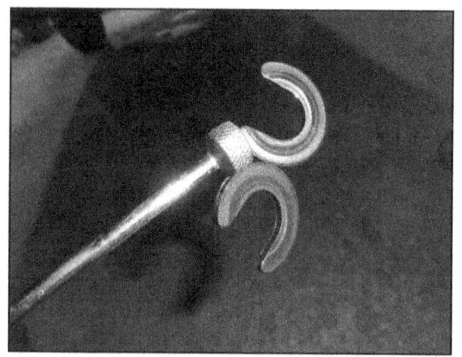

A telescoping magnet is a good thing to have when dealing with fluids. You can get metal shavings out of oil pans or retrieve C-clips on differentials.

Axle Inspection

We haven't inspected any of this yet and there is some inspection to do. First, look at the axle shafts. Clean up the smooth area where the bearings and seals ride on the axle. Check for pits or ridges that could cause seal leakage or bearing damage. If you feel there are ridges and/or pits that could cause seals to not seal properly, use a stainless steel Speedi-Sleeve that goes over that area and makes everything smooth again.

Speedi-Sleeves are not cheap (about $60 each) and they are also not easy to install. The trick is to put the axles in the freezer to get them very cold, then use a long pipe that just barely slips over that axle area to carefully pound the sleeve into place. The option I chose, since my wife does not take kindly to my using her precious freezer for axles, was to take it to a good mechanic who does this routinely and pay to have the Speedi-Sleeves installed.

If there is damage in the bearing area, I recommended replacing the axle.

Axle Housing Inspection

Look around the axle housing for wetness that could be caused by a leaky seal. If the area looks like gear lube has been getting past the seal, replace the seal. To get the old seal out, since it is not reusable, I just pull it out with pliers or jam a screwdriver into it and bend it out, being careful to not disturb the bearings.

With the seal out (or not), let's look at the bearings. Does the bearing race look serviceable? How about each bearing? Does everything spin freely? If there is any doubt, remove the old bearing with a three-jaw slide hammer. Clean the area where the bearings and seals go, then spray some lithium grease in the area to help the new bearings and seals go in smoother.

Clean the axles and ensure the drain hole is clear of dirt and grime. Check the threads on the studs for serviceability and replace them as needed. Brake cleaner spray is a good choice for cleaning these parts.

Remove the pinion nut with an impact wrench and all the nuts around the pumpkin and everything will slide apart. The reason for removing the pinion nut is to inspect the pinion bearings and seal. You may think that going with new everything is a good idea, but that is not necessarily true. There is a stream of really low-quality seals and bearings flooding the market. If you don't see any evidence of leaking and if everything is moving freely, it would be a good idea to leave those parts in place. Besides, rear end repairs later will not be as difficult as it was with the torque tube. If you can find good-quality seals and bearings, replace them all the way around. That is what I ended up doing.

Each axle housing part is scrutinized for any damage or any imperfection and it is dealt with. There

Storing the Differential

In the differential, there are four gears that can fall out if you are not careful at this point. Once the axles are out, I put a block in with the pin to keep everything together. I do not plan on doing any further maintenance to the pumpkin since a visual inspection shows everything looks serviceable. So it will be stored like this until reassembly. ■

The block is shown at the center of the gears. The pin sticking out the bottom locks everything together.

PUTTING A ROLLING CHASSIS BACK TOGETHER

The SuperJig

I am constantly looking for more efficient ways to get things done. So, I made something I call the SuperJig. It was designed to take on these restorations in some very significant ways, allowing for processing doors, fenders, hoods, wheels, etc. throughout the processes from sandblasting to finish paint. You will see it in action throughout this book. To build your own, you can find the plans here: devestechnet.com/Home/SuperJigPlans. ∎

will never be a better time to do this. There is some concern that road gravel and rocks can chip the body filler that is used very sparingly for smoothing purposes, but that is why body filler should never be used for thickness, always very sparingly. I really like Rage Gold Body Filler. It is smooth and applies very easily, drying to a very solid hardness.

The advantage to being so meticulous is the end product will not need any servicing after it is all properly assembled. The time this is taking now will be given back in the simplicity of the installation later. The jig holding the rear end to the SuperJig is merely a few 2x4s with brackets. The rear end is surprisingly lightweight at this point.

Painting Tools and Equipment

When you are ready to paint, the garage needs to be repurposed as a paint booth. After doing a lot of painting over the years, I was able to put this area together with the necessary items for painting. You will need the following.
- A Jenny fan. This 28-inch fan should be placed on the outside wall. It is variable speed and fitted with a filter so we do not foul the fan motor, which is specially made for painting and is sealed.
- HVAC venting. This venting helps maintain a constant

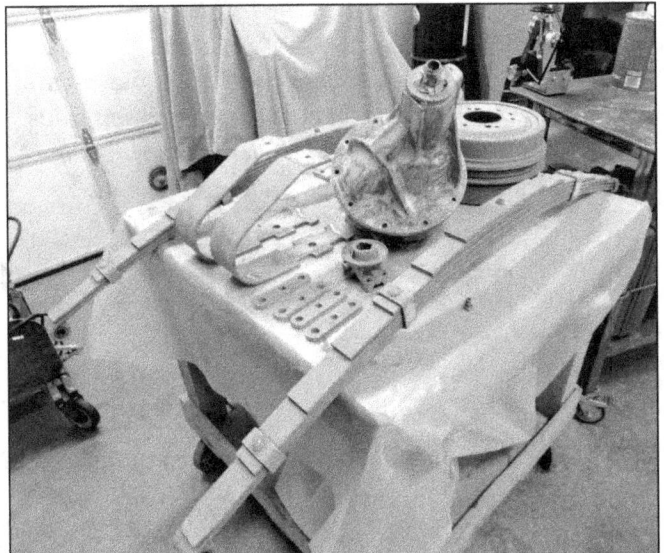

We are going through a lot of trouble to make this truck pristine in every way. This means smoothing imperfections in everything. No exceptions. This batch of parts is ready for DPLF Epoxy Primer then K36 Sandable Primer and Single-Stage Urethane in Gloss Black.

If you are going to fill the primer gun with material, think ahead and prime all of the other parts that you know will need the same treatment. There is seemingly no end to those parts!

Any weld splatter, excessive seam weld, rock dents, rust pitting, or anything that is not perfect gets addressed here. This means a lot of time spent sanding, applying filler, sanding most of it off, and repeating that process.

CHAPTER 4

The outside portion of the kit has louvers that open and close. You have to make your own box with filter channels to mount the fan. When the Jenny comes on, all the doors in the entire building can slam shut from the change in pressure!

Being able to open and close off the large inlet is an energy-saving issue. When open, I can meet any requirements in the paint data sheets.

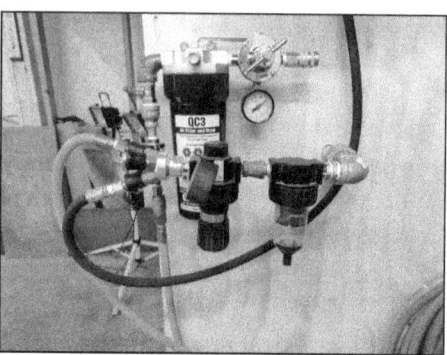

The DeVilbiss QC3 is an economical way to prevent water and debris from getting into your paint. Just be sure to have at least 20 feet of hose or pipeline between the compressor and the QC3.

temperature of my choosing all year around.
- Clean and water-free air lines made possible by using a DeVilbiss QC3 Dessicant Dryer with dual water traps, variable air pressure, and gauges.
- Overhead hooks everywhere to hang parts from.
- Extra sidewall lighting. Using two 8-foot-long fluorescent fixtures adds lots of lighting throughout the space.

This setup allows me to spend a day painting. The air stays clean and clear enough to see through for the entire session. Using box fans under the door just wasn't cutting it!

Having a few 8-foot light fixtures attached to the side walls really helps with more accuracy during painting. Make sure these fixtures can be easily removed and stored away.

Project Build Rear End

In the end, the rear end of my project vehicle was in unknown shape. I had to tear it down and install all new bearings and seals. The axles even required Speedi-Sleeves due to pits in the metal. The pinion needed a sleeve as well. I then put new ARP hardened studs in for an added measure. I don't like things to leak. I used the following parts:

Axle seals	SKF-18695
Axle bearings	MBS C1502
Speedi-Sleeves	SKF-99187
Pinion seal	SKF-17727
Pinion bearings	SKF HM89410 and SKF HM89449
Pinion Speedi-Sleeve	SKF-99170
ARP hardened studs for Ford 9 inches	250-3005
Axle diameter	1.875 (shiny part is 2 inches)

PUTTING A ROLLING CHASSIS BACK TOGETHER

Single-stage urethane paint is leaps and bounds tougher than the old acrylics or lacquers of the past. The paint will really pop for years to come.

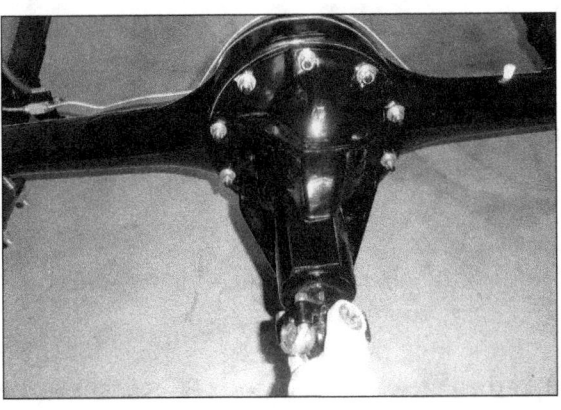

This is why I go to all this trouble. It looks better in person than in the picture!

Brakes, Vents, and Reassembly

Once painting the rear end is accomplished, we can add the brakes, parking brake cables, and the vent and carefully reinstall the pumpkin. All should be installed with stainless steel hardware. Do not overtorque the pinion nut because it was preset with the crush sleeve before disassembly. The brakes are new with all-new springs and wheel cylinders.

I also added speed bleeders to the brake system. These are special bleeder valves with a ball bearing that allows the fluid to flow only one direction, making it very easy to bleed the brakes yourself. I used the 3/8-24 size for this rear end.

Use all-new spring shackles, rubber, new hardened leaf spring perch inserts, and Grade-8 bolts to reassemble everything to the frame. The parking brake cables can even be attached. This was a major milestone! I used the body color to accent the paint scheme in certain places to give this truck a unique look.

Little things that make an impression are the stainless steel hardware, stainless differential cover cap, stainless U-bolts, and those blue Monroe shocks painted body color. All brake lines are stainless as well. This is not just for looks! Stainless will never rust and be around longer than the rest of the truck, which is in keeping with our preservation philosophy.

Front End

The front end will remain its original solid front axle. The original ride is part of what gives these trucks their charm. We will not change that, but we will replace the front drum brakes with front disc brakes. This is a very easy conversion as they go. Everything involved is a direct bolt-on replacement.

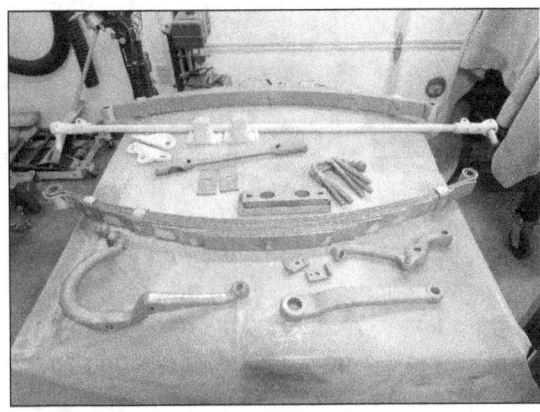

All small parts get super cleaned, smoothed, and sanded. I apply epoxy then high-build primer, do more sanding, and then apply a single-stage urethane top coat.

The new drum brake system on the back will provide plenty of stopping power from the rear.

It is a little-known fact that the overload springs were available as a dealer option in 1950. I am not sure how effective they were, but since I had a set, I wanted to add them in as well.

HOW TO RESTORE YOUR CHEVY TRUCK: 1947–1955

Brake System

The front end gets the same restoration treatment as the rear end and everything else. I replaced the bent tie-rod and added new tie-rod ends. I also purchased kits for the ball joints and checked the king pins. Even after extensive cleaning, there is no play whatsoever in the king pins, so I will leave them as they are.

The front end repairs are more critical because of all the associated systems. The single axle could be bent, which would change the geometry of the steering and disc brakes, so that is checked before paint.

Brakes

To do the brake system right, I researched the available kits and asked around. I ended up purchasing the kit from Brothers Truck Parts. The company was very responsive, even allowing me to change the order a bit. I wanted the rotors drilled and slotted for better cooling and glaze dissipation. They did an excellent job in filling my requests. These parts came from Classic Performance Products originally with used remanufactured calipers from a 1971–1986 C10 truck.

There are a few factors that make this a tricky conversion for first timers. One of them is the original hubs have the brake drums riveted to them. How do we address that? Personally, I do not like destroying vintage parts that are becoming rarer every day. Removing those rivets would mean someone else (or me!) couldn't use them for another truck. So, I opted for brand-new hubs. Brothers calls them 1947–1959 Forged Hub/Roller Bearing Conversion (part number FHA4759).

The next kit needed was the 1947–1959 Deluxe 6-lug Disc Brake Conversion (part number NOFX559). This is the complete kit for converting to front disc brakes. I asked Brothers to drill and slot the rotors when I placed my order. The lug pattern is

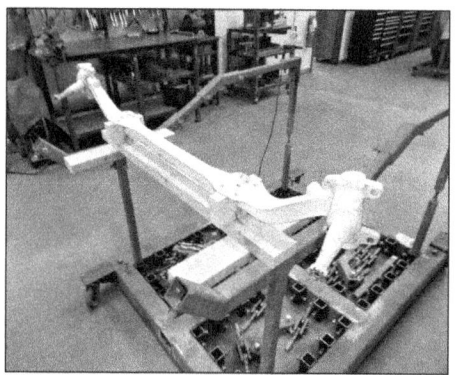

The spindles are taped to preserve the smooth finish. The king pins were checked by a professional mechanic to ensure they didn't need any attention. If you are planning on having a professional inspect yours, now would be the time.

With everything in paint, we can start doing our research on the brake system. It will be a bolt-in replacement for the drum brakes or we will not do it.

Notice the drilled and slotted rotors. This helps with cooling and glaze removal.

I use 30-gauge safety wire and safety wire pliers for making the custom hangers for all the small parts. Batch after batch of these parts were sprayed for the entire truck. No rattle cans were used for painting!

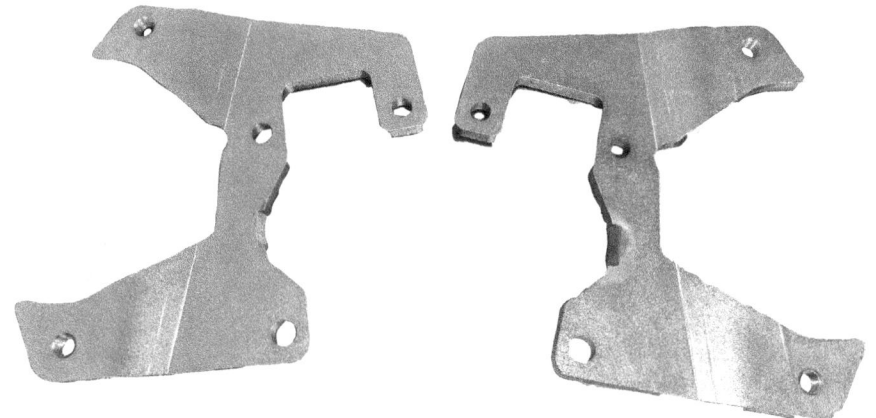

These caliper brackets work perfectly with our front end so it all bolts together easily.

PUTTING A ROLLING CHASSIS BACK TOGETHER

determined by the rear wheels so be sure all four of your lug patterns (five or six) are the same. The brake conversion kit went together perfectly and gets us almost there, but we are not there yet. There is the master cylinder and brake line issue to consider.

For my project vehicle, I am opting for a dual master cylinder. This is to improve safety because the second cylinder will get some braking power as opposed to none should the single cylinder give out. Now is not the time to go cheap, so I purchased more from Brothers Truck Parts. The master cylinder of choice is the 1947–1987 Dual Master Cylinder (part number MSTR900). We then need to adapt that cylinder to our truck, and the 1947–1954 Dual Master Cylinder Bracket (part number DMC5954) will allow us to bolt this new cylinder right up.

But we are not done yet! Due to the difference in pressure between the disc brakes and drum brakes on the back, we will need a proportioning valve (part number VLV4772). I opted to also get the 1947–1959 Prop Valve Under-Mount Kit (part number PVK4759). This allows you to mount the proportioning valve under the master cylinder without problems.

Next, while the Brothers catalog is open, we need two residual valves. These valves are mounted lower than the master cylinder and prop valve to stop the brake fluid from emptying back into the master cylinder when the truck is on an incline, keeping everything working smoothly. You need a 2-pound valve for the front disc brakes and a 10-pound valve for the rear drum brakes (part number RCV7200).

Finally, it occurred to me that I would need to make the hole in the cab floor bigger if I wanted to efficiently top off the brake fluid on a much larger cylinder. So, I purchased a stainless steel door system (part number ACCESS-MC). I also found I needed that 1947–1987 Proportioning Valve Bleed Tool (part number PVBT087).

This is expensive, but it finally allows us to have a truck that stops with the safety and reliability of more modern trucks. I could have added a power brake assist unit as well but decided against it. There were two reasons I decided against it: I wasn't certain it was needed since I have never tried this braking system and I did not want to hack up a riveted crossmember before that question was answered.

There will be a few more considerations. The original brake lines are not configured appropriately for this disc/drum system, so we will make our own stainless steel brake lines using 5/16 stainless. This is where our BrakeQuip Tools will come in very handy. Since the rubber lines with Banjo bolts come with the disc system, we only have to concern ourselves with creating new hard lines. (If the Banjo bolts do not seem to have long enough threads for you, I found longer ones (10x1.5mm [15/16 inch]) at WFO Concepts (part number 494703).

The dual master cylinder with bracket assembly bolts right up without any interference issues.

This shot should help with how to connect everything. The instructions only give you clues. Take your time and it will all come together!

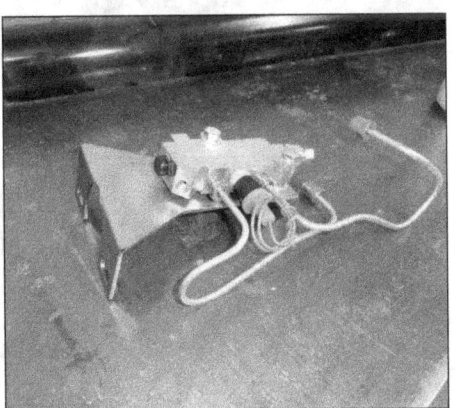

The proportioning valve comes with the bracket to mount it to the underside of the master cylinder bracket. This model comes with a brake light sensor, although I have no plans to use it.

With the accompanying original-style 1950 hubcap that is made for this wheel, nobody will know they are not original.

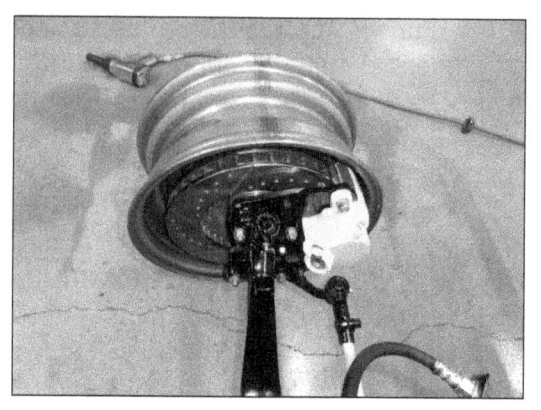

As you can see, the caliper rides very close to the wheel. The original rims will not provide enough clearance.

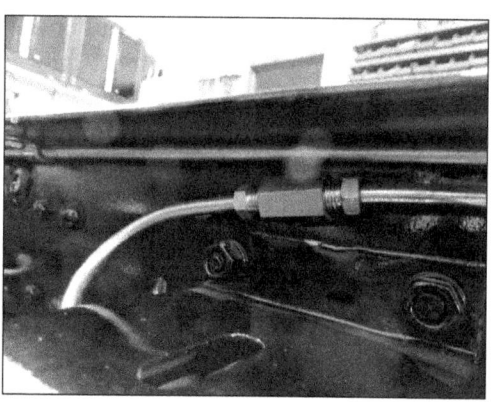

This is the rear line turn to the rear mid crossmember. Rather than using a super long line, I added a connector here, which makes it easier to make that turn.

Brake Lines

I do not know of anyone who makes brake lines for this custom setup, so I made my own. To do the same, you will need a BrakeQuip BQ-351 brake line flaring system, a good bender such as the BQ-613, a good tube straightener (so you can purchase 20-foot rolls cheaper) such as the BQ1028, and a good tubing cutter such as the BQ-602. You will need 5/16-inch tubing and the flare nuts to go with them and the original brass tee connections that came on the truck. I also used some 3/16-inch tube at the proportioning valve. Also, keep in mind we have fuel lines, a vacuum advance line, and PCV lines to do yet. I get my stainless tubing in 20-foot rolls at Summit Racing.

Planning the New Route

The brake line system does not follow the original path to the master cylinder; instead, the "circuits" are separated between front and back. One cylinder of the master cylinder is devoted strictly to the rear (drum) circuit and the other cylinder of the master cylinder is devoted strictly to the front (disc) brakes. I put the two residual valves (the 2-pound front one and the 10-pound rear one) on the crossmember lower than the master cylinder so all the modifications start at the passenger-side frame rail at the mid crossmember.

Instead of teeing the front and back together, the tee is capped at the forward junction and a new line from the master cylinder to the front circuit will be created. The lines will be fastened to the frame with rubberized frame rail clamps.

It's nice that the front and rear circuits are separated because if brake fluid gets low on the front cylinder of the master cylinder but not the back, you will know the front is leaking. In other words, it's easier to isolate the leak.

The brake lines are a breeze to build with the BrakeQuip tools. We can make precise bends and really do a professional job. Remember to measure twice and cut once!

The rear lines are very straightforward and run about the same as original. Where it differs is in the middle of the crossmember. To get from the passenger's side to the driver's side, a 10-pound residual valve is placed in the line. The next segment goes to the proportioning valve.

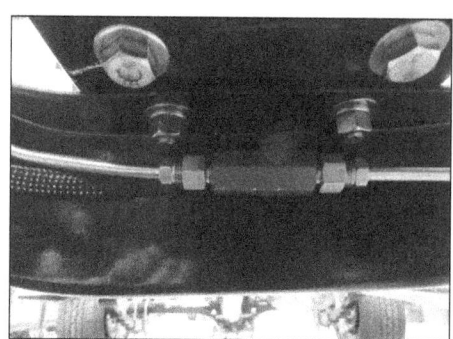

Shown is just after the rear line turn at the bottom of the center of the crossmember. The 10-pound residual valve is placed at the lowest point.

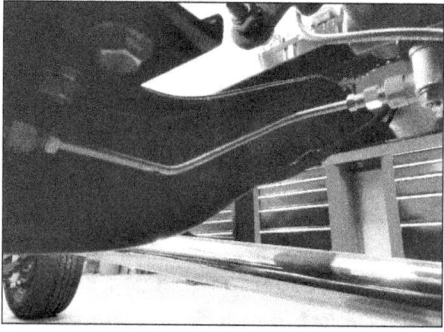

The rear circuit after the residual valve is highlighted here. The brake line continues to the proportioning valve at its end port.

The proportioning valve has two connections to the two circuits. Left is the rear circuit and upper left is the front circuit.

PUTTING A ROLLING CHASSIS BACK TOGETHER

The front circuit leaves the proportioning valve and loops around to the front mid crossmember and over to the passenger's side.

This line goes from the front residual valve to the original tee connection, which is capped off where the rear lines previously met. The line then goes to the other original tee at the passenger-side wheel.

A brake line is routed under the harmonic balancer over to the driver-side wheel, as it was in the original brake line configuration.

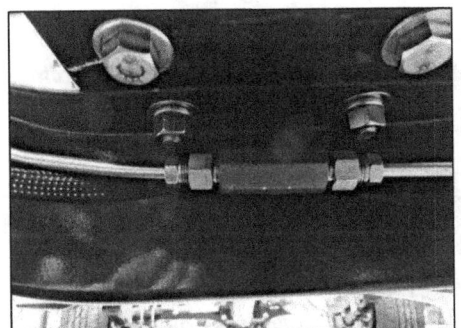

After it leaves the proportioning valve, the 2-pound residual valve is placed at the lowest point on the crossmember.

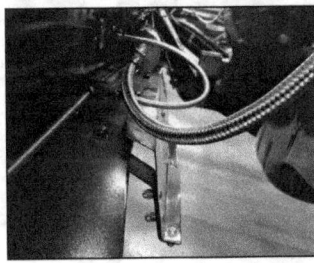

It is hard to see here, but the second tee is used to add the line for the driver-side wheel. The line coming forward is for the driver's side.

The hard line is clipped to the soft line on the driver's side, which is the same as the original.

The front lines are routed similar to the rear; the last place to get fluid is the driver-side wheel. Again, a 2-pound residual valve is placed under the front mid crossmember at its lowest point and then routed to the first original brass tee.

Since there is no rear circuit joining there, it is capped off in the rear port. The line then proceeds to the second original brass tee just inside the frame adjacent to the passenger-side wheel. The other side of the tee goes to the driver's side, which is routed just under the harmonic balancer in the recess of the front crossmember.

After assembling everything, I have no sense of humor about what regular DOT 3 brake fluid does to my precious paint job. So, the alternative is DOT 5 silicon brake fluid.

There are pros and cons; however, the pros outweigh the cons in my opinion. They say DOT 5 rots the 1980s-style rubber seals in the proportioning valve. We will find out over time. I can replace several thousand proportioning valve seals for the same price as repairing the paint! So far, the system is very tight and works perfectly with no leaks.

TECH TIP: Bench Bleeding Tubes

With all those fancy new brake line tools, make yourself a few master cylinder bench bleeding tubes. They allow you to pre-prime the lower fluid reservoir. There are lots of YouTube videos on bench bleeding your master cylinder. ■

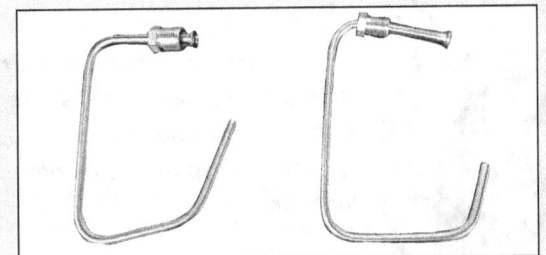

I used 5/16-inch brake line tubing to make bench bleeding tubes. Keep these handy for future master cylinder maintenance.

HOW TO RESTORE YOUR CHEVY TRUCK: 1947–1955

Wheels

Chances are very good that the original wheels will not work with this conversion because they were made before front disc brakes were ever an option. The caliper needs room to work. I didn't regard this as a deal breaker because Wheelsmith makes a wheel very close to the original called the Smoothie that gives us the original look. The company even provides original hubcaps that fit its wheels!

Since the goal is to get this frame on wheels, I opted for 15-inch rims and a special tire (Firestone Destination P225/70R15). The reasoning for this combination is to lower the truck without the truck looking lower than normal. By going to a lower profile and 15-inch rims, the tires look normal, but I get a 2-inch-lower truck without weakening the suspension. With good modern radial tires and front disc brakes, I feel I have the bases covered.

Bumpers

Lastly for the frame, you will need a bumper. With the trailer hitch on and all four bumper brackets taken through the restoration process and ready for the bumper, get shiny new polished stainless steel bumpers for the front and the rear. I cannot tell the difference between a stainless bumper and chrome. But I would be able to tell with chrome in a few years because it begins to bubble from rust!

The SuperJig is shown here in action. The wheels sit on a lazy Susan bearing system, so they spin easily for more precise painting.

Gloss Black urethane and those new original-style hubcaps will make the wheels pop.

This wheel/tire combination lowers the truck 2 inches or more from its original stance (16-inch rims on bias ply tires) by using 15-inch rims and lower profile radial tires. This is tasteful lowering, not outrageous lowering. We have taken nothing away from the utilitarian nature of the truck.

Making a Tow Hitch System for Your Half-Ton Advance Design Truck

Now is the best time to address the idea of a tow hitch. A pickup is just not a pickup without a tow hitch! This design provides additional frame support, better spare tire carrier control (no J-hook slopping around), and very solid anchoring.

Materials List

These bits of metal can be obtained used or new. I get most of my metal from a large metal reclamation yard. It is cheaper, and if you choose wisely, it looks like new. Whenever picking reclaimed metal, be sure to go with thicker stock rather than thinner. Especially for something like a trailer hitch.

- 3-inch square tubing with 3/16-inch walls: 30 inches
- 2½-inch square tubing with 3/16-inch walls: 6 inches
- 2-inch square tubing with 3/16-inch walls: 49 inches
- 1/4-inch plate 5x7½ inches
- 1/4-inch plate 1½x10 inches

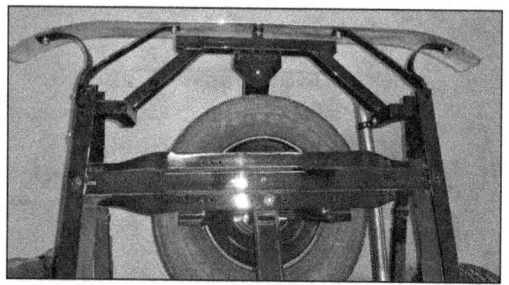

To make a hitch for this truck, a little thinking is in order. For superior strength, we should tie the two rear frame rails together. We should not interfere with the original spare tire carrier. In this case, we made it more stable by eliminating that sloppy J-hook. This is the done deal. It has no effect on the spare tire carrier accessibility and adds a lot of stability in the rear.

Making a Tow Hitch System for Your Half-Ton Advance Design Truck (Continued)

Getting Started

Begin by cutting two pieces of 3-inch square tubing to be 7 inches long. Lay the square tubing inside the frame so they are flush with the frame ending. With a permanent marker, mark the frame rail's contour on the tubing. The top is about 2 inches, but the bottom bevels out farther. Without moving the piece, also mark the holes carefully, including any holes needed for wiring.

With your favorite cutting tool, cut the 3x7 tubing along the cut line. I use a Makita 4-inch grinder with thin cutting wheel. Do this on both sides since they are opposite each other.

Making the Cuts

Use your favorite saw for cutting thick metal tubing (I use a Makita 12-inch dry cut saw) to cut two of the 2-inch square tubing. The overall length is 5¼ inches with one end cut straight and the other cut at a 45-degree angle. We are cutting the piece protruding inward toward the center of the frame. This means the top dimensions is 5¼ inches and the bottom is 3¼ inches.

This piece isn't finished yet. We want to remove the bottom "floor" of that particular piece so it fits into the channel. This effectively drops the piece 3/16 inch. Put the piece where it's going to go, then mark the bottom of the piece with a permanent maker. Cut out the bottom of the piece so that it fits perfectly into the channel. Do this on both sides.

We start with two 3-inch channels (by 7 inches) that fits inside the frame rails. We go on the inside because the bumper brackets go on the outside. One of the challenges in doing this is that not all 1947–1955 pickups measure the same from frame rail to frame rail. The correct number is 45¾ inches inside measurement for half tons.

We have to be sure to leave room for the bumper brackets and the wire grommet for the taillights.

All angles are 45 degrees. Be sure to confine the welds between the holes so there is no interference with nuts, grommets, etc.

When I talk about the channel's floor, notice how the first piece is notched out (near the nut) to share the space with the bottom of the 3-inch frame channel.

Making a Tow Hitch System for Your Half-Ton Advance Design Truck *(Continued)*

On the outside of where this piece goes is a rubber grommet that is used to feed wires through for the taillights. Make that hole bigger on your piece so the grommet will seat inside the hole properly. I drilled mine out to 5/8 inch. Also, drill the two 1/2-inch holes for attaching the bumper brackets. Be precise so you aren't elongating holes, then check the fit to make sure that piece bolts in nicely. You are on your way!

Measure Twice, Cut Once!

Next, cut the pieces that hang downward. These are also cut with one end straight and the other at a 45-degree angle. The dimensions are 6½ inches on the outside and 4½ inches on the inside. Remember to cut two of them, just like before.

Next, we will cut the two that connect to this drop-down assembly. This one measures 12¾ inches on the inside and out, but it's not 12¾ overall. Both ends have 45-degree angles on this one, but both angles go the same way. They also do not perfectly match up on the outside. Take your straightedge and mark that jog with a marker and cut it off. You can then take a piece of some of your cutoffs to cap it off. If both length measurements are 12¾ inches, then you did it right.

Now for the tricky part. It's very important when welding these pieces together that they remain perfectly straight and true so that both sides come together properly. To accomplish this, weld one piece at a time, making sure to square things up as you go. The first piece that protrudes from the frame, inside that 3-inch channel, rests on the bottom of that channel. Set that piece into your little channel piece so that it is 1½ inches away from the front. Mark that, then put a nut and bolt together inside the hole to make sure you can still get a socket on the nut once it's welded. Allow for weld in that area.

I really like my 90-degree welding magnets for this; however you do it, weld it level and square. To prepare for welding, you will need to grind a rounded edge into the bottom so that it fits the contour of the 3-inch channel properly. Take your time.

The Level Is Your Friend!

Weld both sides this way, being careful that both sides measure the same. Bolt the assembly to the frame. If you want it to slide in and out without a hammer, put a washer in

The shop gets dusty fast; it is one of the trade-offs you deal with in a busy shop! This solution is invisible once the truck is back together except for the hitch sticking down below the bumper.

The trick is to keep everything level and straight so when the two sides meet in the center, nothing is cockeyed!

each hole between the frame and the assembly (on one side only) to shorten the hitch for easier removal and installation.

When taking a floor measurement, make sure the truck is sitting on flat concrete. Since the leaf springs could be tensioned differently, *do not* assume your measurements will be the same on both sides. Measure from the top of the frame rail to the floor on each. Record those numbers. If one side is less than the other, jack up the truck on one side until the numbers are the same. Once this first piece

Making a Tow Hitch System for Your Half-Ton Advance Design Truck (Continued)

is welded, measure the end of that to the floor, making sure both sides are identical. Use a level to verify this piece is level with the ground as well as square to the inside. Once you have that welded properly, you are ready for the downward piece.

The downward piece should be just as level all the way around. Measure the bottom of each one after it's tacked to make sure they both measure the same from the floor. I use a grinder to bevel the edges of the angles to be welded for deeper penetration. This is a hitch we are talking about, so good penetration is essential. I even used multi-pass welding techniques for added strength on this project.

Next, prepare the 12¾-inch piece for welding. Remember a good level is your friend here. Weld this piece by butting up the bottom of the downward piece flush with the 12¾-inch angled piece. Tack it in place and measure from the floor to the outward end on both sides carefully. It should be perfectly level across. This particular piece must be level so that it follows the bumper. We will not install the cross piece just yet.

For our next feat of amazement, we will cut a piece of 2-inch square tubing to 24½ inches for our crosspiece. This piece will sit about flush with the bottom of the bumper if you did everything above right. Don't panic if it's just a little low, but it should be very close to flush. There is a lot to accomplish with this piece before we weld it in.

Set this piece on a flat table and cut a piece of 1/4-inch plate steel that is 5x7½ inches. This will serve as our spare tire carrier mounting surface. As shown, round the edges so that the 5-inch dimension bevels down to 2 inches. Mark the center of this plate left to right (3¾ inches) then mark it 3 inches in from the non-beveled side. This is for drilling a 1/2-inch hole for a bolt to secure the spare tire carrier. Drill the 1/2-inch hole then secure a bolt with a weld nut through it to hold the weld nut in place. Weld in the nut on the top side.

Because this piece will have a lot of stress on it due to its association with the spare tire carrier, cut four 1½-inch triangles for supporting this piece. With the entire assembly in the very center of the 24½-inch crosspiece, and both it and the 1/4x5x7½-inch piece sitting flat on the table, butt them together and tack them as flat and as straight as possible. Turn it over and finish the welds, making sure not to warp them. Then, install the triangles for further support. Grind the bottom weld so that everything is flush underneath.

Adding this plate with the gussets makes a very strong place for the spare tire carrier to bolt to. No more J-hook dangling from the bed supports!

The hitch does not interfere with the bumper system, but it sure makes the rear end of this truck stronger.

Make a 1½x4-inch strip out of your remaining 1/4-inch material. This piece will have a 90-degree bend at 2 inches. It will need to be contoured to match the profile of your bumper and drilled in the appropriate place for the bumper bolt. This isn't just decorative, this is part of the support system. The beauty of this hitch design is it uses the bumper, bumper brackets, and spare tire carrier to enhance its strength and rigidity. When you are finished, it will all be a part of the hitch system. Find an anvil, or something to

Making a Tow Hitch System for Your Half-Ton Advance Design Truck (Continued)

beat that contour into that strip in the right place, then set it aside for now. We do not yet know exactly where the hole will be or how far forward to place the strip, so save drilling and welding for later.

Cut a piece of 2½-inch square tubing to be 5 inches long for the receiver. To beef up this piece to meet applicable standards, cut a 1-inch piece of 3-inch square tubing and weld it in place around the 2½-inch piece. Now go to Harbor Freight, Northern Tool, or your favorite trailer supply and get the receiver part with the ball on it. It will have a hole left to right for a large pin that will secure the hitch. Put it in place and measure for drilling the hole in your 2½-inch piece. Be sure to get a receiver that is not too long that it protrudes into your spare tire carrier bolt territory. Once you have everything accounted for, holes drilled, etc., weld the receiver to your crosspiece in the very center.

Now take the entire crosspiece assembly and fit it for welding. Clamp it into place where it is in the very center and matching everything. If everything has gone as planned, it will be almost flush with the bottom of the bumper and will not be touching anything it's not supposed to. Put that 90-degree strip with the bumper contour in place and push it against the bumper. Clamp it in place tightly and mark the hole for drilling. Take the cross assembly off and weld that piece in, then drill the 1/2-inch hole. Remember you must get a nut back there for the bumper bolt. It will be very close.

Final Welds

If everything goes as planned, the final piece will look like it belongs there. Now, put your cross assembly back on and bolt the bumper to it. Tack weld the cross assembly in place, being sure to bevel the welds, clean off the mill scale, and do multiple passes to ensure you have a hitch that will outlast the truck.

Remove the entire hitch assembly as a whole and take out those washers you put between the channel and the frame rail. Reinstall everything. The last small order of business is relocating the exhaust pipe a little. To do this, I drilled a hole in the assembly and attached a new bracket. Lastly, once the hitch was painted with automotive epoxy primer and Gloss Black urethane paint, I put plastic caps in the ends. They look nice and keep the moisture out. ∎

Get a hitch receiver from your favorite trailer hitch supplier. I went to Harbor Freight. Measure the receiver hole for the distance to the hitch pin. This will help you decide where to make that hole.

The spare tire carrier will be dropped down from now on with a 3/4-inch socket. (You could always use a bolt with the proper head for your lug wrench).

This hitch turned out better than I expected. The exhaust system needed to be mounted and my hitch was in just the right place!

CHAPTER 5

The Engine

I will start this chapter by plugging a must-read that will help you to better understand the engine part of this restoration. I wrote a book called *Chevrolet Inline-6 Engine: How to Rebuild* (SA455) that goes into fine detail about these Stovebolt engines. The book should answer all your questions concerning everything about the Chevrolet 6-cylinder for this vintage.

I opted to install a 1964 (replacement block) 261 engine in this truck. I chose the 1958–1962 261 for a few good reasons. In 1958, Chevrolet introduced its first engine that was natively full-flow oiling. Prior to 1958 or if you have a 235, only about 12 percent of the oil is filtered through the canister oil filter. (I have always wondered which 12 percent.) General Motors decided that full-flow oiling allowed for cleaner and longer lasting engines. Since 1958, all GM engines are full-flow oilers. This is why I recommend 1954–1962 235 or 1954–1957 261 owners to get their machine shop to modify the engine at rebuild time. The 1958–1962 261 does not need any modification. It has a dowel pin that acts as a switch for either bypass or full-flow operation.

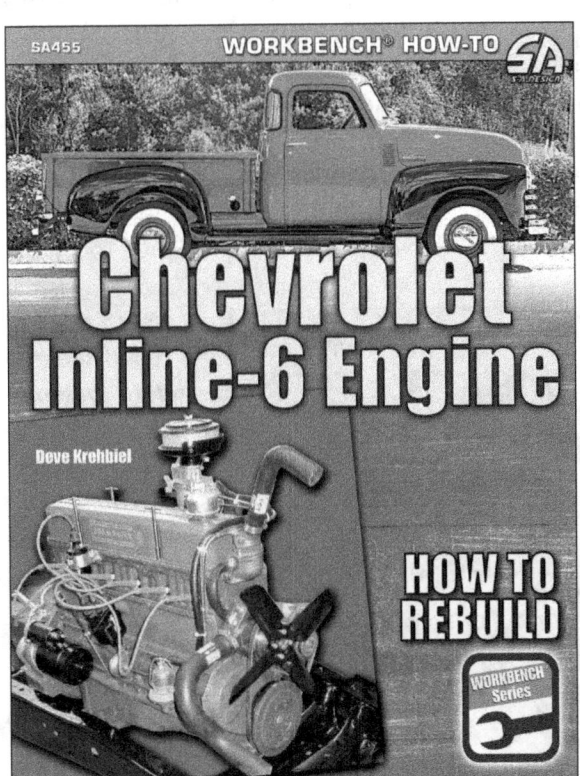

Check out the book Chevrolet Inline-6 Engine: How to Rebuild. *It is your one-stop shop for complete teardown, examination, and rebuilding information for the 1954–1962 Stovebolt engine.*

This is the best combination of engine block and head in the Stovebolt era: a 1958–1962 261 with an 848 Head.

CHAPTER 5

The 261 is shown here during its post–machine shop runup. With hydraulic lifters, it's a very smooth-running engine.

Here is another 1950 project that is 100-percent stock. This one features the 216 engine.

The 1950 216 engine that was original to this truck was a babbit bearing engine and thus very expensive to rebuild if you can find anyone to do it at all. The art of pouring babbit into forms then align boring is an almost dead art, and it's very hard to get your 216 rebuilt properly. The next generation 235/261 has insert bearings and bolts right into the truck, so an engine upgrade is highly recommended.

Engine Improvements

Since our engine has full-flow oiling, we are adding a spin-on adapter for easier and cleaner oil changes. We are also doing a whole lot more! Just by changing from the 98-hp 216 to the stock 148-hp 261, we will see performance changes, but we are not going to stop there.

Don't get too excited. We are not going with dual exhaust and dual carbs because the performance advantage is minimal due to the design of the head. The air intake is restricted by valve diameter, chamber volume, etc., so there is no benefit to adding more air/fuel in or out of the engine. They look cool, but they are not worth all the regular maintenance of adjusting dual carbs or the problems associated with dual exhaust getting in the way of crossmembers, shifter rerouting, etc. I admire the guys who love to play with that setup though!

Positive Crankcase Ventilation

I have more subtle improvements in mind that will increase performance and add longevity to that expensive engine rebuild. I am starting with adding positive crankcase ventilation (PCV). PCV was first introduced by General Motors with the 1954 261 engines in larger trucks. These original PCV systems are very rare because they were only offered on large trucks that chugged up slopes with heavy loads at low speeds. Little did they know that all GM engines would have it starting in 1962. This is because crankcase gases are responsible for a great deal of sludge buildup in the engine.

Chevy used a road draft tube on the old Stovebolts to attempt to fix this issue. The road draft tube has a beveled end that is shaped to invoke

The spin-on filter is more reminiscent of modern systems and will make oil changes much easier. Thanks to Chevy putting motor mounts on the side of the engine that we do not need for our pickups, we have a nice place to mount the adapter!

THE ENGINE

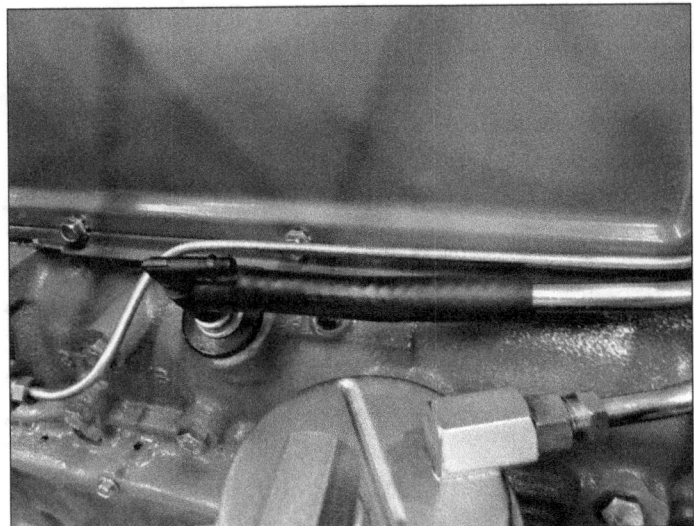

The V-237 valve with a 3/8-inch stainless line to the intake manifold on the other side coupled with a vent-type breather cap on the valve cover makes for a great PCV solution.

Under this voltage regulator cover is the high energy ignition (HEI) module. The coil is a high-performance MSD 8202 45,000-volt model. This combination makes for a wonderful alternative to a stock ignition system.

the Venturi effect. At speeds of 30 mph or more, the road draft tube pulls crankcase gases out of the lower engine. The problem with that is, you must be doing 30 mph or more for the engine to get any benefit. To resolve this issue once and for all, all that is needed is a few fittings, some PCV hose, and a PCV valve.

High Energy Ignition

Another upgrade that is very exciting is installing a high energy ignition (HEI) using the stock distributor! This is an amazing upgrade that makes the engine run at its best all the time with no need for points. What's so innovative about this offering is that it uses the stock distributor so there is no large, out-of-place-looking distributor mucking up the underhood vibe!

High-Compression Head

The engine I am installing has the preferred 848 high-compression head. It was the standard head that many 235s of that era came with, but its compression numbers are better than the other two heads that were offered. Since this is a 261, we must drill six holes for water cooling, but we have the best combination possible.

Exhaust System and Air Cleaner

We will add a stainless steel exhaust system as well. This is for longevity more than it is for looks. We will also use an air type of air cleaner on top of the Rochester B carb. General Motors came out with two stock air cleaner types, but they touted the oil-bath air cleaner as better, so they sold many more of those. This makes a good air type from 1950 rather hard to find. If you find one, you can use a standard air filter (Napa part number 2373) for the element. No more oil sloshing over the top of your precious engine!

When we refer to an 848 head, we are referring to the last three digits of the head's casting number, which can be viewed without removing the valve cover on the driver's side.

CHAPTER 5

The original filter was brass mesh. They are still available, but the more modern, pleated filter is easier, and I do not feel it takes that much away from the appearance. This one was original in 1950.

Hydraulic Lifters

Another upgrade, though controversial, is using hydraulic lifters. I had the 261 specifically machined to accept hydraulics. I like quiet engines, and if you have a hydraulic 235, you can relate to what I am talking about. In addition to the quiet, it is also much easier to adjust the valves. The engine runs so nicely! The controversial part is that it is said by some that hydraulic lifters rob the engine of horsepower. I have not noticed this; instead, I notice how quiet and nice the engine runs at all speeds. Even at top speed, this engine smoothly handles it.

Fuel System Upgrade

A few years ago, I designed a fuel system upgrade that I am also incorporating. I am augmenting my mechanical fuel pump with an electric backup. In addition, I created an electronic circuit that automatically primes the carburetor for instant starting. You know how after the truck has been sitting awhile it takes longer to start because the carb's fuel bowl is starved, and it takes a while to fill the bowl? This eliminates that problem by running the electric pump for 10 seconds prior to start-up.

Cooling System and Related Issues

It is also a must to talk about the cooling system. Your original radiator may be good, but it is still a two-row, single-core radiator from 1950. It will work nicely if you do not run at high speed in midsummer, but what if you wish to add air-conditioning at some point? It turns out that US Radiator makes a nice original replica of the 1950 pickup radiator that has four rows and two cores and is a great upgrade.

The replica radiator uses late 1980s/early 1990s vintage technology. It will cool substantially better than the original and allow you to add air-conditioning without worry. For about $600 you can have one shipped to you.

I decided on the 261 engine and a better radiator, so I also need to be thinking about driving the AC. The single-belt harmonic balancer may not be the best choice for this. There are options that allow you to use the single-belt harmonic balancer,

My backup system uses an electric pump with a glass filter that is mounted to the frame rail. Then, soft hose connects the electric pump to the mechanical pump, which augments the mechanical and acts as a redundant system.

The original 1950 radiator (left) is shown with the new four-row, dual-core radiator available from US Radiator (right).

THE ENGINE

This Chevy small-block harmonic balancer was machined for the 261 with the addition of a dual pulley cover. The jury is still out, but it was a cost-effective solution.

Another rare option is to use a dual pulley that was found on larger trucks. It just bolts to the original harmonic balancer. But good luck finding one!

but they are either astronomically expensive or kind of poor in performance. Instead, a dual-belt harmonic balancer is an option.

Vintage Air sells a dual-pulley harmonic balancer for about $450. Another option is to get a small-block Chevy balancer and have it machined to accept your crankshaft/seal setup, then add a dual-pulley cover that bolts in three places to the balancer. A third option is to find a very rare antique large truck balancer with a second pulley that bolts to it. The machine shop had no qualms about charging me $50 to machine a small-block Chevy balancer and selling me a $20 dual-pulley cover that bolts to it. I am skeptical about its ability to run true at high speeds due to the three bolts that do not attempt to self-center. The jury is out until we take this machine out on the road and give it time.

To get this 261 into the truck properly, a short-shaft water pump is needed, but I still have an issue. The original 216 had the water pump mounted in the exact center of the radiator. The 1955–1962 235/261 engines have the water pump located about 3 inches lower. This means your fan is not cooling at its best. To resolve this issue, install a Dave Folsom Water Pump Adapter Plate and then go with the recommended 1953 water pump. You will also need a 216 fan due to the bolt pattern on the water pump.

All trucks prior to 1954 have the water pump mounted high. This is to put the fan in the center of the tall radiators of the time (look at the space between the pump and thermostat housing).

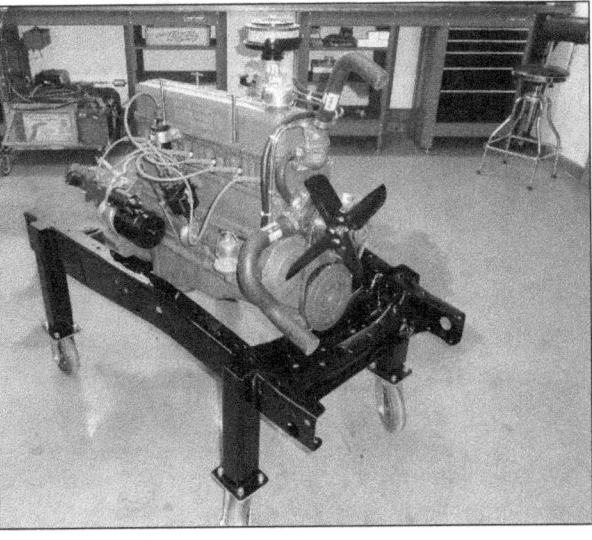
The 1955–1962 235/261 engines have the water pump mounted 2 1/2 inches lower because the radiators were not as tall those years. A Dave Folsom Water Pump Adapter Plate and a 1953 pump with a 216 fan combination resolves this issue.

CHAPTER 6

Transmission and Drivetrain

The Saginaw SM318 was GM's go-to 3-speed transmission available from 1955 through 1969. It was a very reliable and solid transmission. BorgWarner introduced the R10 in the 1950s for the higher-end cars and a whole host of auto manufacturers, including Ford, Packard, Willys, Rambler, Studebaker, and General Motors.

General Motors accommodated by making the SM319 so the R10 could be a bolt-in upgrade. The main difference between the mass-produced SM318 and the SM319 was the addition of four bolts for bolting on the R10 Overdrive tail assembly.

For a half-ton pickup, the BorgWarner R10/SM319 transmission is a great solution because it bolts right on the bellhousing and fits perfectly. The BorgWarner R10 Overdrive gives basically six speeds and really extends the speed range. By using the R10 as intended with a kickdown switch on the carburetor (GM style) and the electric solenoid to engage the Overdrive at speeds above 30 mph, I have an amazing solution for my project pickup.

BorgWarner R10 Overdrive

The R10 overdrive system is comprised of an electrical control circuit that consists of a centrifugally operated switch, a relay, a kickdown switch, and the overdrive solenoid. With the control lever inside the truck in the overdrive position (pushed *in*), overdrive is automatically selected when the truck's speed exceeds about 30 mph. At this speed, the centrifugal switch closes and overdrive engages if the driver momentarily lifts a foot from the accelerator pedal. At speeds below 30 mph, the transmission will revert to direct drive. However, because the sun gear was not locked to the planet carrier, the transmission will "freewheel" on the overrun clutch.

The SM319 Saginaw transmission with the BorgWarner R10 Overdrive unit as the tail assembly as a bolt-in upgrade is shown here.

TRANSMISSION AND DRIVETRAIN

The Freewheel Effect

The freewheel effect means that when the vehicle is just sitting there, parked and turned off, the transmission will not be in gear the way you would expect. When putting it in first, second, or third gear, the vehicle will roll as if the clutch is pushed in. This is perfectly normal. A good habit for overdrive-equipped trucks is to put the vehicle in reverse when parking. Doing so will lock the transmission in both directions. The only way to get around this is to pull the overdrive handle completely out every time you park. ■

If engine braking or reverse gear is required, the control lever has to be moved to the direct drive position (pulled *out*). Another feature of this overdrive was that if direct drive is required for acceleration or overtaking while in overdrive, the accelerator pedal could be pushed all the way down to operate a kickdown switch in the solenoid circuit and give direct drive. When the kickdown was used, the ignition was momentarily cut to take the load off the locking pawl and to allow it to disengage.

BorgWarner first introduced Overdrive in 1934, so this is proven technology. The last production car to have a BorgWarner Overdrive was an AMC in 1974, when the technology was discontinued in favor of concentrating on automatic technology. My late great friend John Erb drove his 1951 half-ton Chevy from Hesston, Kansas, to Anchorage, Alaska, and back with a 261 engine and an R10 Overdrive. I really enjoyed driving his truck. I was sold after that!

The only drawback to having one of these transmissions is you really need to have two of them. The R10 is very difficult to come by, and if you do not have replacement parts, chances are you won't find them. This is indeed a very rare transmission. There are a few vendors who sell some of the parts, but the most important wear items, such as the planetary gear system, are nearly impossible to find.

That said, if you are planning a full restoration, the way to approach this in today's world is to adapt a Tremec T5 5-speed with Overdrive from the late 1980s so it has the mechanical speedometer gear system. There is a lot of material on the internet that covers how to do this. If you can get a T5 from an Astro Van, that is said to have the gearshift closest to the original 4-speed location on Advance Design trucks. The T5 requires an adapter plate for bolting up to the bellhousing and possibly a shaft length adjustment, but it is a very good choice for highway speeds.

My friend John Erb also helped me rebuild my SM319/R10 unit. We spent a few days working together on this, and it is time I will never forget. In his honor, this truck will have this combination in it!

Driveshaft

When putting together a custom driveline, the driveshaft is really the last thing to look at. The engine, transmission, and differential should be solidly bolted to the frame so you can take measurements for a custom driveshaft. I removed the driveshaft from a 1962 Suburban and took it to a local speed shop that chopped it for use in my project. Most people just

The R10 had three planetary gears, while the R11 had four. This is an insignificant difference for a half-ton pickup.

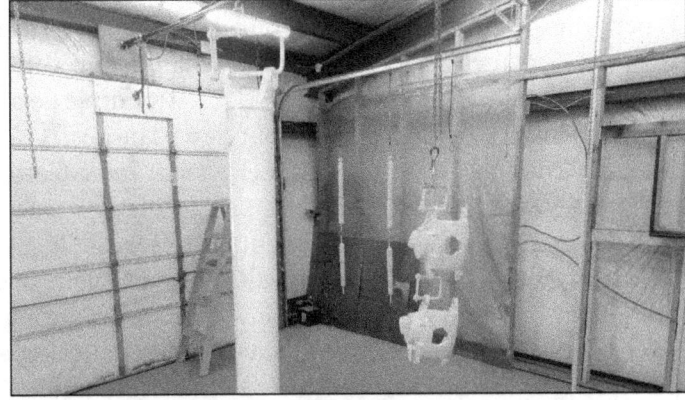

A 3-inch driveshaft out of an early 1960s Suburban will give you all the parts you need. It will have to be chopped to the correct size.

call the driveshaft customizer and tell them what they need.

For this truck, a 3-inch tube driveshaft is good for strength. The U-joints are 1330 for heavier duty and the driveshaft is balanced. The company runs it on a machine and adds weights to balance it.

The length is determined when the truck is sitting on its own weight and fully assembled so it's at its constant gross weight. Measure between the end of the transmission tailshaft housing and the leading edge of the rear end housing. Tell the driveshaft maker this is how you measured it. He has the necessary computations available to provide the perfect length driveshaft. He knows from that information to make the shaft shorter so if the truck bottoms out, it doesn't break anything. This worked out really well for me. By giving him the 1962 Suburban shaft, he had the correct spline gear end and everything he needed for a vintage Chevy build.

The driveshaft is on the frame. You will feel a great sense of accomplishment when your project gets this far! At this point, all mechanicals have been thoroughly addressed.

Flywheel and Clutch Assembly

The driveline starts at the flywheel, *especially for this vintage*. It was late 1955 when Chevrolet first introduced the 12-volt electrical system. When the original engines on our 1947–1955 AD trucks were replaced, it was normally with the post-1953, newer-style 235 or 261 engine, but typically (not always) the flywheel that came with the truck was used. So, why does this matter you might ask? Turns out, it matters a great deal.

All pre-1955 flywheels are considered 6-volt flywheels, and all post-1954 flywheels are considered 12-volt flywheels. The difference is a problem when you go to purchase a starter. The pre-1955 flywheels have 139 teeth or 4 teeth per inch. Matched to this pattern is the 6-volt starter drive gear, which has 9 teeth.

The post-1954 flywheels have 168 teeth or 5 teeth per inch. Matched to this pattern is the 12-volt starter drive gear. It also has 9 teeth! This is a problem because if you try to install the wrong voltage starter, you will get binding and severe problems when trying it.

So, the question is, which starter do you have? If the starter has a black ID plate on it, it is probably 6 volts. If

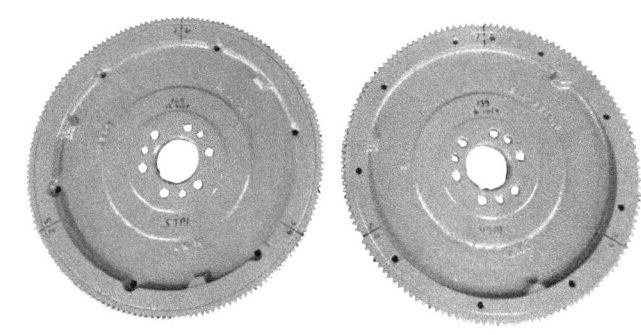

Compare the 12-volt, 168-tooth flywheel (left) to the 6-volt, 139-tooth flywheel (right). Though describing a flywheel in terms of voltage is kind of bizarre, it is quite accurate for this vintage.

it has a red ID plate, it is probably 12 volts. The *probably* is because those ID plates are available from our vendors and hopefully the replacement one is the correct color. A better way to know for sure is to count the teeth on your flywheel. You only need to count to five for a 12 volt and four for a 6 volt. Measure off 1 inch on the flywheel and make a count. It turns out that my 261 uses the original 1950 6-volt flywheel. This means when it comes to starter purchasing, I need a pre-1955 6-volt starter.

TRANSMISSION AND DRIVETRAIN

6-Volt Versus 12-Volt Starters

It turns out that the 6-volt starter has beefier windings than the 12-volt starter because 6 volts requires twice the current flow of a 12-volt starter. So, you can run a 6-volt starter on a 12-volt system without problems. In fact, I prefer the 6-volt starter because it turns faster and responds better. The important thing is to match the starter with the flywheel's ring gear.

If the teeth are getting a little worn on your ring gear but are perfectly okay on the non-contact side, flip the ring gear around the other way! Ring gears are pressed on. There are two ways to remove them: heat them with a torch until they almost fall off by themselves or use a brass hammer or brass punch and slowly work your way around prying it off, being very delicate so as not to warp or damage the ring gear. To reinstall it, put the ring gear in the oven at 400°F until it's thoroughly hot, then very quickly put it back on before it cools. Ring gears are not indexed in any way, so you do not need to worry about how it's placed. You can even swap ring gears to get the proper tooth pattern for your starter. ■

Measure the clutch surface to determine clutch size. Never assume your truck has the best combination clutch system since the previous owner could have swapped them out without knowing which is best.

In addition to the considerations above, it's also a good idea to know what clutch size is correct for your flywheel. On the back of the flywheel is the clutch plate mating surface. If the surface of the flywheel has a mating surface of $9\frac{1}{2}$ inches, you can only install the 9-inch clutch. If the flywheel has a mating surface of $10\frac{1}{2}$ inches, you can install a 9- or 10-inch clutch. It needs a mating surface of 11 inches for an 11-inch clutch. Clutch discs commensurately come in 9-, 10-, $10\frac{1}{2}$-, and $10\frac{3}{4}$-inch-diameter sizes. Pressure plates came in $9\frac{1}{2}$-, 10-, $10\frac{1}{2}$-, and 11-inch diameters.

When purchasing new clutch parts, be sure to get the proper throw-out bearing for your clutch assembly. Tell the parts department the size of your flywheel mating surface to get the proper parts. Don't assume the correct parts were already in there. The previous owner could have installed whatever parts were available.

Taking the time to do these things will give you more information about your vehicle and take a lot of the guesswork out of it. In this case, I am putting in an 11-inch clutch because my flywheel has the 11-inch surface. The larger the clutch, the more pressure is required to engage it, but also the more holding power it has. You can also get your flywheel resurfaced at any automotive machine shop if necessary.

HOW TO RESTORE YOUR CHEVY TRUCK: 1947–1955

CHAPTER 7

PREPARATION, PAINT, AND COLOR SANDING/FINISHING

By far the most difficult and time-consuming process is paint and paint prep, especially if you have no experience with it. This job takes patience and the willingness to put in the time. It is a very difficult task because what may look great in primer can look horrible in gloss paint. Since it has to be done right, let's examine how to make that happen.

Prep for a Perfect Paint Job

You simply do not know what you have until you get down to the bare metal. I have found poor repair jobs using brazing, fiberglass patches, holes just covered over in body filler, etc. that I wouldn't have known about otherwise. When you consider it costs upward of $5,000 in just primers and paint to do this job right, you do not want it ruined prematurely because of something you didn't know. Sandblasting is the best way to get that knowledge.

You can't sandblast everything and then store the parts right away because of flash rust. The humidity in the air will start to rust right away, so we need to decide how to protect the metal until you are ready to process each part. I personally use PPG paint products because of the consistent quality.

The first order of business is to clean the sandblasted parts. Use PPG's SX330 Metal Prep Cleaner and clean the metal thoroughly. It is also known as Wax and Grease Remover. The PPG website discourages the use of self-etching primer because the acidity of its self-etching nature does not play well with epoxy primer. So, no self-etching primer, rather we will go with PPG's DP40LF Epoxy Primer. Apply two good coats on all parts on the truck. You want to do this right away after sandblasting, to prevent the flash rust.

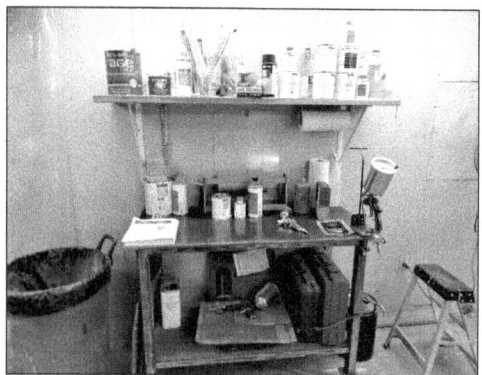

A painting area should be equipped with a gun holder and a shelf for frequently used items. You want these things to be handy when the time comes.

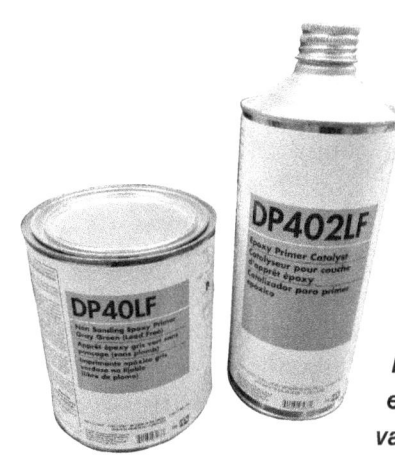

I used PPG's DPLF Epoxy Primer and hardener. It comes in various colors.

HOW TO RESTORE YOUR CHEVY TRUCK: 1947–1955

PREPARATION, PAINT, AND COLOR SANDING/FINISHING

Paint Guns

So, you are not a professional painter. In fact, this is the first time you have ever tried this. You have questions about paint guns, specifically the quality of them and which one is best. You will be asking the same question about the paint brand you purchase.

Do you want an inferior tool or a product that you will be fighting against on top of trying to learn a very difficult task? Your head is already spinning, and you are already anxious doing something this hard in the first place, so why add a crappy paint gun into the mix so you can ask yourself "Was it me or was it the gun?" I think not. While a professional may have no problem adjusting the Harbor Freight $9.99 special, you may not be so lucky.

Get a nice DeVilbiss gun from the StartingLine Series, the FinishLine Series, or the Techna Series. I used a DeVilbiss Finishline for the primer and sealer steps and a Tekna Copper for the base and clear. Being an amateur, I just don't have the desire to sand everything down and do it again because my gun wasn't up to the task.

The same thing goes for paint products. Right now, I use the best of the best. Later, after I am more comfortable, I may go to PPG's Shopline Series and save a lot of money. If there is any difference in the way these chemicals lay down, now is not the time to find out. Besides, PPG's top-of-the-line paint adds more UV protection and I want the best for this project.

Don't get the wrong idea, I don't have a money tree, but there are other places we can save money. This just isn't one of them for the first outing. ∎

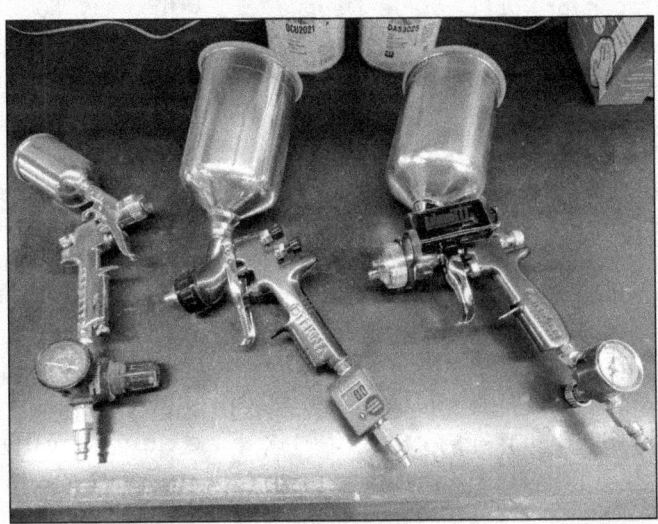

DeVilbiss is well known as the industry standard for paint guns, so I can't blame the gun if things go wrong!

My process is to sandblast the frame, get it in epoxy primer, sandblast a few fenders, primer, etc. But it is also a bit more complicated than that. The problem with epoxy primer is it only allows for a seven-day window. What this means is, you *must* paint another product over it within seven days. If you fail to do that, you have to scuff up every square inch of the piece prior to adding anything. Do you want to risk missing a spot? This creates work that can be avoided if you preplan a little. To get past this seven-day window without the chore of scuffing first, add PPG's K36 High Build Primer. Epoxy primer is not to be sanded, so you need a sandable primer anyway. Once you apply K36 over the epoxy primer, there is no window and you can store your parts until you get to them.

Because everything is in sandable primer at this point, we can start making repairs as we have time. This is where common sense comes into play. If you have brazed (brass looking) patches in the metal or something that will be covered and

PPG's K36 High Build Urethane Primer goes on thick and builds for a very nice, sandable substrate.

HOW TO RESTORE YOUR CHEVY TRUCK: 1947–1955   57

then unviewable after primer, cut out or repair those pieces prior to applying any primer but only if you can do it quick because of flash rust! The reason we are primering everything is to stop rust. The repairs that come later will be addressed as you have time.

Assess for Rust Damage, Dents, Etc.

Assess each part for rust holes and rust pits. This may mean cutting out the bad parts and replacing with fresh metal. A Makita 4-inch grinder with a thin metal cutting disc is a good way to cut out the bad parts. A body saw can be used to finish up corners. Have the appropriate patch panels on hand prior to cutting so you know that you have the proper shape metal for replacement.

Use a flap disc on your Makita 4-inch grinder (120 grit or lower) to remove enough primer around the edges to get a good weld.

Assess for dents and dings. The questions here are: Do you have access to both sides of the metal? and Is the plan to make both sides look perfect? If so, then whatever you do to one side of the metal, you will be doing to the other side. While that seems obvious, keep that in mind because things like the hood that will be seen on both sides need to be treated carefully. Pounding out a high spot will cause a high spot on the other side if too aggressive. Back your hammer up with a dolly on the other side and use proper technique. This means, use the appropriately shaped dolly that conforms to the shape of the metal and start around the edges of the damage first.

If it's a large dent, remember that metal is now stretched, and it needs to be shrunk back into place. Take it slow! It won't take very long to learn how hard to hit to move the metal. There are many tutorials on metal working on YouTube, and weldingweb.com forums is a very good resource for metal fabrication, welding, etc.

One-Man Show

This book is written for the one-man show. If you have 20 people standing around with welding experience, you can attack all of the metal damage quickly and not have to use primer first. But since you are doing this all by yourself and you can't let these parts sit more than a day or two without flash rust problems, get them in both primers. The other alternative is to sandblast a part, address the metal work, primer, then continue with one part at a time. The problem with that idea is that sandblasting is a nasty job and a real mess that I personally feel you would be happier having over and done quickly.

Body Filler

Keep in mind the cardinal rules of body filler: never go beyond 1/8-inch thickness and never have body filler near holes that are used to bolt things up. With practice, you will learn to stay within 1/16-inch max thickness. The standard procedure for applying body filler is to skim coat the entire part with a 1/8-inch-thick coating then sand it all off again with 36-grit paper until every dent and ding repair is smooth. This is how the professionals do it.

I abhor sanding, so I keep the metal bare around the good areas and skim just the damaged area, feathering the body filler into the good area. Once it's dry, I use 80 grit to sand it smooth to the rest of the undamaged metal surrounding it. It will be low because body filler shrinks just a little. So, I add another real thin skim over it, let it dry, and use 80 grit to smooth again. Once it is within a few millimeters of being perfect, I move on to the next problem dent or ding. Never mind the areas where you sanded into the bare metal, but make sure you get in the habit of stopping at the epoxy primer. Avoid going through to the bare metal wherever possible.

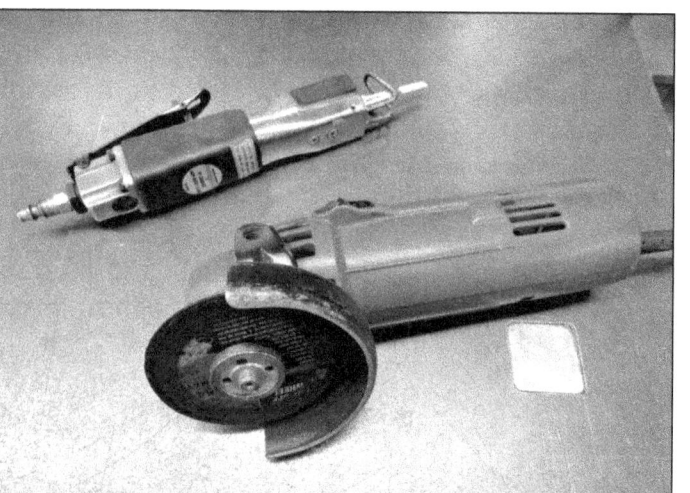

A Makita grinder with a thin cutting disk and an 80- to 120-grit flap disk and an inexpensive body saw will get most of the cutting done without acetylene.

PREPARATION, PAINT, AND COLOR SANDING/FINISHING

I only use three sandpaper grits before color sanding: 80, 220, and 400. This homemade dispenser is equipped with a hacksaw blade to smoothly cut the paper to length. The brand I use is Dura-Gold PSA self-adhesive in rolls.

Understand the Paint Products

Now is a good time to understand the product datasheets that come with your paint materials. If your supplier does not provide datasheets, you must get them because those datasheets tell you some very important information. They tell you the ambient temperature you can successfully apply the coating at, how much of each chemical to mix, etc. In the case of DPLF Epoxy Primer, it provides the induction time, which is the time it takes after mixing the chemicals together before the chemicals are bonded properly for spraying. The sheets also tell you dry times, which fluid tip to use on your gun, etc.

In addition to having the correct datasheets, you will want to make sure you have the correct tools for the job. A strong two-stage compressor with a good water catcher (such as the DeVilbiss QC-3 placed at least 20 feet away from the compressor), a hose to paint with, and a good paint gun with the proper tip (as printed in the datasheet) is a good start. Your paint supplier will also have incidentals such as mixing cups, stir sticks, tack cloths, and mixing funnels and filters.

While you are at it, think of your health and get a good mask rated for this sort of work. Paint in a well-ventilated area. This first attempt at coating will teach you a few things about applying automotive coatings without doing any damage. We do not care about runs or sags because all of that will be sanded off during the prep. But remember, you are practicing your technique, so the goal is no runs or sags.

As far as which paint gun to use, HVLP is best with a gravity-fed gun. In this type, the cup is above the nozzle, so you are using a higher volume of paint but lower pressure. Most coatings say 10 psi at the nozzle, which translates to 26 psi or so at the gun's inlet gauge. Setting up your gun properly is very important. Hang a piece of cardboard on a convenient wall and shoot (8 inches or so from the wall) a quick burst just to make sure you have a nice 6-inch or so symmetrical pattern and your paint is not dripping off the cardboard. Do an internet search on how to set up your gun so you fully understand how it works.

After the Sheet Metal Is Reworked

I have a method of finish work that works well for me once all dents, dings, and repairs are made and the part is relatively smooth. To start, I shoot K36 High Build Primer on the entire area again. You are building on the substrate, which needs to be even, so go way beyond the damage. If you have repair areas you suspect are a little low, hit those first, then go over it again with the entire area, essentially putting two coats in the low spots. Using a guide coat, sand

Keep Moving

The best advice I can give a novice is to keep the gun moving. If you move too fast, you will just be putting on less material with one pass, but if you move too slow, you can be sanding it all off and starting over. You will learn quickly what speed the gun needs to move at in order to give yourself a comfortable safety zone between running the paint and getting the perfect coat. The hardest parts of spraying is to be consistent with the speed of movement in your passes and perfecting the 50-percent overlap. Once you have determined how fast to move, you will have far less chance of runs or sags. Be consistent with gun speed and observe a 50-percent overlap and before you know it, you will be painting just like a pro. ■

CHAPTER 7

down the entire part using 220 grit and a long board.

Guide Coats

The guide coat method is the most significant way we can make our work look like a professional did the job. Using sandable dark primer in a spray can, dust on a very thin coat, just so the K36 (which is whitish) looks like it has dust all over it. This contrast shows high or low spots in our panels so we can sand them more or add body filler. The professionals can feel it with their hands, and you will get there too, but this is the best insurance you can get. Be sure to always use guide coat.

Use the guide coat to see what is in front of you. For small dings or low spots, use filler; high spots that are too high to sand down require the hammer and dolly. If you find yourself needing to hammer and dolly, apply body filler again, shoot the entire panel with K36 again, sand with 220 grit, apply a guide coat again, and sand the entire panel. Rinse and repeat until everything is perfect. Then shoot K36 one last time, apply a guide coat, and sand using 400 grit.

At this point, you should have a perfectly smooth and perfectly straight panel that is ready for the next procedure. I find sanding distasteful and time consuming, but I still recommend using the Armstrong method of sanding and avoid using air or electric equipment. This will help you get the feel for the work.

Long Boards

A very important sanding technique to master is long boarding. I feel the best purchase I made was the long board kit. Use the longest board that is practical with PSA sticky sandpaper so that your board follows the proper contour of the surrounding area. Sand using an X pattern with the ends of the long board always setting on the proper contour of the piece with the damaged area in just the center.

With bendable long boards, we can sand using the natural contour of the piece you are working on. This is a real game changer because now you can develop a technique of blading off the right amount of primer based on the larger contour of the piece. ■

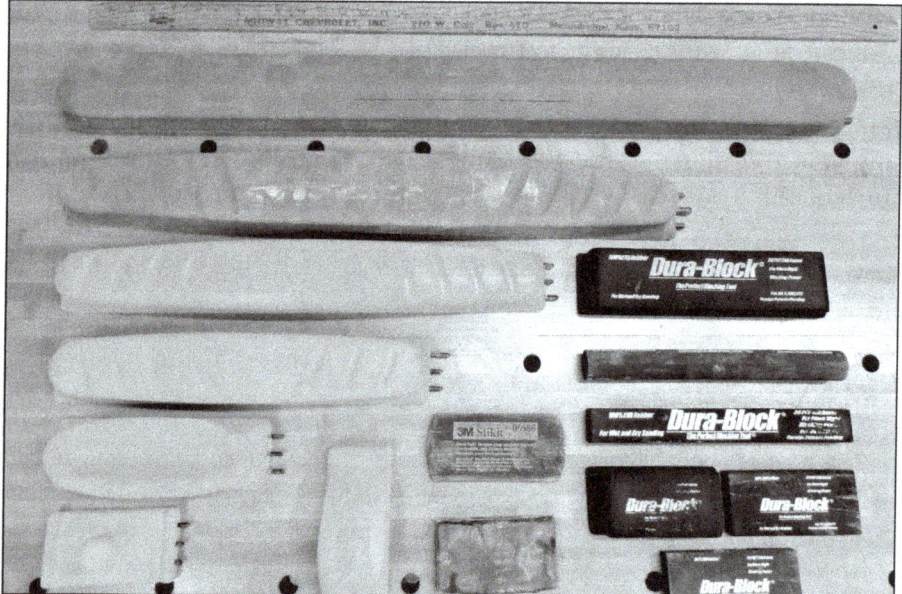

These are the sanding boards I use routinely. The long ones are used for the back of the cab to ensure absolute flatness. The black Dura-Blocks are used a lot too but only in perfectly flat areas. The beauty of the red and green long boards is their ability to perfectly conform to curved surfaces. That is a real game changer!

Simply remove the three rods and your board goes from perfectly flat to conforming to your panel. The versatility is amazing!

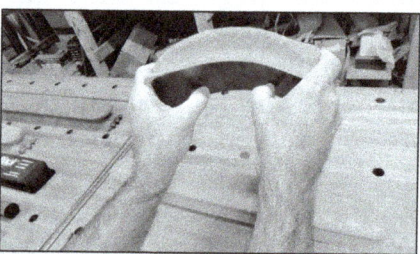

This green long board is my favorite for conforming to the dash, around the outside cab corners, roof line, etc.

PREPARATION, PAINT, AND COLOR SANDING/FINISHING

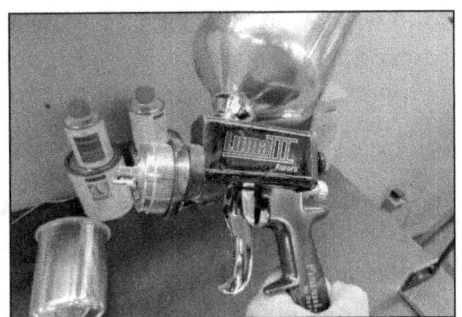

I used to have to go around with a shop light in one hand and the paint gun in the other, which meant I was always tangling cords and using inferior light. Thanks to LumaIII for creating the Aurora^2 paint gun light.

The Aurora^2 paint gun light uses 9V rechargeable batteries that last for a few hours. The light is very bright and eliminates the light issue completely!

A paint shaker is nice for automotive paints, unless you want to stand there and follow the data sheet, which says to agitate for 15 minutes. The K36 requires a lot of agitation.

Finish Coats

We can now apply the finish coats. Things get a little more urgent from here on. There are two or three different coatings required, depending on your needs. The reason I mention them here at the same time is because one sealer has a 72-hour window. You can shoot the sealer on one day and then the base/clear on the day after, but the window is short, so keep that in mind. The base coat and clear coat are shot on the same day.

One option is a single-stage urethane method that is not to be confused with base coat/clear coat. It's a one-shot paint that has the color and the clear coat built in. You would not color sand this, so it should be used only in places that will not receive close scrutiny.

This two-coating method is PPG's DAS3025 sealer, a urethane that seals in all the chemical substrates you used previously, and PPG's DCC Concept urethane top coat. This is used for small parts, places that will not get a lot of damage, or places that are unseen.

The other option is to apply a sealer, a base coat color, and a clear coat. This method is sprayed with PPG's DAS3025 Urethane Sealer, then its DBC base coat (the color), and then its DCU clear coat. The sealer can be applied over bare metal (in very small places) if necessary, so don't worry if you have a few small exposed areas. I prefer to use three coats of the sealer to make really sure I have every square inch properly sealed. This sealer heals 400-grit scratches, so your finish comes out perfectly smooth.

The base coat is only for coloring the vehicle. There is no need to get it too thick. Three good coats of color is enough, but because I am new to this and I am unsure that I am getting the precise 50-percent overlap, I gave it four coats. When I am better at this, three will be more than enough. The base color has no hardener in it, so it depends on the clear coat to chemically react and bond to the color. This is why they are done in the same day.

Get in the habit of waiting 10 to 15 minutes between coats. After all coats of the color are applied, use PPG's DCU2021 Clear Coat. For areas that are not seen but still need to be covered, apply three wet coats. For areas you want to show off, apply four to six coats of clear. The areas you are showing off need to be color sanded and will likely be exposed to the sun, waxing, etc., and need more protection.

> **TECH TIP — Dry Sanding**
>
> During the past 15 years or so, the idea of epoxy sealer was introduced to eliminate the need for wet sanding prior to applying a top coat. The idea of introducing water into your substrates prior to fully sealing them turned out to be a bad idea. The old procedure was to wet sand with 600 grit prior to a top coat. By using epoxy sealer, the manufacturer says we can dry sand only and stop at 400 grit to get the exact same result. This is true if using 400 grit on a DA sander; however, if you are doing it by hand, it is a good idea to go to 500 or 600 grit for final dry sanding. ■

Color Sanding to Perfection

Color sanding is the process of removing the orange peel effect of the entire process. During the standard painting process, the paint does not lay down perfectly smooth; there are hills and valleys. I want the finished paint to look super smooth and shiny. To do this, I will have to color sand and then buff to a perfect shine.

Color sanding is done very carefully with the appropriate coats of clear (so you do not sand through the clear). Gather color sanding pads with 1000-grit paper and a squirt bottle filled with water. To begin, wet the area completely and wet the paper. Sand the area with a light hand to remove the orange peel and create a flat surface. This step should be done slowly. Take the time to shine a light on the paint as you go so you can see the hills and valleys and how much progress you have made.

Once the hills and valleys are barely gone, move to 2000-grit paper. Wipe the 1000-grit surface down so you can see the difference between the two grits to gauge your progress. Sand with 2000-grit, making sure to keep the panel wet. Each pass is smoothing the deeper scratches of the grit before.

When there are no hills and valleys at 2000-grit, it's time to use the electric buffer at about 1,000 rpm. With a nice high-density foam pad (the black one in the kit), buff the paint with either Meguiar's Professional Ultra-Cut Compound 105 or 3M's Finesse-It Machine Polish 39003. Either of these products will heal 1200-grit scratches and bring out an astounding shine. Do not concentrate on any given area too long to prevent heat buildup and let the machine do the work. Stay at least 1/8 inch away from any edges.

It is critical to stay away from the edges or sharp corners. Only sand to within 1/4 inch of any edge. It may even be a good idea to tape the edges within 1/8 inch just so you can't mistakenly run your paper over the edge. That would ruin your day. Remember, it is imperative that you do not sand through the clear coat. This is why I err on the side of more coats of clear when I know the work requires color sanding.

Next, use a nice glaze compound that is made for smoothing. I use Meguiar's Show Car Glaze #7. I got a nice buffer (Dewalt DWP849X) to do the buffing and waxing. Once the glaze is applied, you will be impressed, but finish the job with a good carnauba wax such as Meguiar's Professional Hi-Tech Yellow Wax #26. Always make sure anything you are using says "Safe for Paint Shops" somewhere on it. This is critical because some compounds can contaminate paint environments and ruin your day.

And that is the basic gist of how it's done! I encourage you to do a search on the internet for YouTube videos on how to do all the steps and learn the nuances before attempting this, but as complicated as it seems, it's not all that daunting after you get a few parts behind you. Of course, a professional will read this and have coughing spasms, but that is because they are far removed from amateur status and I have written into this instruction added caution. Just be sure to use common sense, and do not take what you see on YouTube as gospel before getting corroborating evidence!

This is an inside door after color sanding and buffing. It looks amazing!

The Dewalt DWP849X variable speed polisher with soft start is the ticket when doing entire vehicles. Be warned that learning about all of the various pads and what they are used for takes a while.

 **Armstrong Method**

The Dewalt buffer is a great option for large surfaces, but it is not a good idea to use it on the dash or most interior surfaces where there are too many odd shapes for it to be useful. The fact is, if you have sanded the whole cab and all associated truck parts before, this is a cakewalk. I ended up only using the buffer on the rear, the roof of the cab, and larger parts such as the fenders and the hood. It's just too easy to use the "Armstrong" method and hand sand the rest. There was no air-powered or electric mechanical sanders used in this process. The Armstrong method is the only good way to actually feel where you are in the process. ■

CHAPTER 8

The Cab

The cab requires really careful consideration. Before doing any work on it, we should identify our goals for this project. For example, are any patch panels required, are there changes you wish to make to the structure, or do you wish to make improvements? All of these things should be considered before beginning work.

With the condition of my project truck, I needed several patch panels to replace rusted-out ones. I am very grateful that they make good-quality patch panels for this vintage. In this case, both cab corners, both full front cowls, both front inner cowls and supports, an entire toe board, both left and right floor panels, both inside kick panels, all under-floor structural supports, and various odd pieces of 11-gauge sheet metal were needed. I told you, this cab was a mess!

Now is also the time to decide what other things you want to do. For example, my project truck will have a dual master cylinder and the round hole is simply inconvenient. Now is the time to make a plan to address that issue. Part of the support structure needed to be cut and boxed back in, and I didn't have much space between the center floor pan and the new cover to say the least. I preplanned and addressed changes before proceeding.

This upgraded opening for the master cylinder required measuring several times and being really sure before cutting. I am positive the stainless steel door will be a very nice addition.

Also, I have never liked how hard it is to access the space under the seat. I decided to fix that by adding two independent locking drawers with heavy-duty slow-slide ball bearing sliders made specifically to hold a fire extinguisher and jack on one side and miscellaneous items on the other, making that space usable again! While I am at it, an electrical system cut-off switch will be located between the drawers. It will be wired to the positive side of the battery and will kill all power to the truck from inside the cab with one turn of the switch.

Someone thought this change was a good idea. They needed a bigger radio than would fit in the hole, so they took a pair of tin snips and remedied the problem. Only a restorer can appreciate the anxiety! It was fixed with donor cab metal and a little (upside down) intricate welding.

HOW TO RESTORE YOUR CHEVY TRUCK: 1947–1955

CHAPTER 8

The sheet metal drawers were made at the local plumbing and heating shop. I used the cut-outs for the front of the drawers, so they look like they belong there and nobody will know they are there! Here is what it looks like with the drawer system roughed in. More finesse is still required.

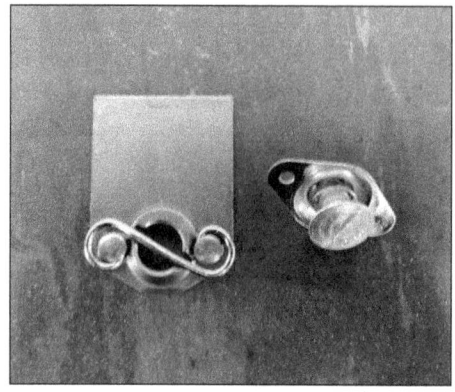

Sheet metal screws are an abomination to me. They are pointy, so they tear you up if you are not careful; they rust to the metal they are holding down; and they make it hard to remove the panel. We can fix that with Zeus fasteners!

Seat belts are a must-have addition, so I went about designing a solution for our Advance Design cab.

I also mentioned that I do not like sheet metal screws in the center floor panel. I made a plan to put in quarter-turn fasteners to make it secure and easier to remove. This is part of my aircraft industry heritage. These fasteners are not hard to weld into place if you can get the measurements exact enough. Precision measurements are a must! It isn't easy, but it's worth it in the end.

I also knew I needed to add seat belts to my pickup. When I started on this cab, there were not a lot of options available, so I went about designing my own. We needed three-point belts for the left and right. They must be safe!

Lastly for the planning stage, you can't take for granted that miscellaneous holes that are present in the dash, side panels, and anywhere really are factory. After consulting with many people, I was able to determine which holes did not belong. There was also damage to the dash where the steering column was fastened. All of this became very apparent after sandblasting every square inch of the cab.

Let's Get to Work!

Once preplanning stages are complete, it is time to get down to the actual work involved. The first step is sandblasting everything. Once we know what metal is good and what is not, we can decide what to do next.

In the case of my project vehicle, so much metal was rusted away that I had to be very careful. There were structural supports either missing or severely damaged, so I could

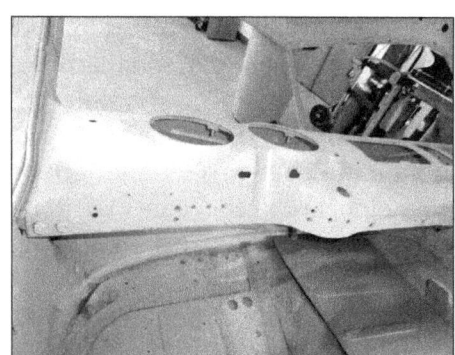

Miscellaneous holes needed to be closed, damage repaired, and some areas even reinforced to provide additional strength.

Shiny new metal is the only good way to assess the damage. Even though sandblasting is a messy job, it is the foundation of a proper frame-up restoration.

easily make it worse by welding a patch panel in wrong, which could cause permanent damage. Before doing anything, I welded a cross brace inside the door openings. It doesn't have to be pretty, just tacked in enough to hold the opening straight while removing the metal below. Any time you feel extra bracing is needed, add 1-inch angle iron across those gaps. It can make all the difference.

Before moving on to repairs, protect the bare metal from flash rust. Take all the parts that were sandblasted and give them a coat of

THE CAB

This is the common condition of a 1950s pickup after sitting for many years. If you see this, there's a very good chance the supports under the floor will be rotted as well.

epoxy primer; I use PPG products. Clean the surfaces thoroughly with SX330 Metal Prep Cleaner and then shoot the surfaces with two coats of DPLF40 Epoxy Primer, waiting at least 10 minutes between coats. See chapter 7 for details.

Start by assessing the damage to the floor and under-floor supports. If the supports look good, leave them in place and remove the spot welds holding the floor. You can easily see the spot welds after sandblasting. When replacing a floor panel, it's a good idea to keep the transmission cover in place on the other three sides to keep everything straight. I use a cheap spot weld cutter in my electric drill to drill welds out, then I use a 4-inch Makita grinder with grinding wheel to smooth each area off.

Just because you purchased an entire patch panel does not mean you should use the whole thing. Assess how far the rust has done its damage, then go a few inches beyond that, making sure you are past all the rust. Cut the hole in the cab first, making sure the hole is smaller than the panel on all sides! The hardest part of all this is figuring out how to transfer that hole size to your patch panel. Use a piece of cardboard to cut a template to exactly the same size, then transfer it to the patch panel. Once you have it marked perfectly, add 1/4 inch all the way around and then cut your patch panel. Add the extra because being too large is bad, but too small is *really* bad! It's easy to trim off a little excess, it's harder to add metal to your patch panel because you didn't measure twice and cut once.

During this process, be sure the cab is sitting the same way it would on the frame (or leave it on the frame to do the repairs). This keeps everything in its natural position. Once the structure is sound, remove the cab for the rest of the restoration. In my situation, there was no floor or supports, so I took the cab off right away, designed a cart that would emulate the frame, and hoped for the best.

In case it is not obvious, only do one patch at a time. Cutting too much of the metal away is dangerous in that you can possibly warp the cab structure. With your patch panel cut to fit the hole exactly, use the butt weld method to burn it in. This takes finesse in recessed areas, but with a little practice, you will get the hang of this process quickly. Use Vise-Grip clamps or butt-weld clamps to hold the patch panel in place all the way around. The panel must be straight, flat, and clamped in many places prior to welding.

Tack the piece in by welding a small area (1/8 inch or less) in each corner. Next, weld in the middle between where you tacked the corners, then in the middle of that, etc. The reason for doing it this way is because of the very good possibility of warping the metal due to excessive heat. Weld in one spot quickly, then completely move to another spot. This dissipates the heat and prevents warp damage. Sure, it looks terrible when you are done, but it's nothing a grinder won't resolve.

But, warning again! You just welded the panel in correctly, so be sure to grind the metal the same way, moving from one place to another to keep the metal cool as much as possible. I learned this the hard way, so I hope you don't have to!

I will not bore you with pictures of every panel I replaced on this truck,

I purchased the entire toe board, but that doesn't mean I have to use it. If some of the more intricate areas do not have rust, save them. The holes are in the correct place already and have served this truck well for 60 years; let's not add potential problems.

CHAPTER 8

Butt welding in new patch panels means removing all spot welds and customizing the size of the patch panel to fit. The outer skin of the cab is completed last, after replacing the affected toe board, inside kick panel, and inside cowl supports. There is a lot happening here that will be noticed if not done right. Check door fitment prior to welding and then again after.

but I made the vendor's day with that order. I assure you, it doesn't take long to learn how to weld thin sheet metal. There is an art to it, but you will get the hang of it pretty quickly because you have to! Just turn down your welder's heat and wire speed and take your time. There is a reward for doing all of this in a meticulous, careful fashion.

Seat Belts

Before starting on a project, consider your safety and reliability requirements. How are seat belts anchored in modern vehicles? What is the shoulder harness distance that is the most desirable for this installation? We are starting from scratch and putting a safety system in a truck that was never designed for it. Turns out Juliano's Hot Rod Parts has a nice kit that gives us a good place to start.

We will use the Retractable 3-Point Shoulder Harness with Soft Arm (JU016300 Series), which comes complete with all of the necessary hardware to mount the system securely. The hardware kit is also sold separately. Survey the kit and read the accompanying document to familiarize yourself with the parts.

After measuring several vehicles to determine proper height placement for the top pivoting shoulder harness bolt, it was determined that 41 inches off the floor of the cab was the proper height to ensure the harness isn't too low or too high for the average person. This number is variable, however, due to the height of the person. Vehicles measured from the top of the seat bottom to the bolt hole varied anywhere from 26 to 30 inches. Most trucks are at 28 inches, which equates to 41 inches off the floor. For our trucks, this is about the perfect location for providing the best structural support.

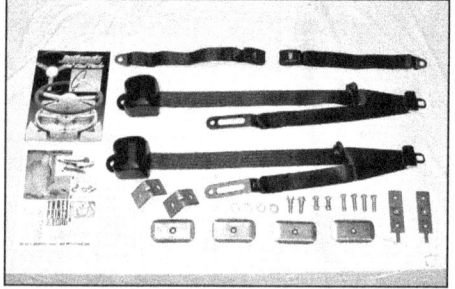

This is a great seat belt kit to use because it comes with all of the support metal needed to reinforce the cab for safe installation.

Seat Belt Installation

Shoulder Harness Instruction

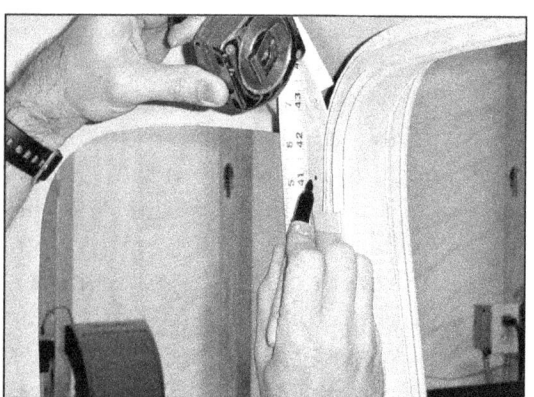

1 Make a mark at 41 inches off the floor of the cab as shown. Center the mark on the post as much as possible. As you can see, the five-window cab complicates matters, so we will use a five window for our install. If installing the seat belt in a three-window standard cab, you can just put the plate behind the sheet metal in approximately the same position without cutting. You will have to remove or at least loosen the back corners of the headliner because you will be installing a plate behind the dual layered area of the post.

2 Make a cardboard template that can fit behind the sheet metal. Clamp the template in securely, then drill a 1/8-inch pilot hole on the 41-inch mark, making sure to drill through both the metal and the cardboard. Be sure the hole is centered from side to side.

THE CAB

Seat Belt Installation *(CONTINUED)*

3 I use Vise-Grip welding clamps a lot during these restorations. This clamp is holding the template behind the post. Don't drop it!

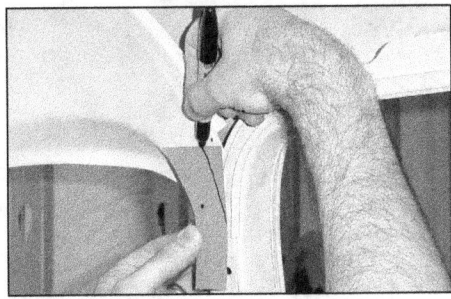

4 Because of the headliner screws, taper the template (and the metal plate) so it doesn't interfere with the headliner installation.

5 Remove the template and lay it over the provided metal plate as shown.

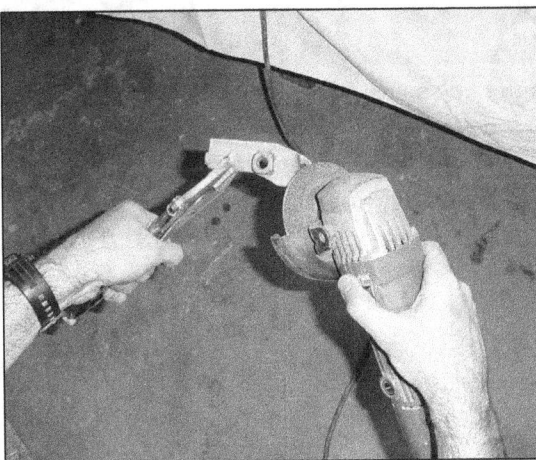

6 When the plate is properly marked, make the cuts. I like to cut a little big. You can always grind it down if it doesn't fit. I used a thin cutoff wheel on my 4-inch Makita grinder to make the cuts and then a standard grinding wheel to round the edges of the metal slightly all the way around the piece.

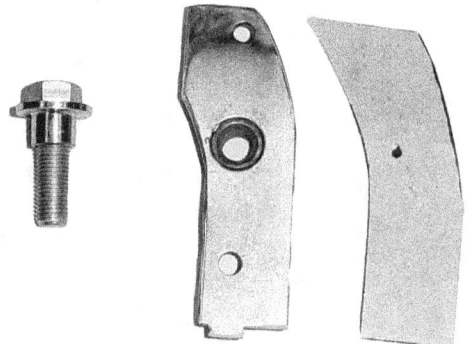

7 Here is the sculpted piece ready for welding in place.

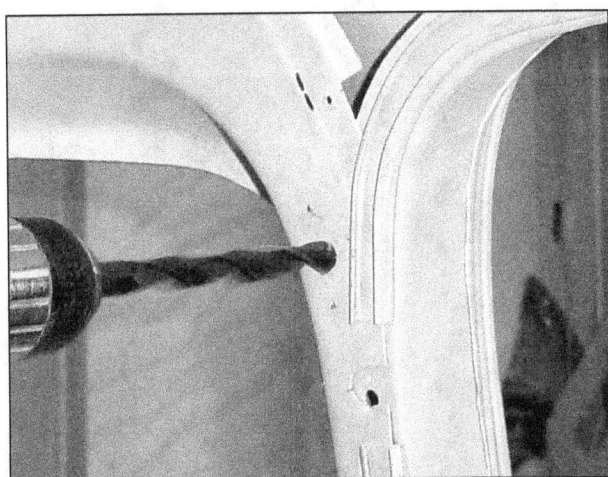

8 Test fit the new plate by placing it behind the post and eyeballing the pilot hole to be sure it appears to be centered. If you like what you see, drill out the pilot hole with a 7/16-inch drill bit and test fit again, putting one of the provided short bolts into the hole and tightening it.

9 Determine where you want to drill two more holes in your cab sheet metal, one above the 7/16-inch hole and one below for spot welding the plate in place.

HOW TO RESTORE YOUR CHEVY TRUCK: 1947–1955

Seat Belt Installation (CONTINUED)

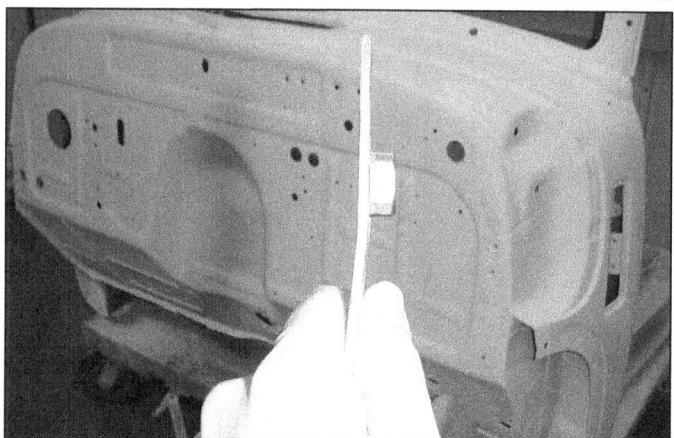

10 It's also necessary to slightly bend the custom plate to conform to the contour of the cab.

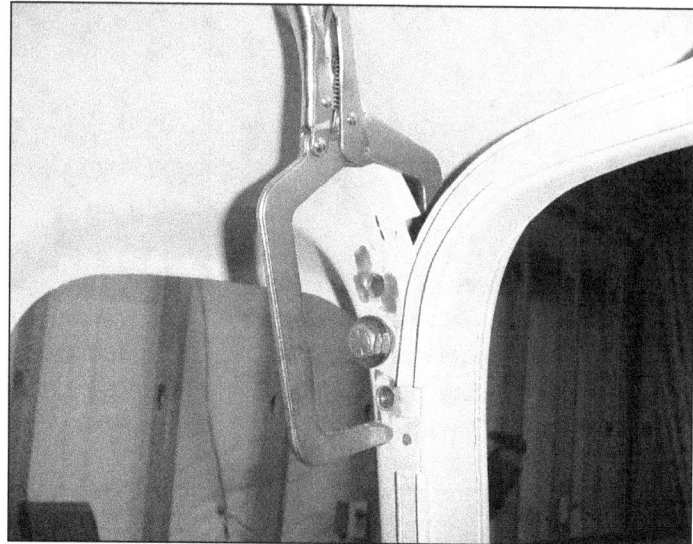

11 Once the holes are drilled and properly dressed, install the plate using one of the provided shoulder bolts and tighten snugly. I augmented the pressure with a welder's clamp to keep up the pressure for welding.

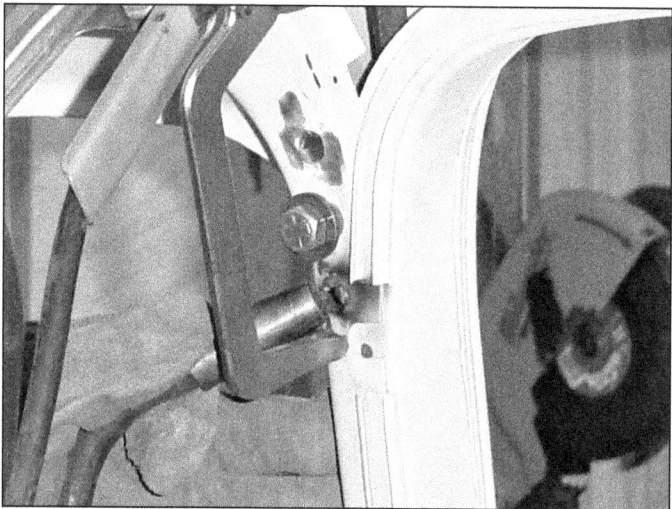

12 Weld the plate in place by applying enough heat and material to ensure a secure weld.

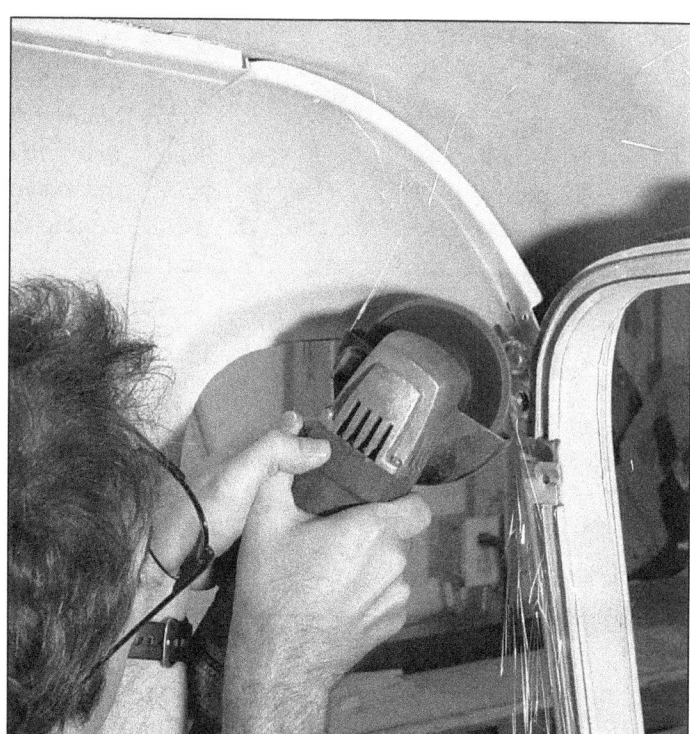

13 Dress down the weld and smooth it out. I like using a 120-grit flap disc on my 4-inch Makita grinder.

14 The 120-grit flap disc is a wonderful accessory for the Makita grinder for a lot of this type of restoration work.

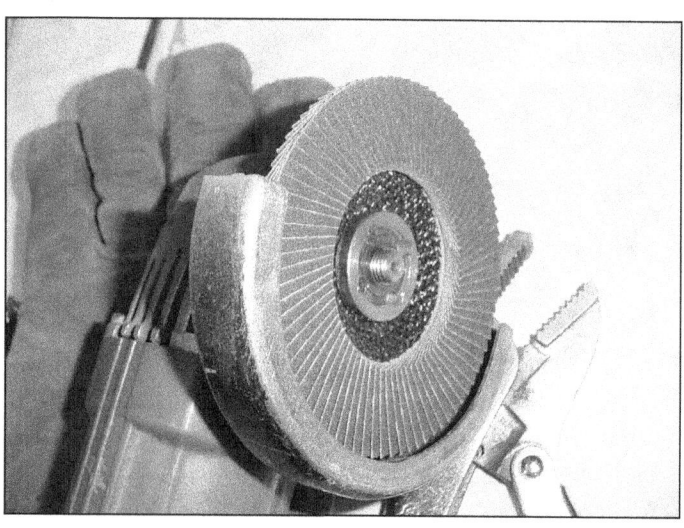

THE CAB

Retractor Assembly Instructions

I have a great location for the retractor assembly that is already spot welded in the cab's structure. All I have to do is drill and reinforce for safety. This makes the cab corners a bit more inaccessible after everything is installed, but that is a very small price to pay.

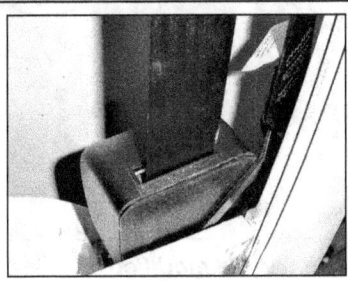

1 Due to the gas tank, the gas inlet tube, and the chassis connections, there is only one logical place to put the belt retractor assembly. This placement meets the strict requirement that the top shoulder post be directly above the retractor while keeping the belt assembly out of the way.

2 Since the chassis/cab mounts are in our way, we need another solution to make the belt retractor assembly solid and secure.

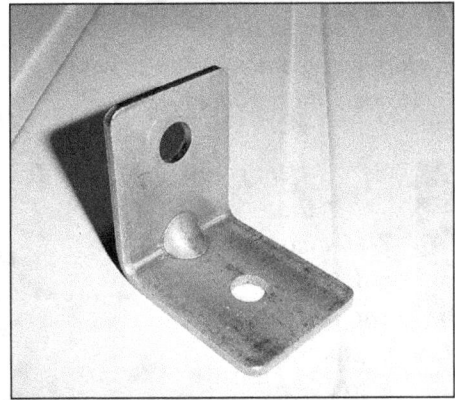

3 Locate the angle bracket in your kit as well as the $2^{3}/_{8}$ x $4^{1}/_{2}$-inch metal plate as shown.

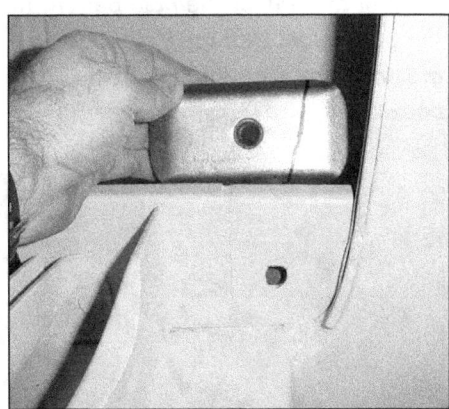

4 Weld both brackets into place to use the seat pedestal back and the cab floor for a very secure mounting.

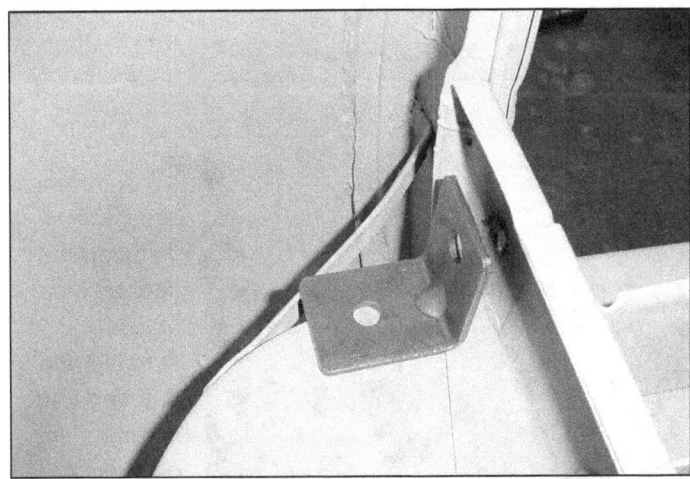

5 Cut the $2^{3}/_{8}$ x $4^{1}/_{2}$-inch modified plate as shown. Drill the 7/16-inch hole accurately by setting in the angle bracket so it's set properly flush with the lip of the seat pedestal back (leaving 1/2-inch gap). This is so that we have room to slide in the modified metal plate. The corner of your angle bracket should sit flush on top of that little support beam.

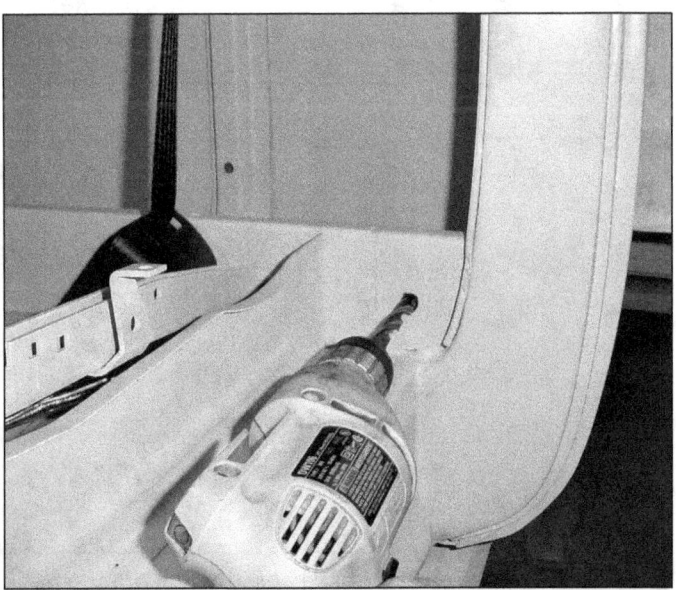

6 With a pencil, carefully mark the hole going to the seat pedestal back from the inside. Use a small taper punch and a hammer to tap the center of it so you know where to drill the hole on the outside.

Seat Belt Installation (CONTINUED)

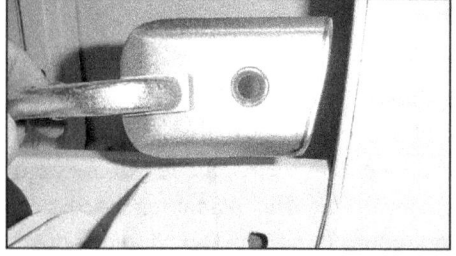

7 You can use whatever other ingenious method you can think of to transfer the hole pattern to the other side. Drill the 7/16-inch hole, making sure everything lines up correctly.

8 Place the modified $2^3/_8$ x $4^1/_2$-inch metal plate behind the seat pedestal. Bolt the plate securely in place with the provided 7/16-inch short bolt.

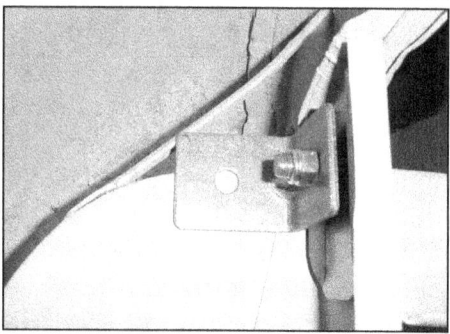

9 You will want to sand off the weld area so welding goes smoother. Weld the plate in place securely from behind.

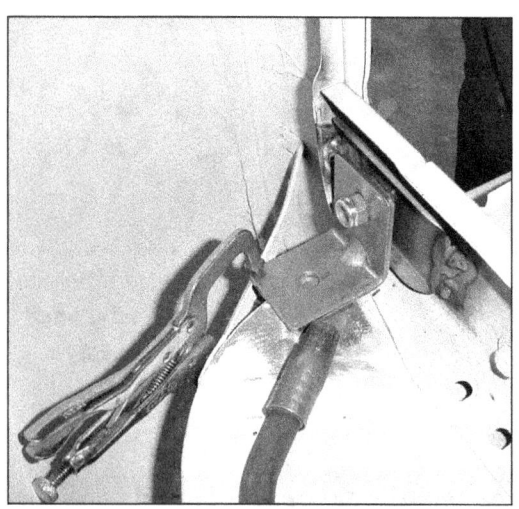

10 Using the 7/16-inch nut, bolt the angle plate in place. I also use a welding clamp to hold the angle bracket securely to the floor.

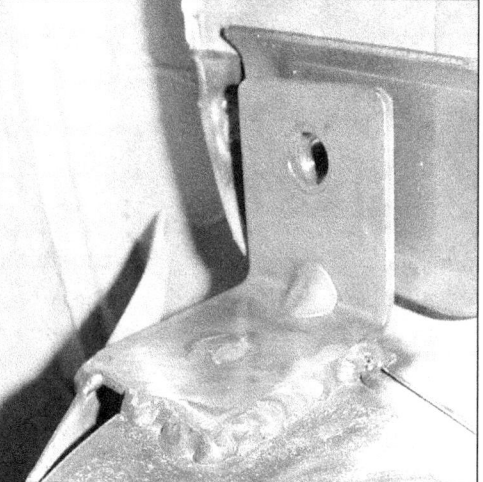

11 Weld the angle bracket in place and then grind off the area for a clean install. Remove the short bolt and nut and replace it with the long bolt with washer through the assembly.

12 Install the retractor assembly and the other end onto the bolt and tighten using the 7/16-inch nut. Install the belt assembly so it is not twisted or binding in any way. The belt should not chafe on the sides of the retractor assembly and the system should work smoothly.

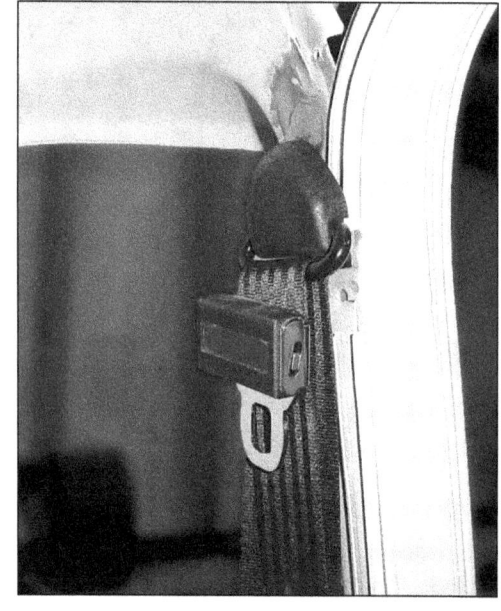

13 The retractor assembly is installed. Of course, there is finishing sanding and painting to do, but mechanically, everything should work great.

THE CAB

Latch Assembly Instruction

The latch assembly is the hard part in that it requires a reinforcement piece under the cab. You don't want to skip that reinforcement because you do not want the mount bolt to pull right out of that thin sheet metal if it is ever needed for its purpose.

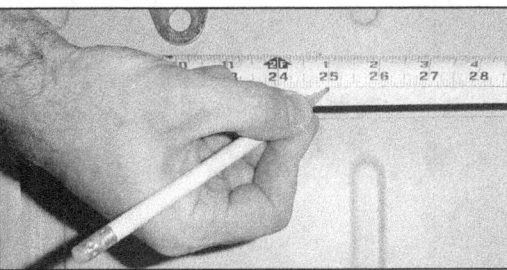

1 I determined that 25 inches (approximately) from the rear panel of the seat pedestal nearest the door inward is the best place to install the latch belt anchor. You can decide what fits you best.

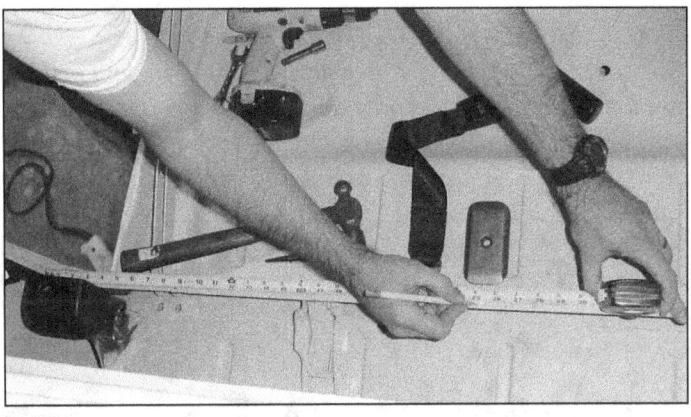

2 This distance gives the rider a comfortable width if they are average size, and we have a recessed area in the seat pedestal pan that is in the way of making it longer.

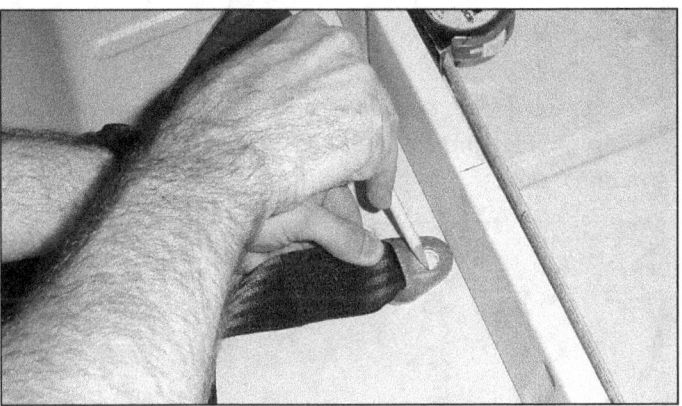

3 Mark the anchor hole in the bottom of the seat pan at the 25-inch mark, making sure the $2^{3}/_{8}$ x $4^{1}/_{2}$-inch metal plate will ride just shy of that recessed area in the pan.

4 This plate goes on the underside of the cab and will prevent the belt from pulling out in case of a jarring pull.

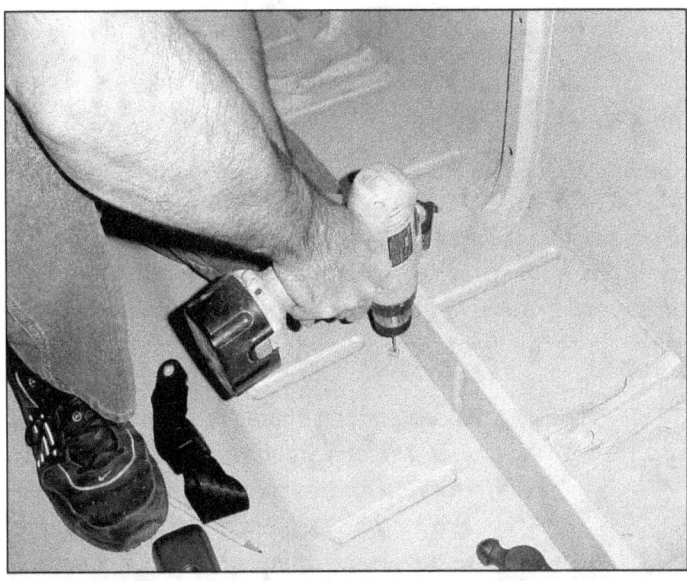

5 Drill a pilot hole and then a finished 7/16-inch hole on the mark. Place the plate under the cab and bolt it into place. You can see how it just misses the recessed area.

6 I do not like the way these unsightly plates look from the underside of the truck, but it's a small price to pay for safety.

HOW TO RESTORE YOUR CHEVY TRUCK: 1947–1955

Seat Belt Installation *(CONTINUED)*

7 Drill two additional holes for spot welding purposes: one at the top (just behind the seat pedestal) and one below.

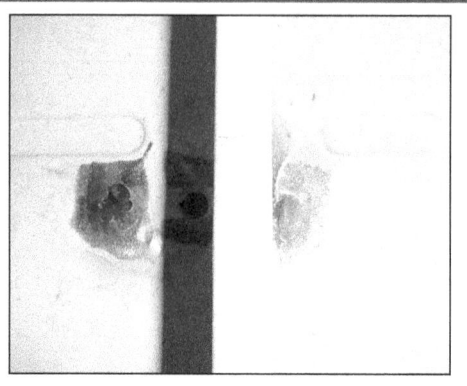

8 If your gas tank is in the way of the top weld, you could forego that one or weld it from the bottom of the cab. Weld the plate into place and do the required grinding.

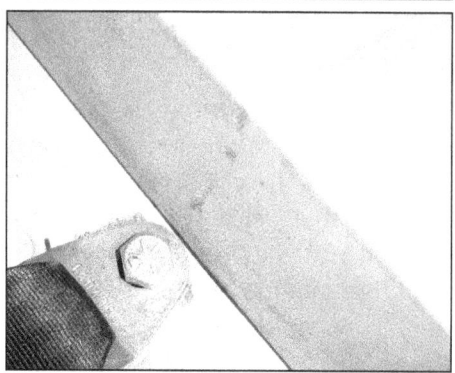

9 This ends the latch assembly instruction. During seat installation, I decided to go with a bracket that extends this to the top of the rear seat pedestal.

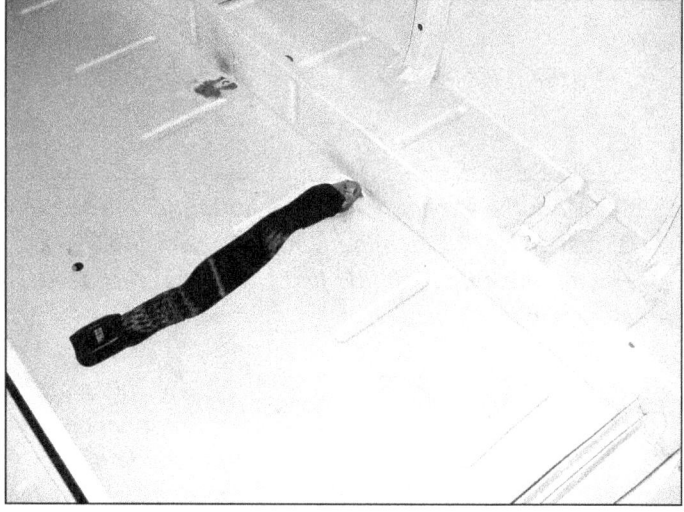

When you are done, it should look like this. Some suggested a better way would be to make an angle bracket that follows the seat pedestal back and connect the belt on the vertical plane so it's closer to the seat and possibly prevent the seat squashing it during use. That was not all that difficult to make and bolt in using the same bolt.

Because the drawers that I added were in the way of this area, the angle bracket was necessary anyway. Turned out this small bracket in both places solved a few issues! It anchors to the lip of the seat pedestal for added strength.

Final Thoughts

After actually driving the truck, I was very happy with the dimensions and the installation. This was well worth the effort and I feel confident it was built to exceed the standards of even more modern vehicles. The Juliano's Hot Rod kit turned out to be a very solid solution.

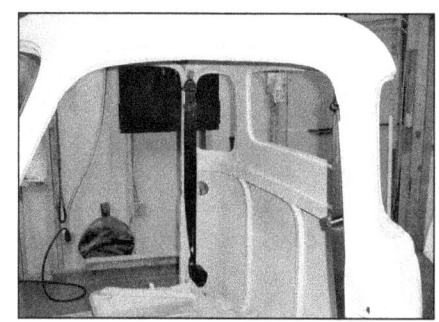

When done, it should look something like this. The only things left in the Juliano's Hot Rod kit that were not needed were two long bolts. I was impressed with the relative ease of installation. Of course, I did it in an empty cab, but I still feel that it would be well worth it even if I would have had to remove the seat assembly and part of the headliner to do it.

A Unique Drawer System

The next cab modification I made was adding a drawer system. The space under the seat is even harder to get to when you have seat belts laying across the seat, so I wanted to remedy that problem. I have always thought it kind of a waste to have all that space under the bench seat and not be able to get to it easily. Most truck owners store the jack under there or maybe some things they don't need to get to frequently. This will change all that. The goal of this endeavor is:

- Maintain the structural integrity of the seat pedestal
- The end result must look like it was always there
- All safety concerns must be thoroughly addressed
- No shaking, rattling, or any obnoxious sounds should come from under the seat
- Stock the spare tire jack, a trailer receiver, and a fire extinguisher in the drawers

I wanted maximum depth, so I cut the openings 4 inches high, leaving 3/4 inch off the floor so the floor mats wouldn't rub. The 4-inch drawer height happens to be the perfect height for the truck's jack and even a normal size fire extinguisher. Other considerations in deciding the width of the drawers were the floor shifter and leaving about 4 inches of untouched steel in the center of the pedestal to retain its strength.

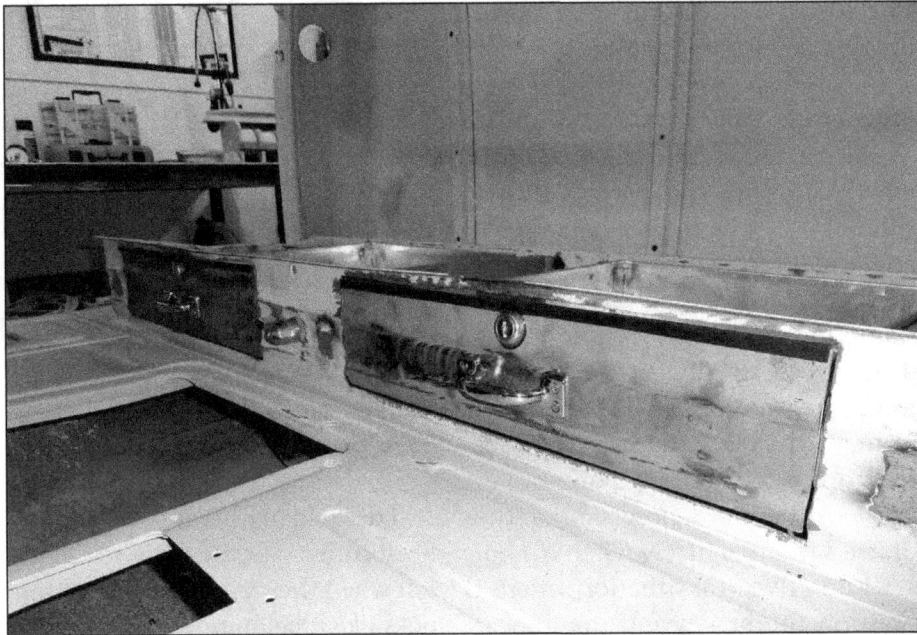
Very carefully cutting out the drawer fronts will allow me to reuse those pieces as the drawer faces. I used a thin cutoff wheel and went slowly.

Here the drawers are roughed in with all hardware and locks installed.

Materials List

- 80 inches of 1x2-inch rectangular tubing
- Four 18-inch slow-close drawer slides (150-pound capacity)
- Two lock mechanisms (toolbox type)
- Two window sash handles (four-screw type for solidity)
- Two 16x18x3-inch 24-gauge galvanized tin drawers
- Miscellaneous scrap metal

I sourced out the creation of the drawers to a local HVAC contractor. The locks, sash handles, drawer slides, and hardware were purchased from a local hardware store.

I decided on 16 inches wide by 18 inches deep for the drawers.

Preplanning for Success

There are a few considerations when choosing the proper drawer slides. I want them to be heavy duty and slide very easily, but I do not want a situation where the drawer is slamming against the stops during driving and creating noise. To eliminate the shuffling when closed, I went with slow close drawer slides that are rated at 150 pounds per drawer. The slow closers hold the drawers in place nicely when closed.

I don't want a situation where I slam on the brakes and the drawer slides open real fast and jams against the gas pedal and keeps the brake pedal from going down. No, sir, I don't think so! We need to secure those drawers, so they simply can't come open during driving. I solved this by putting toolbox locking mechanisms on the drawer face.

Due to the slow closer slides, handles were also necessary. Since the pedestal sits inward from the actual bench seat a bit, you can't see them unless you get out of the truck and look. I also put foam in each drawer to capture and secure heavier items.

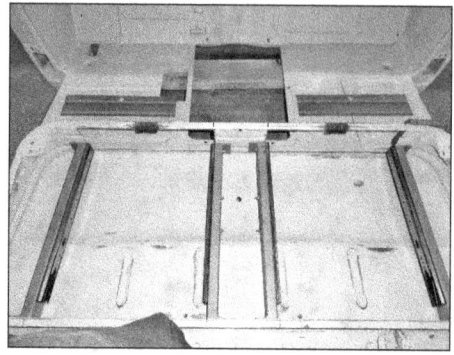

The 1x2 steel tubing really makes the seat pedestal a lot stouter while serving its primary purpose very well.

I decided to use the seat pedestals' metal cutouts for the drawer facing so that when they are closed, everything looks like it belongs there. To do this, I used a very thin grinding wheel and stayed on the straight line I drew. If you take it slow and steady, it will come out fine.

Measure Carefully

I made the drawer slide mounts out of 1x2 rectangular steel tubing. I then made 2-inch square ends to weld onto the rectangular tubing for either bolting front to back on the pedestal or welding them in place by spot welding. I drilled two 3/8-inch holes for each spot weld through the pedestal so it looks really nice. It's very tedious work because you can't mess up the dimensions one little bit. Since it's metal, it is not forgiving, and your drawers will be either too tight or too loose if you don't measure a few times before welding.

As any drawer installer knows, when installing the drawer slides, even though you leveled the mounts perfectly, install the slides tilting backward by about 1 to 2 degrees. That is about the thickness of the screws you use to mount them. This makes the drawers almost close themselves when extended; you want just a slight tendency for them to close, not full-on closing.

The drawers themselves are made from 24-gauge galvanized tin. The place to have tin drawers made is a plumbing and heating contractor because they have all of the bending and cutting equipment already since they make duct work every day. This made for some irregular painting prep but was necessary. I ended up sandblasting the drawers in my blast cabinet to eliminate the galvanization and then sanding each surface smooth with 220 grit. Epoxy primer stuck very nicely then.

The cutouts for the drawer fronts are 4x16 inches, but the drawers are only 3 inches tall. That seemed to work out the best. Because the HVAC

With surrounding foam inserts, heavy items will be readily available and not bounce all over the place.

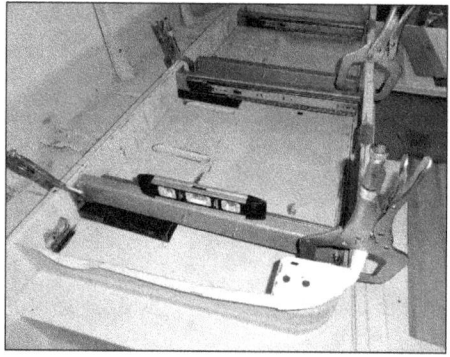

You want to balance the sliders so that the door has a tendency to close on its own, but not too much.

I added an electrical cutoff switch that will be easily accessible by the driver to kill power to the truck.

THE CAB

The foam can be cut out to hold anything you wish while keeping everything secure.

contractor may make the drawers a tad smaller or larger than asked for, wait until you have the drawers in hand to make the front cuts or add the 1x2-inch slide mounts.

Dimensions and Hardware

To review, I used the following dimensions for each part:
- The drawer opening is 4 inches tall by 16 inches wide by $19^{1}/_{2}$ inches deep.
- The four drawer slide mounts made from 1x2 rectangular steel with 2x2 (10 gauge) plates on each end are exactly $19^{1}/_{2}$ inches long, the exact distance from the front of pedestal to the back of it.
- The drawer slide mounts are placed in the center of the opening (on each side) in the front and are level front to back. They are exactly $19^{1}/_{2}$ inches long total.
- The drawer slide mounts are exactly $15^{7}/_{8}$ inches apart from each other (per drawer).
- The drawer slides take up 1/2 inch on each side, so the drawer itself is $14^{7}/_{8}$ inches wide by 3 inches deep by $18^{1}/_{2}$ inches long. The drawer face will cover the slides if you cut them out carefully.
- The drawer slides are 18 inches, are slow closing, and have 150-pound capacity total.
- The lock mechanisms can be found at any local hardware store and are the typical locking mechanisms found in toolboxes everywhere.
- The handles are window sash handles because they are stronger than typical drawer handles. They look nicer to me too.
- The latching mechanism needed a beefier center on the pedestal in the middle top, so I measured what was lacking and put a small block of metal (about 3/8x1/2x3 inches) in the center for the lock. I added shims as necessary to ensure the drawer was tight.

Since I have a floor shifter and about 6 inches of separation between the drawers, I decided to put a master power cutoff switch in the center. Nobody will notice it and it's relatively easy to get to that way. If I had any words of caution, they would be to be very careful how you cut the openings if you plan on keeping the cutouts and using them for the drawer face.

Final Thoughts on the Drawers

In the end, I have a nice way to access the things under the seat. After this restoration was fully over, I tested the drawers several times and I would not do anything different if I had it to do over again. I can tell you that if you are set on using carpet on the floor, you may be smart to sacrifice a little drawer height to keep the drawers about 1/2 inch higher off the floor. This will restrict what you can put in the drawers, but the carpet would mean that is your only choice. I feel the stock rubber mat looks better and wears better in the long run.

Cab Paint

This cab has been through the ringer and was in very bad shape when I started. It took a lot of metalwork to get it ready for primer and paint. There are lots of videos out there to help you with this step. I certainly watched my share!

There is a lot to this procedure and it is very time consuming. See chapter 7 on exactly how to prepare for paint. You can feel with your hand for any bumps, ridges, valleys, etc. and then mark them with a lead pencil. Add more filler, sand, re-primer, rinse, and repeat!

Even after this, most of the filler was taken down further and more added.

CHAPTER 8

Exterior Color

The cab is on its cart, so we can easily move it around in the paint booth to get the best lighting. But the bottom of the cab needs paint too! To do this, I slid the cab off its cart temporarily and added a rubber mat to the pedestal so when it rests on finish paint, there is no damage. I then situated the cab on its firewall (on the cart) to paint the underside. It is now ready to apply the PPG DAS3025 Sealer and a single-stage urethane to the underside only.

I went with PPG Concept DCC Acrylic Urethane in Sunblast Yellow 82960 for the cab underside. This is single-stage urethane and very tough. I do not feel there is a need to go with more expensive base coat/clear coat on the cab's underside as long as it matches.

The rest of the outside will get base coat/clear coat. Again, the best PPG products are used in Sunblast Yellow 82960 in DBC (base coat) with DCU2021 Clear to finish it off. I did not opt to add any sound deadeners or any undercoating to the bottom of the cab. If I change my mind later, I can still do this.

Interior Color

Next, we will paint the interior of the cab. This means masking off all possible avenues for paint products to get onto the outside surface. Tape all holes from the outside using Scotch Green Masking Tape. Green is made for automotive surfaces and sticks well even on the edge. Get a roll of at least 12-inch masking paper. It is essential to use whatever combination makes sense to you that completely seals the inside of the cab from the outside.

Of course, you need access and the ability to see and breathe, so leave the door openings open. Mask

After most of the sanding, the cab is in a new coat of epoxy primer. The primer seals in the other substrates so they will not chemically affect the outcome.

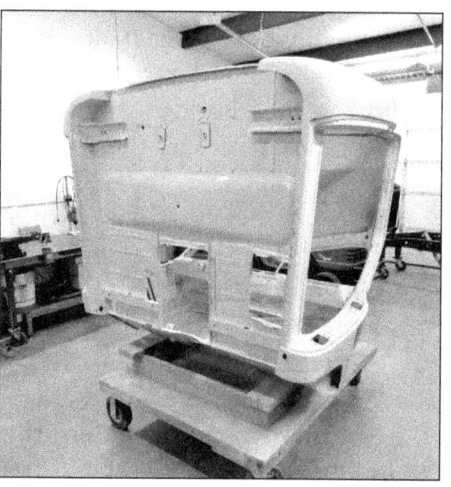

The bottom is complete, so now it's time for the hard part!

It is best to paper around the windshield and rear window openings so we do not trap overspray inside the cab. The more breathable the better.

To keep paint from places I don't want it, I applied masking paper liberally over a large area of the outside and sealed the holes to the interior well from the inside.

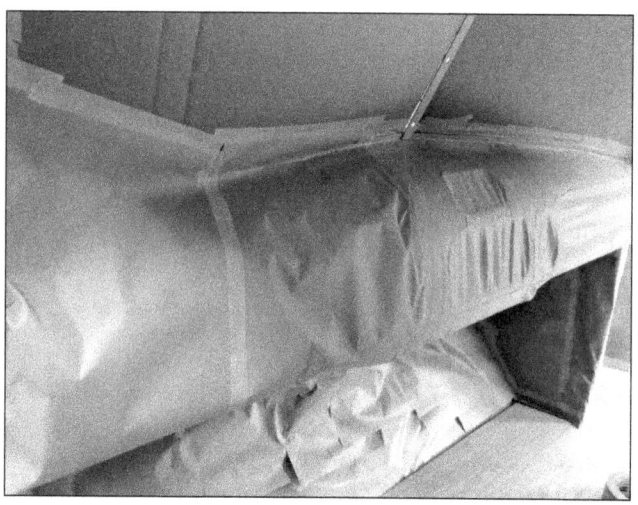

To make this step more manageable, I taped off only the underside of the dash and painted it separately. This was the hardest part of the entire process. Getting into all the nooks and crannies proved to be very hard! I used a cheap mini siphon gun so I could reach into places better.

THE CAB

off at least 24 inches all around the outside of those openings to protect from overspray. All windshield openings, floor openings, and all other openings must be totally sealed. Urethane is sticky, nasty business to remove after the fact. Since we are painting the interior first, if you get a little overspray on the outside, it is not the end of the world.

The next step is a bit more complicated. You will be staring at an almost white (K36 is semi-white) cab that is very smooth. The next thing on the agenda is to use an epoxy sealer. This is how we get by with stopping at 400-grit. Epoxy sealer is made to fill in any scratches left over by 400-grit sandpaper. It is made to final seal the entire substrate and make everything very solid and durable.

Consider Carefully Before Pulling the Trigger!

It is important to apply two to three coats of epoxy sealer. You have 72 hours to coat this sealer with base coat. Once you have done this, shine bright lighting on the surface and check for any runs or sags. If you find them, sand them down with 600 grit, run a tack cloth over it to remove dust residue, then reshoot that area with sealer.

For the interior, I used urethane base coat/clear coat in DBC 915784 (with the variant B Bluer) in a color they call Gray Ash Rose, which is a medium to darkish gray with light metal flake. This gives UV protection for the dash and interior paint. I have used it successfully before with great results. I also had the paint supplier mix a quart of single-stage urethane DCC in this same color for under the dash and some small parts.

The cab is sealed and ready for the interior base coat. Once the interior is sealed, be sure to use a tack cloth on every surface to get rid of any dust prior to the next step.

Be sure to have a well-thought-out plan as to exactly how you are going to proceed with painting. Write it down: 1. Under the seat pedestal lip, 2. Behind the door openings, etc. Failure to do that could result in you forgetting to hit a very important spot until it's too late.

You can use less clear coat in some areas you won't be color sanding, such as the interior back of the cab. Three coats are all that is necessary in those inaccessible areas.

TECH TIP: Keeping Clean

Keeping the dust out when your paint gun is creating it via overspray is difficult, but it's critical to keep everything clean!

You do not want any bugs, dust, or debris in your paint. I am assuming you do not have a paint booth, as I do not. So, the first step is to do some serious cleaning. I use a very long reach air nozzle to blow every piece of dust from the rafters all the way down to the floor. I do this over a few days, cleaning surfaces, walls, etc., and trying the best I can to mitigate the dust issue. I then lay large rolls of plastic to cover the entire floor, using duct tape to secure it. Anything you do not want covered in very sticky urethane paint you want to cover with plastic as well.

Also clean air hoses and anything that you will use. On paint day, be sure the temperature in the space is in the middle of the paint datasheet range. The best time to paint without a paint booth is in the winter after the bugs have gone dormant and there can be a regulated temperature within the datasheet specification. I painted in November after a thorough cleaning of my paint area, ensuring a constant 68°F. Everything came out wonderful. ■

This is the interior after painting. Now I have to be really careful to make sure it stays this nice!

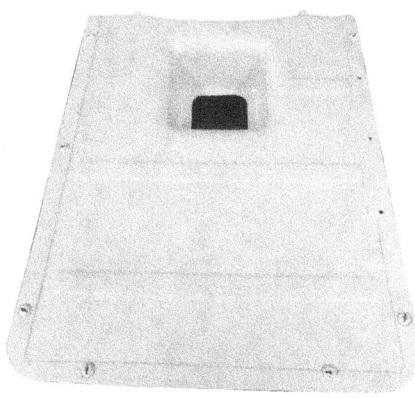

This custom panel made from the 3-speed version will protect the lower shift mechanism and adds some style while still allowing the drawers to come out all the way.

The part that makes me nervous is if you get a run in the sealer, be sure you find it and sand it down before applying the other coats! If you discover the run in the sealer after all three steps, you will be starting all over again! You can't sand the run down without going through the base and clear. Anything you do wrong will show. The clear can be repaired, but once you have the clear on, the base is done.

I am not trying to scare you, but it *is* important for you to take these steps very seriously. Especially when you see the prices you are paying for automotive paint products these days.

Meticulous Prepping Is Essential

Lastly for the cab prep, there are many small pieces that require the same attention. The transmission cover is one of them. Since I added my custom floor shifter, I wanted to make the cover worthy of installing in this truck. The cab itself has new quarter-turn Zeus fasteners, so we need to add those to the cover as well. Then, even though a stock 4-speed transmission cover would work, I wanted to bring the cover up higher to cover more of the lower shift mechanism before adding a fabric boot. This requires a lot of hammer and dolly shaping to make a custom box and add it to the cover. The idea is

THE CAB

It's critical that all avenues for overspray be completely sealed so that exterior bold yellow color does not leak into our newly painted interior. Use plenty of tape and really think things through.

The exterior has several means to ruin your interior paint job. Take special care in the front cowl areas on both sides and door hinge openings. Check and triple check them.

Here is the finished and color-sanded cab from the front/side quarter. This Sunblast Yellow base/clear combination really stands out.

The finished and color-sanded cab is shown from the rear/side quarter. Wow! If you did the prep work correctly, there will be nothing but smooth, clear surface.

The color choices for interior and exterior really make this thing pop! The medium gray with a touch of metallic looks like it belongs with this vintage interior and does not look out of place with the Sunblast Yellow exterior.

Thanks Troy, Josh, Jordan, and Jacob for the help in getting this cab back on the frame. It is always a good idea to have one person on each corner and a supervisor after all of the work that has gone into it. Wear gloves and take your time.

This is indeed a major milestone. Marrying the cab to the frame gives me a clearer picture of the next steps to putting it all together. It's all downhill from here!

that in the end it should look like it was made for its application.

The exterior of the cab is much easier to paint than the interior, even though it uses the very same steps: sealer, base, clear. The procedure is top down, so we will start at the top then go downward. We must make very sure to get the inner cowl areas and under the corners, door, and firewall areas with each pass. Have a clear, well-planned system decided on prior to starting. See chapter 7 for painting details.

This is the culmination of hours of watching videos, reading books, and trial and error. I am very pleased with how the job came out. I waited about seven days to ensure it was plenty dry, then I enlisted the help of my brother-in-law, Troy, and my three nephews to help me get this cab mounted on the frame.

With the cab on the frame, I can look back and critique my work. The paint job is not perfect, but unless you have a small dental mirror and a light, you will never see the minor imperfections. A lot of that can be attributed to dust falling on wet paint. A paint booth is preferable, but all in all, I am very pleased so far.

I am always very critical of my work. If it isn't exactly perfect, then I am not really very happy. But in the case of painting and finishing this cab, I have to say other than a few dust specs that are very hard to find, I have achieved a level of perfection that even I can live with. This was my first attempt at show-car quality finish work, and I believe it came out way above average.

In the end, I learned that it is imperative to use about five coats of clear on anything you will be color sanding. This is because about one-and-a-half to two of those coats will be sanded and buffed away during the process. There is no need to stress over not having enough clear.

With the cab on the frame, I have a milestone to celebrate! What a relief and lots of anxiety behind me from doing something extraordinary.

Cab Glass

With the cab on the frame, I like to work from the back of the cab to the front. With that in mind, we have several things to do before getting to the dash. One of them is installing the glass. I have to install two corner glass pieces and something special: a rear sliding window. I want to be able to reach the cooler in the bed! We will then install the windshield so we can test the wiper system that is installed later.

Rear Corner Glass

The rubber for the corners and the rear are not the same. The glass for the corners is made from tempered glass and is thicker than the rear safety glass. I chose smoked (gray tinted) glass for everything but the windshield. Cab corner glass is nice, but a deluxe cab does get hotter in the summer because of corner glass, so I am trying to mitigate this issue.

I also chose the chrome lock strip for the rubber to give the outside a little more class on both of the corners, the rear window, and the windshield. I used Bowtie Bits Smoked Corner Glass (WW-475-T), Corner Glass Rubber with Chrome Insert (AD-475-GCRC), Rear Glass Rubber with Chrome Insert (AD-475-BGRC), Deluxe Windshield Rubber (Stainless Trim ready) (AD-473-WSRD), and Stainless Exterior Trim (AD-473-DWS). The windshield glass is standard flat safety glass available anywhere, including Bowtie Bits.

The Process

Installing the corner glass, like every other rubber gasket installation, requires patience. The rubber is looped to fit in a bag, and rubber has memory. Begin on the bottom of the opening in the middle so the seam is on the bottom of the glass and the insert faces out.

Start fitting the rubber around the opening. Knead the rubber into place with your fingers; there is no need for lubricant. I thought it would go easier with a smear of petroleum jelly, and I was wrong. Be sure it is dry, even though it seemingly makes it harder.

When you get to a corner and it refuses to stay in place, use masking tape to hold it. Did I tell you this is a two-day affair? You want the rubber to reset its memory to the opening before you cut the end to fit. Knead it in place, tape the corners if necessary, and wait until the next day

Glass Tinting Laws

In case you are wondering if smoked glass is legal in your state, which is a good idea, I went to AAA's site to check. The smoked glass I got from Bowtie Bits uses a 30-percent tint, which is legal in my state. This means as long as it is registered and legal in Kansas, I can drive it anywhere and not have to worry. That is my story and I am sticking to it. Check drivinglaws.aaa.com/tag/glass-window-tinting/ for up-to-date information.

This is the corner glass installed but without the lock strip. I did this myself without help. The key is patience!

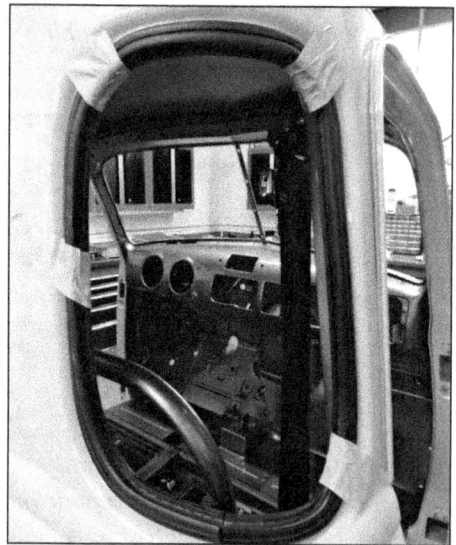

Tape the corners if you have to. I didn't need to tape the driver's side but ended up taping the passenger's side.

THE CAB

before cutting. You can do this all by yourself if you wait.

Cutting the rubber right is essential. It will shrink over time, so it is important that you cut the corner rubber about 3/4 inch longer than will initially fit. The vendors sell this rubber in one long piece that they expect you to cut in half, so be careful to cut it long enough but not too long or you will make the other side too short. Once you have a nice 90-degree, perfectly straight cut using a sharp knife, and it's 3/4 inch too long, put the ends together and knead the rubber into place. Now I know it doesn't look like there is anywhere for that 3/4 inches to go, but the rubber *will* smooth into place.

Once the rubber is sitting in the channel all by itself with no tape or anything in the way, grab the appropriate corner glass and set it into the bottom channel area first. It will go into the bottom fairly easy. Use either of the hook tools to carefully pull the rubber lip over the glass, pushing the glass inward just a little. Do not use a lot of pressure, just enough to get the job done. Be careful to not let the hook tool slip and ruin your precious paint or shove it into the rubber too hard to create a hole or tear. This is a finesse job.

The Rear Glass

The rear glass needs a similar technique. I opted to install a sliding rear window, but the process is exactly the same. Place the rubber in the opening first, like you did with the corners. This time, cut the rubber at a perfect 90-degree straight cut and 1 inch longer than will comfortably fit. This will allow for the shrinking of the rubber over time. Use masking tape at the corners until the rubber remembers where it belongs, then start the window at the bottom, applying even pressure as you use the hook tool to get the glass into place.

Lock Strip Installation

Get a lock strip tool with a nice handle. This is essential because you will be doing a lot of pushing. Place the lock strip in the tool. Then, start the end of the strip that is nearest the tool in the channel even with the rubber seam on the bottom of the

Insert the lock strip into the tool then start at the rubber seam at the bottom of the window opening.

glass. Push the lock strip tool into the channel.

Once the tool is completely in the channel, it must stay there until you are finished. This may not be as critical if you are not using the chrome lock strip, but it's just good practice. It is very hard to tuck the lock strip in once it gets out of the channel. It's much easier to start over.

Since we do not want to scuff the chrome, use soapy water to lubricate the entire channel and the outside of the chrome lock strip. Since the chrome lock strip has a blue covering over it for protection, lubing the top of the chrome strip will help prevent scuffing the chrome. Pull off the blue

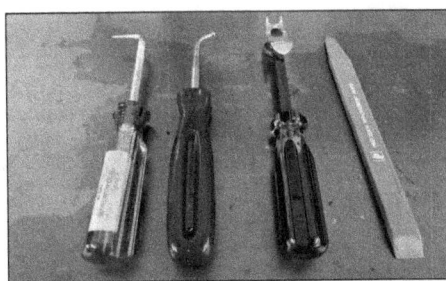

The hook tool (left) is essential and will help you with all of the rear glass and the windshield. The ball hook tool (center left) is used for pulling the rubber into place. The rubber insert insertion tool (center right) is used for pushing the lock strip rubber into the channel. A tapered stick (right) helps with kneading the rubber into place.

To get the lock strip in, push the lock strip ahead of the tool into the channel. It's not hard once you get the hang of it. Remember, if the tool comes out of the channel by accident before you are done, start over!

CHAPTER 8

Here is a shot of the completed rear window installations. The chrome lock strips go with the stainless steel surrounds around the windshield and side glass to give the truck a more balanced look.

Cover the entire back of the cab and floor, including under the seat pedestal but minus the corners. Sound deadening has no effect on the drawer action. I used an aluminum tape by Dynamat to cover the seams.

covering as you go. It is not hard to do these window installations all by yourself, but it does require patience.

Sound Dampening

With the rear of the cab glass installation out of the way, let's look at the possibility of adding some sound deadening material to make the cab quieter than normal. The idea is to dampen the vibrations caused by the metal as the truck moves. You do not have to cover the entire inside of the cab to get the best result. A good rubberized stick-on material that is about 1/8-inch thick added in places that are the most susceptible to vibration will do the job just fine.

The Advance Design cab has three support posts along the back of the cab that used to have a strip of tar paper behind them to prevent the metals from coming together. I ordered 2 feet by 12 inches of Buna-N 1/8-inch rubber mat from McMaster-Carr. I cut it into 3-inch strips and inserted them behind those supports. It will do the job even better than stock.

I chose Kilmat, a product from Amazon (Kilmat 80-mil 36-sq. ft. Car Sound Deadening Mat, Butyl Automotive Sound Deadener), for the stick-on rubberized mat with aluminum backing. You will need 38 square feet to do the entire truck and then some. I did not want this product to show anywhere, so I left the cab corners without deadening. It will have no effect on the quietness because the mat is dampening the entire back of the cab anyway. See the YouTube video using the cymbal test put out by Boom Mat to better understand the principle.

Clean the surfaces thoroughly with alcohol or metal-prep cleaner. Cut the mats to fit and pull the paper off only in a small area. Attach to the floor and then reach under and pull the backing paper off as you go. This gives the control you need to get it on straight the first time.

The cab's interior roof gets its own sound deadener piece that covers the entire top. I purchased it from Amazon as well (Guteauto 236-mil 15 sq. ft. Sound Deadening Insulation Mat). It is a one-piece affair and it is hard to center. I cut a slit from

Notice the seam in the center. I cut this seam to help pull the paper off in the very center front and slowly take it out. This took two people, so we could keep the seam in the very center. Cut to fit the profile using the headliner as the template.

front to back in the very center, almost cutting the sheet in half but leaving about 6 inches at the front of the cab. This allowed me to reach under to pull the paper out slowly. The stuff sticks really well as long as you have a clean surface. As with any mat of this kind, use alcohol or a good metal-prep cleaner to prepare for this job.

THE CAB

> **TECH TIP — Cutting Template**
>
> The best way to cut the self-adhesive sound deadener to fit the roof of the cab is to use the headliner as a template. There is plenty of material to make that profile and even tuck the deadener as far forward under the lip near the windshield opening as you can. ■

Grommets press into the hole in the support as shown. It is easiest to lube the rubber with soapy water before pushing them in.

For the front floor area, we will use a sound deadening product from Bowtie Bits (part number SD-475). It is a tar product that is precut for most of the cutouts needed for the parking brake, pedals, etc. Just like cutting carpet to fit, this product requires some patience and measuring several times before cutting, but a nice drywall knife does the trick easily. Once the floor is covered, we can decide if we want carpet or the stock rubber mat to go over it. We need to keep the thickness total of everything under 3/4 inch so the drawers will slide out properly.

The firewall cover I chose (Bowtie Bits AD-473-AWP) is not the roll-up kind. I chose the solid ABS/jute cover because that is the more stock solution. Although it does come scored for the deluxe heater, do not think it will be easy to install. The jute is very hard to drill through and patience will be required. I opted to go with 1/4-inch screws, washers, and nuts to hold down the cover. I put flat washers on both sides to protect the paint on the firewall and to give the ABS more holding power on the inside. Remember, for each hole needed on the firewall, a subsequent hole is required through the jute!

Before you put the firewall cover in place, study the firewall carefully. There is a lot happening here. I drilled the two top holes for mounting the cover first, hung the cover exactly where I wanted it, then went around to the firewall outside and marked the cover with a marker. I removed the cover and drilled the holes off the truck. No new holes are necessary to drill through the firewall itself. This made the job much easier.

Gas Tank

Installing the gas tank is pretty straightforward, so I won't go into much detail. The tank requires several gaskets, grommets, clamps, etc. You can get all of the parts needed from Bowtie Bits or your favorite vendor. Install the three grommets in the rear cab supports to act as bumpers against the tank.

The original pins to hold the straps in were kind of cheap, so I decided to use a $1^1/_4$-inch clevis pin with pin clip to keep them in place. The tank has a wire grommet underneath it (in the cab floor) and a spongy rubber donut where the fuel pipe protrudes through the floor. The tank then sits on two tar paper pads to keep from metal to metal contact. The air vent hose and fuel filler hoses are then connected with hose clamps to the fuel inlet pipes. There is not much to it.

I went to a little trouble of scraping some paint off the top of the tank and the strap so there is intentionally metal-to-metal contact for grounding purposes. One of the biggest problems with the fuel gauge reading correctly is an improper ground. Since the straps are so tight, they will never cause noise or rubbing problems.

The installed gas tank is shown. This $17^1/_2$-gallon tank is new as original and fits perfectly in its designated place. It is necessary to install rubber pads and a rubber donut under the tank prior to installation.

HOW TO RESTORE YOUR CHEVY TRUCK: 1947–1955

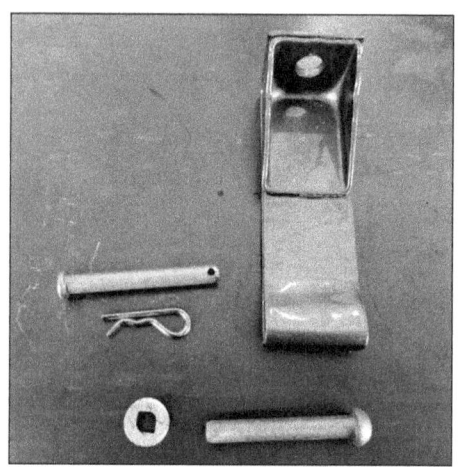

The original hardware is shown here versus the clevis pin and clip. This solution will hold without me having to worry that a 65-year-old clip is working its way out.

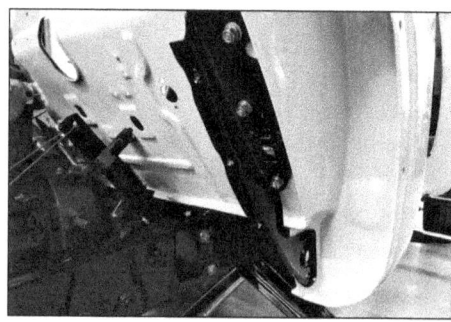

I like to use contrasting colors for these parts, so they are easily picked out when describing them. This bracket is a cause of the rust on the toe board!

to the local hardware store and got some 1/8-inch cable and a few clamps, then watched the video.

The reason I am punting on showing you exactly how to do this is because even when you are through doing it completely correct, it takes two people's butts to push the seat forward because it requires balance in the center. I look at the whole engineering effort by General Motors to be highly flawed in the first place. Maybe it is just me, but I will never use it. It works as advertised, sorta!

With the seat pedestal properly installed, we have completed the back of the cab (minus the seats). I left the seats for later because I need access under the dash and felt they would be in the way. Now it's time to address those things that are *very* hard to get to under the dash.

Seat Pedestal

This seat pedestal has the ability to move front to back using a cabling system. The joke is, you would have to be about 4 feet tall and change to need it. I am still perplexed as to why they made these cabs so tight for a 6-foot-tall person. There is a YouTube video on how to string the cable that is much clearer than I could explain here, so do a search and you can learn exactly how the cabling is routed. I went

Electric Wipers

Now is the time to install the electric wipers. The instructions are in chapter 13, the electrical chapter. Be sure to check it out before populating your dash!

Parking Brake

The parking brake assembly includes a large bracket with accompanying rod and foot pedal assembly that mounts to the underside of the cab on the outside. It also serves as an anchor for mounting the driver-side inner fender.

Once you have the main bracket and assembly mounted, add the spring and hold the pad from the outside to insert the large curved rod as shown. The main rod is held in place with a special shoulder bolt and acorn nut.

Here is the pedal assembly minus the rod that pulls from the dash. Since I am using a special dash panel, I had to make another pull rod out of 1/4-inch rod to accommodate the new location.

The seat cable routing is best shown in a video. Go to YouTube and search for 1947–1955 Chevy seat installation. Those guys did a good job!

This is the assembly from the outside. The pad is necessary to deaden the sound and keep the paint from exploding when using the lever!

Miscellaneous Items

I won't go into detail on the small stuff. Anyone can attach the clutch, brake, and gas pedals. Just be sure to use the padding in the appropriate holes. The heater is installed just the way it came out. Be sure to start the back screws first, then slide the heater in place. The Ranco valve is held in by two screws on the firewall. I go into detail in chapter 13 on electrical systems for most of the rest of the interior.

Seats

Now we can install the seats. Short story of significance: My dad was an upholsterer and ran his own business. About four years before he passed, I asked him to make me a set of seats for this build, knowing I would eventually need it. When he died in 2008, they sat another 11 years in bags and now I finally get to see them in the truck! Thanks, Dad!

Cab Windlace Rubber

I like to do heavy research before attempting to do stuff I know little to nothing about. The problem with cab windlace rubber is that the experts do not agree on how this is done. The people who manufacture the rubber tell you it's *hard* and it requires a special tool to knead and push (sideways) at the channel to get it into place. The question to ask is, how did General Motors do it on the assembly line with very limited time (probably a few minutes) to get this done? There is really only one choice: you slide it down the track! The problem, of course, is that it binds and gets so stuck you are lucky to get it back out to try again! But imagine a stock new truck with no arbitrary bends from people hitting it, no crap inside the channel, and no overspray that acts like sandpaper.

Clean out that track properly before even attempting to install the windlace rubber. Fit some 220-grit sandpaper into that channel and start scrubbing it out. Once the channel is clear inside, use lithium grease in a spray can to lubricate the track really well. Also use a very large screwdriver to lift the channel wherever it is improperly bent inward. Be sure it is shaped correctly along its entire length. This is key.

You must give that rubber a place to go and there can be no binding. Take a close look at an undamaged portion of the channel. It is squarer on the inside than it seems right away. Every inch of that channel needs to look that way or you are creating a choke point. Clean and bend everything back into shape.

Once you do that, you are ready to spray the rubber with the lithium grease and start at the top frontmost divide, pushing the rubber downward through the track. We start there because that downward push is the hardest because of the dash being in the way. Keep going until you have 3 inches sticking out of the bottom near the floor. The extra is to trap the rubber when you add the floor metal retainer.

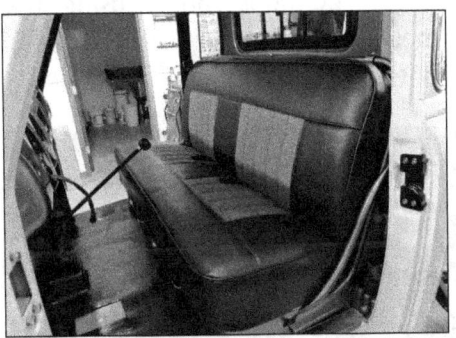

My dad made the seats, which makes them all the more special. Little did we know the interior color would match the inserts perfectly!

Use sandpaper to smooth all the overspray and crud inside the channel, then lubricate with lithium grease to smooth the way for the rubber.

This break in the channel is stock and put there for a reason! My bet is the newbie at General Motors was the poor soul who got this job back in the day!

This is how to thread the rest of the rubber through the channel. Be sure it is not twisted.

The floor windlace retainer, in this case stainless steel, clamps down the rubber and holds it into place.

You want to leave about 2 inches sticking out on the floor so the retainer can do its job.

Next, take the other end, make sure you don't have a twist anywhere, and start it going across the top of the door opening the other way at the break in the channel. Push, knead, push, knead until you have it sticking 2 inches out on the floor near the back. If you run into any major obstructions, remove the rubber and start again after fixing the problem. Once it's in place, cut to length, being sure to have 3 inches sticking out on the floorboard. You will trim some of this later, but it is essential to trap the ends with the lower cab windlace retainer. You see, there was a reason for that channel to have breaks in it near the top!

The lower cab windlace retainer is screwed into place with six sheet metal screws, and the lower cab windlace strip is pushed into place before tightening. This will become a juggling act when you decide to clamp down the floor rubber using that metal strip. For my project vehicle, I purchased a stainless steel retainer.

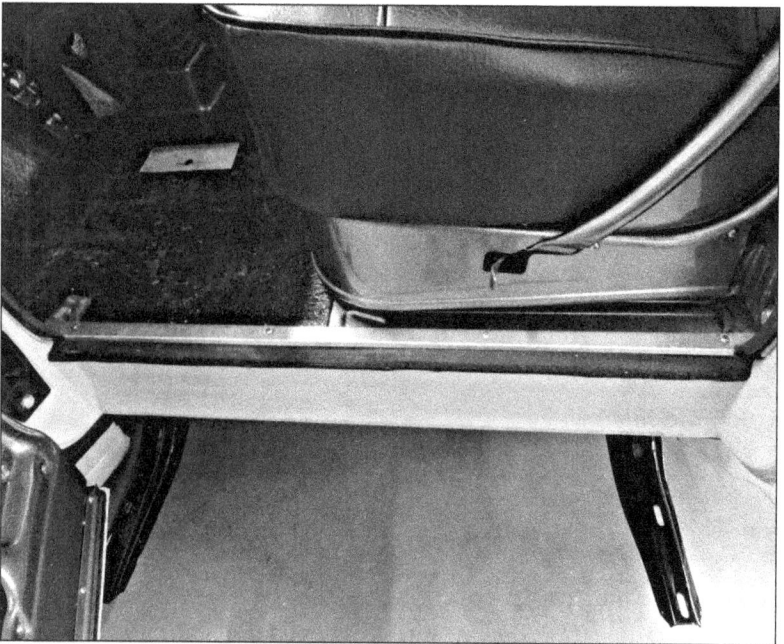
The retainer strip holds the lower cab windlace and is also popularly used to hold down carpet or rubber matting.

On both ends, the retainer is made to hold down the ends of the cab windlace. It can be trimmed as long as there is enough under it to hold it down solidly.

THE CAB

This isn't possible without some assistance from time to time. My friend Mike Fahrbach is a kind person with an AD of his own, and he understands the procedures. Thanks, Mike!

The Windshield

My windshield is getting a stainless steel molding around it, so it uses the deluxe molding rubber. This rubber has an extra groove in it for this purpose. Other than that, the windshield goes in very straightforward. Again, this is about doing your research. Precision Replacement Parts (PRP) is the source for very good rubber for our trucks and also the tools needed for the install. There is a nice YouTube video from the folks at Precision at youtube.com/watch?v=MqcW5QyatIo.

The trick is to do everything on the table beforehand. Spread out the rubber and install the glass by hand. This is not that hard to do without tools or anything. Then, tape it in place at the bottom. Because of the way the glass is shaped, the bottom will want to pull away from the glass. Next, insert the stainless steel molding in its groove, which will allow you to remove the tape at the bottom. After that, flip the entire operation over and install the 1/4-inch rope into the bottom groove, starting at the bottom center and ending at the bottom center. I purchase 12 feet of rope to do this.

Prior to walking the assembly over to the cab, the last thing you do right before that is to apply 3M glazing compound (3M Auto Bedding and Glazing Compound #08509). It is a compound that does not dry but seals the rubber to the

I think the stainless molding really adds to the look of the truck. It's a tougher install and the stainless is pricey, but this is the result.

You can remove the tape after the stainless molding is in. If you don't use the molding, keep the tape in place. It will break as you pull the rope during the install.

opening. Use a caulking gun and set a nice bead all the way around the rubber's outside opening where the rubber meets the cab.

With everything assembled, place the entire assembly over the windshield opening in the cab and have a friend push gently to start it near the bottom. Have him or her follow you around the glass, putting pressure in the same place as the person on the inside is pulling on the rope. Stop at each corner, especially when using the stainless molding, to ensure the outside rubber is not bunched up inside the groove but is spread nicely outward like it's supposed to be. Failure to do so will result in new rubber and another try. Ask me how I know! The stainless molding was the complicator and the YouTube video didn't use that molding.

The 1/4-inch rope thickness helps spread the rubber as you go. Anything thinner would not be an advantage. You will find, especially with the stainless molding, that the window will not go in easily. Tamp it down, being careful not to break the glass. This is a balancing act, but done carefully, the window goes in relatively easy. Rubber has a memory and it will be easier to get the rubber in after it has been sitting on the table for a day to two retaining its new shape.

Lastly, to eliminate the possibility of leaks, press the caulking tube between the rubber and the glass (cut the tube for about an 1/8-inch hole) and bead around the glass using another compound, 3M Windo-Weld Super-Fast Urethane (part number 08609). Be sure to get the tube end stuck inside the rubber, which is not easy for best results. Use a razor blade to clean around the glass after.

Headliner Installation

For this project, I went with the two-piece cardboard style in gray. I wanted to use the trim that came with the truck and I had the center bow and the rear trim.

In doing research on this, the first things that hit you are: it's difficult and it takes two people. Well, I beg to differ. It's not that tough and I did it all myself. You also do not have to wet the cardboard. Start by deciding if you want the passenger to have a sun visor. The headliner does not have cutouts for the passenger's side because that was not an option back in the day. I wanted a sun visor for the passenger. Besides, it makes the headliner installation easier.

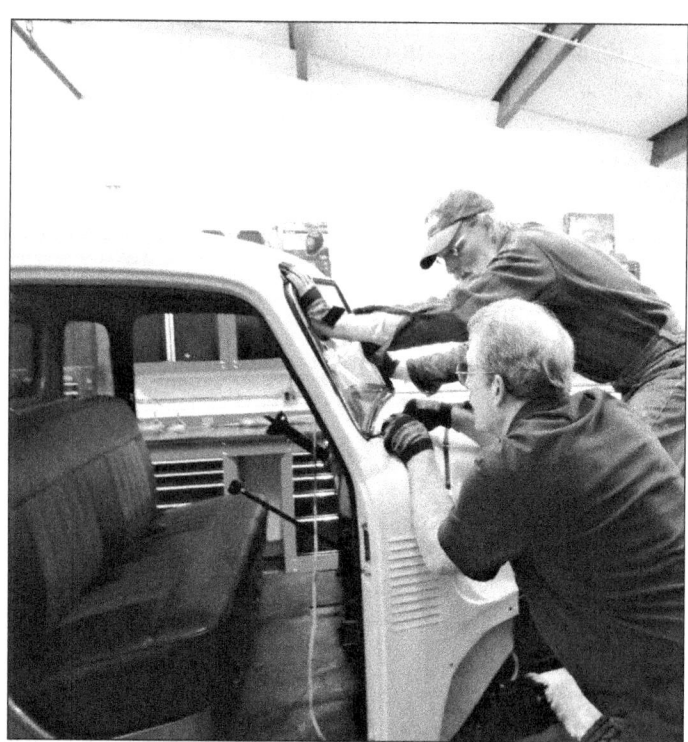

There are certain things you cannot attempt by yourself. In this case, there is a lot of pushing and pulling from both sides that is necessary to get the assembly in place. Thanks for your help, Pat!

Cleaning off the windshield glaze compound is done best with a dry towel. It comes right off.

THE CAB

Installing the Headliner

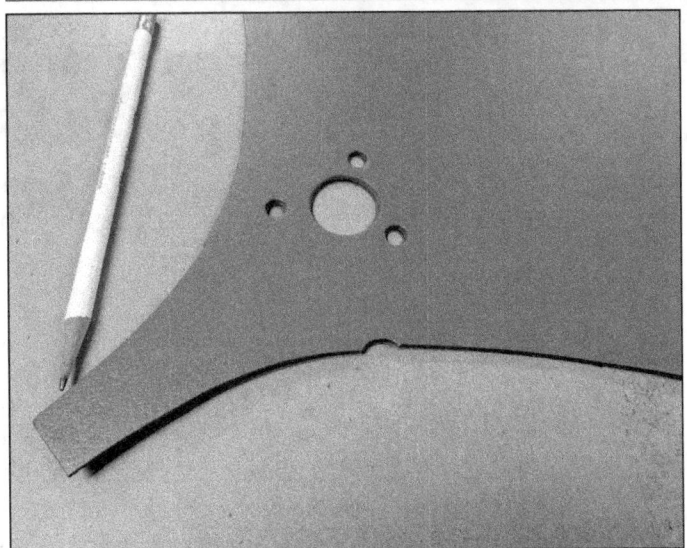

1 With a piece of chipboard, trace around the front left corner of the new headliner, trace around the three holes and the center hole, and cut out a template for marking the other side in the exact same place as shown. Use an X-Acto knife and a steady hand. This also makes the install infinitely easier!

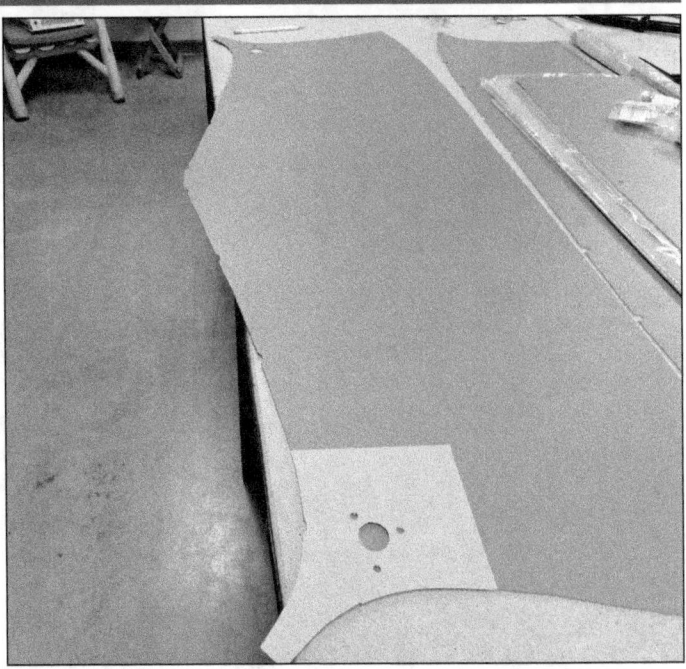

2 With the cardboard template, trace onto the passenger's side the exact hole pattern from the driver's side.

3 The trick here is to place the front section onto the door windlace rubber on top and tuck the front edge into the windshield rubber. Once you have that done, you can easily see where the two sun visor brackets go. Jostle around the headliner and screw in the sun visor brackets using three #10 sheet metal screws. With those visors in place, the front headliner piece isn't going anywhere. With the front headliner piece bolted down, we can attack the rear piece without juggling.

4 Put duct tape on the top inside of the rear piece to tape the rear headliner piece to the bow. This helps keep the shape and allows for a much easier installation. Since the rear piece somewhat conforms to the rear of the cab, the rear piece will sit on the door windlace and then slide right into the bow channel. Be sure you opened the channel sufficiently beforehand, so you aren't struggling with that. There is no need to remove the tape since it's on the inside of the bow/headliner.

Installing the Headliner (CONTINUED)

5 With the tape securely on the top inside, take the assembly over to the cab and slide it into place. The cardboard conforms to the bow this way, so there is no need for struggling.

6 With the two pieces in the bow's channel, all we have to contend with are the screws on the back trim. The cardboard is cut perfectly front to back. It may be a little tight, but if you start the front correctly, the rear piece should go right in. If I had to criticize the headliner, I would ask the manufacturer to make it 1/4 inch wider (1/8 inch on one side of center and another 1/8 inch on the other) so it tucks into the door windlace better. Other than that, this installation was pretty easy. The key is to take your time and concentrate on the little stuff. Once the headliner is in place, all that is really left is adding the windshield trim, mirror, and sun visors. With the back screws in place, the job is done. Not bad for about an hour's work.

Steering Wheel

After everything else is in place and completely squared away, install the steering wheel. Because I chose to use the self-canceling turn signal cup from a 1955 First Series truck, the steering wheel itself is the newer 1954–1955 model. The 1955 steering wheel is designed for very easy installation with a spring-loaded horn switch, a preinstalled self-canceling plate, and a large nut. It is topped off with the horn button. This is another major milestone!

Besides the electricals, explained in chapter 13, that about does it for the cab.

Installation of the steering wheel consists of a spring-loaded horn switch that goes into the steering wheel's side hole, a self-canceling plate on the underside, and the horn cup prior to bolting it down. Then the horn button finishes it off. There's not much to it, and it looks awesome!

CHAPTER 9

Fenders, Hood, Doors, Etc.

Each piece of sheet metal on my project vehicle has damage of some sort that requires either hammer and dolly work or outright metal replacement. I did not look for better ones because that would mean I gave up on fixing what is broke. With all sheet metal properly sandblasted and inspected for damage initially and with epoxy primer and urethane primer coats in place, it's time for another good inspection.

Inner Fenders

We are starting this chapter with the inner fenders because they will be installed on the truck before anything else. The two inner fenders get a lot of abuse. Often, they have rust holes through them, someone added an accessory so there are holes that don't belong, or there are many small dents. Just like everything else, address these problems.

First, weld the holes closed that don't belong. Grind them smooth and tap out the dents with your body hammer and dolly. Any metalwork needs to be done at this stage, then a coat of epoxy primer and K36 will be applied so we can smooth the surfaces as usual. Once the threads have been chased, the staples removed, and the metal has been smoothed to 400 grit, we can apply epoxy sealer and a good high-gloss urethane top coat.

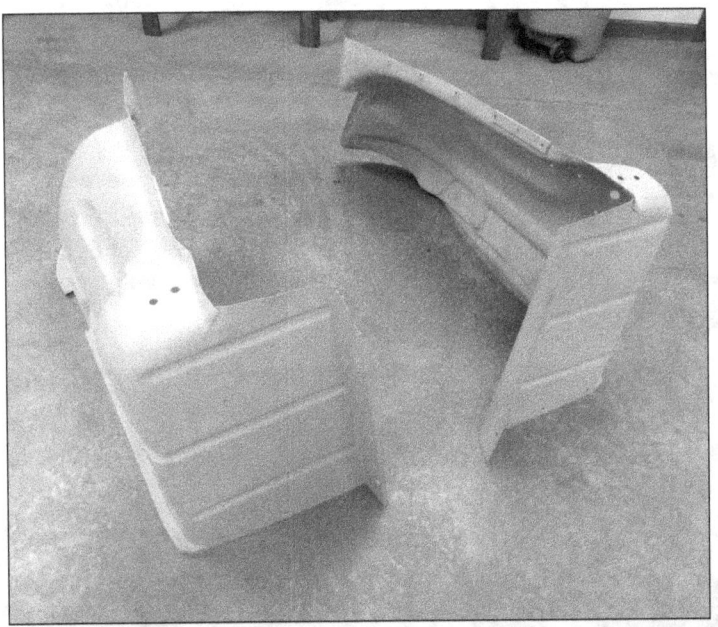

The inner fenders are shown here after the metal work is complete and the epoxy and high-build primers are applied. There is still lots of sanding to do from here.

The completed inner fenders have a coat of PPG premium Gloss Black base/clear on them.

The inner fenders do not just bolt right up; there is the matter of installing gaskets on them. The gasket kit (Bowtie Bits AD-475-FFGS) comes with new staples so you can use the original holes. The problem with that is my inner fenders were done on a Friday afternoon and the staple guy missed all but a few holes. In some places there was one hole, others there was a hole and a half! So, no go on the staple idea. I don't like it anyway. Better to use Permatex Ultra Black Gasket Sealer and glue them down. Clean the rubber groove with alcohol before applying the sealer.

Masking tape does the job of holding down the sponge gasket that saddles over the top of the front area. I used masking tape to hold down the other flat ones too. It helps to put bolts in the holes just to keep the holes aligned. Let the gasket sealer sit for 24 hours before installation on the truck.

In addition to the gaskets, install a three-screw terminal strip (some have four screws, but the inner fenders are made for one or the other), the inner fender grommet for the headlight wires, and the 5/8-inch heater hose hold-down on the passenger's side.

Fenders

The project vehicle's fenders were in bad shape. The rear fenders were badly creased, and the rust damage was extensive. I had to do a lot of welding and hammer and dolly work.

Once you have things pounded out close, apply body filler to the outside of the fender first. This is because you can't pound out the dents perfectly. A skim coat of filler on the entire outside sanded with long strokes in all directions will reveal high spots. Now take the body hammer with the pick end and tap down the high parts just a bit, which further corrects the metal's position. Back the area with the curved heal of the dolly so things stay put. Sand it smooth and reapply filler. Rinse and repeat until only a very light coat of filler is present on the metal, if any at all.

Next, address the inner part of the fenders, but remember that you can't pound anything out anymore. Do the best you can at filling pinholes in the filler, low spots, etc. Because you did such a good job on the outside, your inside doesn't need much work. Use a skim coat of filler on the inside, but be sure to sand most of it off. The entire purpose of a fender is to prevent rocks and mud from flying up. The problem is, the inside of the fender gets damaged easily from normal driving.

Without undercoating, a rock can kick up and cause a star on the outside paint job, ruining your day. So, we will be undercoating the inside of the fender. This is done for

Use masking tape to pull down the sponge gasket that saddles over the front of the inner fenders. This method works very well!

The fenders get beat up pretty bad over the years. A lot of reshaping and repair work is needed.

The inner fender is ready to be installed. The gasket goes the full length of the inner fender and prevents metal-to-metal contact between it and the fender.

FENDERS, HOOD, DOORS, ETC.

protection (preservation) and to create a quieter ride. After all that work, no undercoating will mean a short-lived high-quality paint job.

The front fenders were rusted through at the eyebrow area of the headlight sockets along with the usual dents, metal cracks, and rust damage. Now it is possible to just order new metal fenders, but where would be the fun in that?

All the work described above is accomplished the same way as with everything else. Once the high-build primer is properly sanded to 400 grit, we will apply epoxy sealer and then a premium Gloss Black base coat/clear coat combination. Of course, the color scheme is a matter of choice, but I feel the black fenders, running boards, and grille inserts will tie together nicely.

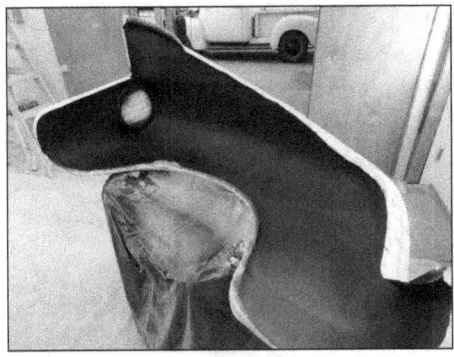

Each fender gets undercoated to prevent the inevitable stars that occur when a rock kicks up off the tires.

This is the stuff I used for the undercoating. It gets good reviews and I now understand why. It goes on very smoothly and looks awesome when done. I used about $1\frac{1}{4}$ cans per fender, so 5 cans total for the four fenders.

The SuperJig is a great way to stabilize the fenders for paint.

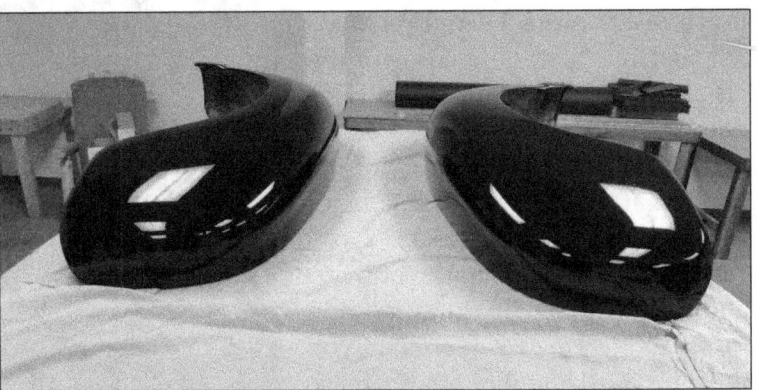

Here is the exterior of the completed rear fenders. The insides are undercoated to protect the paint.

I have a son who is a very talented artist. Kelly was able to capture the intent perfectly! I can only hope to do as well on the actual truck! This was done years before the truck became a reality.

Hood

The AD hood is interesting. I would be willing to challenge just about anyone who has a pristine restoration of this vintage to remove the hood and tap the bracing that holds the hood panels together from the underside with a soft rubber mallet and not have rust come pouring out. The reason for the rust is because it is very hard to disassemble the hood completely. It means removing spot welds and sandblasting then welding together all the parts associated with the hood. Most people do not take the hood apart because it is so finicky to get back together perfectly. Of course, in this case, there was so much rust damage, I had no choice.

General Motors used two rivets and then spot welds to hold this bracket in place. The only reason for the rivets was the manufacturing process. It needed to set this brace in place for the spot welder. So, you can remove the rivets and spot welds and then just spot weld everything in place. But when you do that, you must be very careful to put the brace in its *exact* perfect position. I used 1/4-inch Cleco fasteners for this.

Drill out the rivets with a 1/4-inch drill bit and go all the way through both the skin and the bracket. This allows us to hold the pieces together on reassembly with 1/4-inch Cleco fasteners and gives us a nice size to spot weld shut.

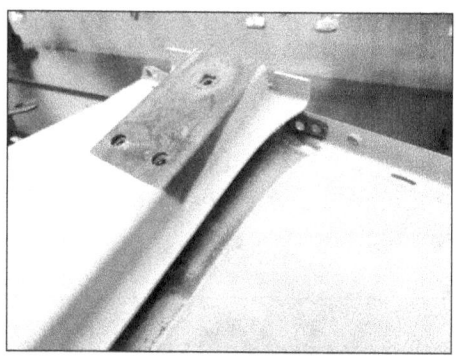

The other end near the center of the hood is spot welded. Drill out the spot welds and the brace will come right out. Be prepared for lots of internal damage.

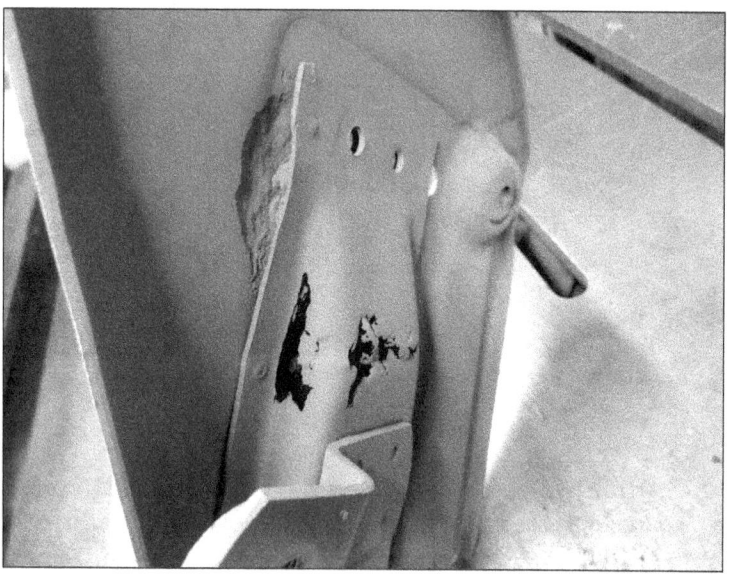

In case you were wondering why I went to all this trouble, here was the common condition of most of the entire truck. No shortcuts!

The damage inside the cavity of the bracing is not accessible without going to a lot of trouble, but this cannot go undone. This is after sandblasting and epoxy primer. There is just no good way to get inside!

This is what is under that bracing. It is normally not addressed unless there are big holes in the bracing. I feel better knowing this hood now has no rust inside its inaccessible places!

FENDERS, HOOD, DOORS, ETC.

> ### TECH TIP: Cleco Products
>
> One of the nicest tools you can have around the shop for the spot-welding process are Cleco pliers and Cleco fasteners. The fasteners are very strong and hold two parts together very tightly. They come in various sizes for hole sizes of 1/8, 3/16, and 1/4 inch. Another type is used for edge clamping. ■
>
>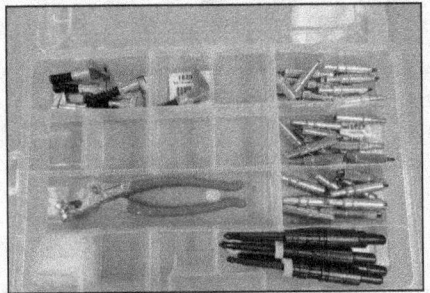
>
> *This Cleco Fastener Deluxe Kit is available from any tool supplier for about $65 and comes with everything you will probably need. I purchased this one on eBay.*
>
>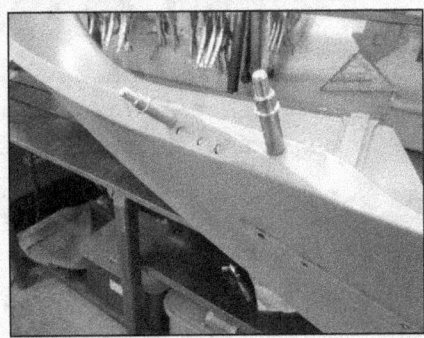
>
> *The holes have to be drilled all the way through, and then the pliers allow for ideal placement and hold everything together very nicely.*

The air flanger has a nice hole cutter for the spot weld holes that are necessary for reinstallation on the hood.

With epoxy and high-build primer on the two halves of the hood, I will sand and primer and sand some more, then add base/clear finish coat. The last thing to do is reassemble the hood halves. This allows us to paint the hard-to-reach areas.

Here is a shot of the completed hood. It is a huge and unwieldy piece alright! I prefer the 1955 emblem design.

By cutting out the spot welds and removing the cross bracket from the main brace, I was able to cut and square up the damage. I installed small pieces of metal shaped appropriately and butt welded the work so none of the repair can be seen. By adding weld into the deep pits and smoothing it, we have a very solid fix.

Once the piece is repaired, we have to spot weld it back to the main brace. I use an air flanger/spot weld hole cutter to accomplish this. Using a few more holes than original, I can be assured this connection will be more solid than before. A little weld-through primer to protect the inaccessible inside of the brace will keep this from happening again. This brace is then epoxy primered separately from the hood panels so there is a layer of protection between the brace and the hood panels. This problem will likely never come up again.

Once the hood halves have the brace welded back in, epoxy primer is used once again to cover all the bare metal of the welding. Then, sandable primer is applied for the finish work. I used stainless steel hardware and did not paint over it, so it is featured.

All small parts will get this same process. I do not use rattle cans! The hood bracketry, supports, and even the springs get the full process.

The emblems on the side of the hood have capture nuts to hold them in. The one behind the bracing is not long enough. I used JB Weld to hold the pin in the hole. This works out very nicely if used sparingly. A dab of paint over the JB and no one will even see it.

The center strip is stainless steel and goes on the same way as the old one. Tines push through each slit and are then twisted from underneath to hold it on. The front emblem is bolted in place with 1/4-inch screws.

CHAPTER 9

The underside of the hood is shown here after all the support bracing is reinstalled. There is a lot going on here, so think the process through, especially if you want to feature the hardware.

This hood was originally a 1950 hood, so there were two sets of holes here. I welded the bottom two shut so I could use (what I think of as) the cooler badging.

Clean the slits up the hood's center of paint with an X-Acto Knife so you don't have larger paint chips from becoming a problem. A 45-degree twist is all that is needed to hold the strip in place.

The new stainless steel front emblem is held in place by four 1/4-inch screws.

Install the six rubber bumpers in the three larger holes on each side of the hood. The hood bumper kit (Jim Carter FP113) comes with rubber pads or bumpers. The four thick ones go on the hood latch plate above the grille and the other six thin ones go on the hood.

Doors

The damage to the project truck's doors was pretty extensive at the bottom. I purchased new patch panels and some sheet steel to make areas from scratch. This is easy enough to do. Shaping metal is really a matter of finding the right profile and hammering against this profile to create any shape you wish. To do this work, I broke out my SuperJig. You really only need a foldup workbench, but the SuperJig provided more stability.

The idea is to have stability while sanding and repairing the sheet metal. Any way you can, you just need stability. The SuperJig is equipped with a hinged stanchion that allows for work on both sides by simply flipping it over at the hinges.

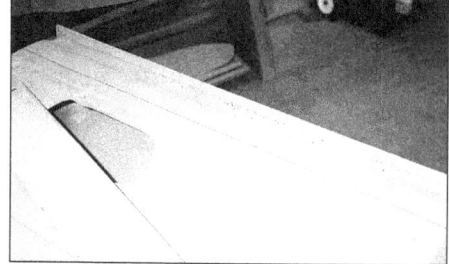

Both doors had substantial rust-through damage on the bottom inside. Many vendors sell patch panels for this. With a patch panel, all you do is put them in! However, if ever there was a reason to worry about warpage, this is it. The distance across these doors is not very stable. Take only the amount of the patch panel you need. In this case, I marked the area I would cut out, placed the patch panel over the hole, then reached in and marked the profile from inside.

FENDERS, HOOD, DOORS, ETC.

Door Repair and Test Fitting (Add Support Where Needed)

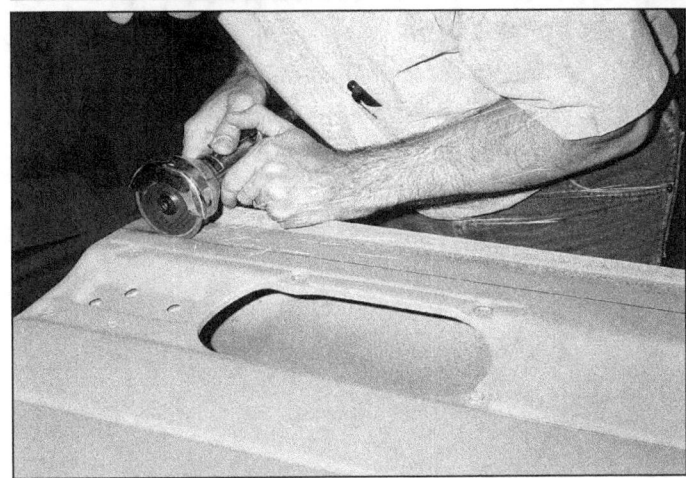

1 I added a piece of angle iron the length of the patch panel to use as a flange under the panel. This added the stability needed to keep the panel from warping as I welded. I learned this the hard way. I had to remove my first attempt due to warpage, and I followed the rules! It's tricky, so be careful. I did both doors, and in the end, they came out looking absolutely perfect. You simply can't tell where the panels were patched. Time and patience is key. The 3-inch die grinder was the weapon of choice for this task. All that matters are good, clean, and straight cuts. Stop from time to time to keep heat from building up.

2 This is a very long span to weld without warping. Adding a piece of 1-inch angle iron under the weld across the entire span will add strength and help prevent warpage. The die grinder was the perfect tool for the job. It created straight cuts that left the edges nice and smooth. Bending the crimp over was a bit tricky (at the bottom of the door) but was necessary to get the patch panel under it. I ended up cutting that crimp over off completely and welding a strip back on after the panel was installed. The job came out looking really good and removed all the rust-through and pitting.

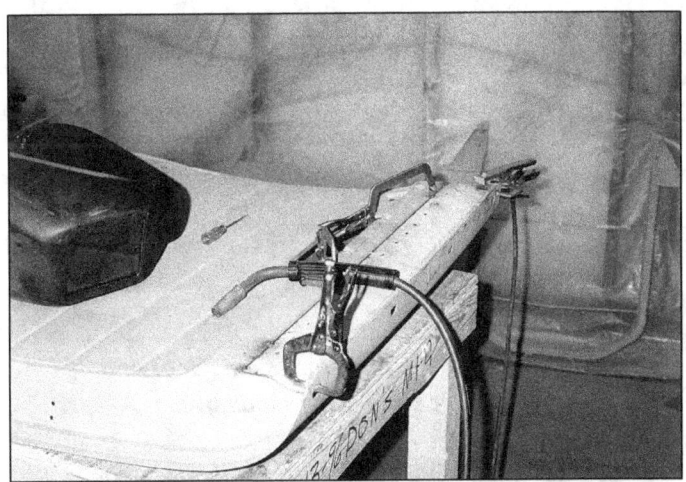

3 The patch panel is installed and fitted. After clamping, there is nothing left to do but weld it in. Tacking it on opposite ends until the weld is complete isn't all; you also must be careful how much heat you use when grinding the welds smooth. You can warp the metal during the grinding process just as easily. You want to fit the panel completely in with butt-weld clamps and Vise-Grip clamps to ensure proper fit.

4 Weld slowly, jumping around to prevent warpage. Stop and let things cool, taking your time for the best result. The hard part of this is getting everything smooth again. After carefully and slowly grinding off the weld, skipping around to prevent warpage, we need to add a 5/8-inch strip across the very bottom to emulate the fold from the top skin since that was bad too. Then there were holes on the door sides that needed to be patched. All of this follows the same basic procedures.

CHAPTER 9

Prep for Paint

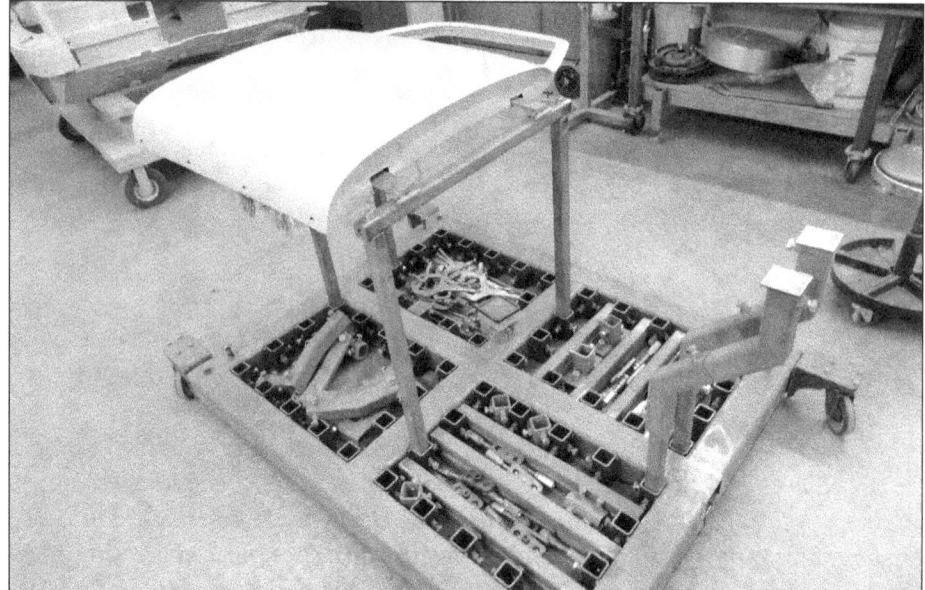

After skim coating with filler, a lot of sanding, adding K36 high-build primer, and more sanding, the doors are ready for sealer and paint.

Paint

The doors are painted gray on the inside and yellow on the outside. This is accomplished by masking the outside and painting the inside then doing the opposite to finish them. I used the pinch weld as the demarcation line between the colors. With the doors painted per chapter 7, we can move on to assembly.

Since the paint is metallic, the doors need to be oriented upright as they would be on the truck. This helps the metal flakes align on the correct plane.

The paint looks amazing! And this is before color sanding.

The completed doors are ready for assembly. The doors should be installed prior to adding anything but the hinges. Tape carefully around anything that could come into contact during assembly to save the paint! It is not a bad idea to have a helper when doing this to ensure the paint surfaces remain intact.

98 HOW TO RESTORE YOUR CHEVY TRUCK: 1947–1955

FENDERS, HOOD, DOORS, ETC.

Vent Window Restoration

To replace all the rubber and moldings and do this right, remove the rubber retainer and latch rivets and replace them with new rivets. To remove the old rivets, drill them out with a 1/8-inch drill bit and punch them out with a punch. I also removed that chrome vent window latch because I want to shine it up a bit. New ones are not available; however, the handle side is available. Once everything is apart, sandblast, primer twice, sand, seal, and paint.

With the assembly ready to start putting back together, let's look at the parts we need to get. I will include the vendor I used and the part number here, but you can use any vendor you wish.

- Vent Window Assembly Rivet Kit (Bowtie Bits part number AD-515-825-KIT): This kit comes with everything you need to re-rivet everything necessary.
- 1951–1955 Vent Rubber Kit (Bowtie Bits part number AD-515-VWR): This kit comes with a set of two each of the outside rubber and the small straight piece that rivets to the inside flat.
- 1951–1955 Felt Window Kit (Bowtie Bits part number AD-515-FWK): This kit takes care of all the rest of the doors' felt and rubber parts for the windows.

Start by replacing the riveted rubber seal to the vent window assemblies with six rivets from the kit. Be extra careful to fully understand the orientation of the vent window assembly as it goes in the truck. You do not want to install these seals backward.

Check the frame to make sure it is completely undented and serviceable. Take care in removing the rubber retainer rivets to tear down the old assembly.

These vent window frames are especially hard to paint because of all the angles.

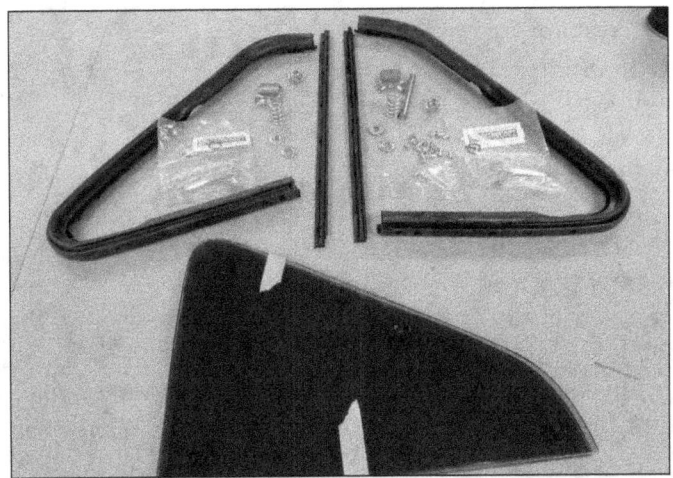

Here is a look at the parts you will need for this task. All these parts are readily available at your favorite vendor.

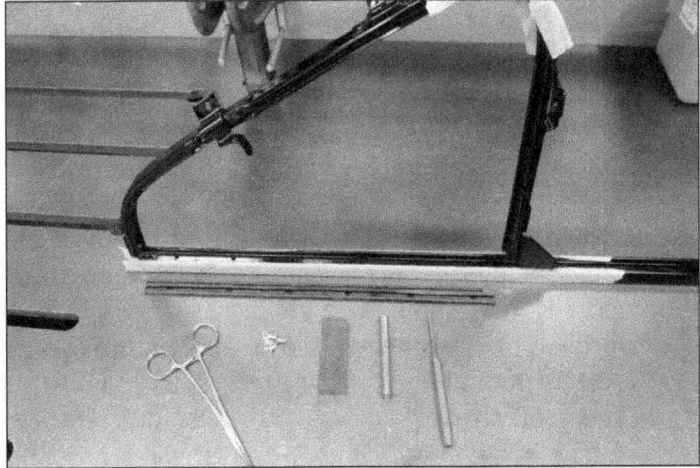

The chunk of 3/8-inch-thick steel is about 1x3 inches long. It is used to back up the rivet heads inside the channel.

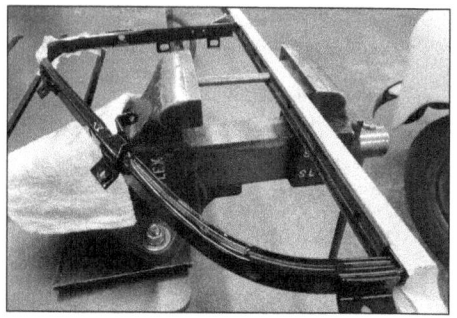

Be sure to juggle everything together straight! You want the rivet to squash evenly. Be sure to tuck the rubber back out of the way so you do not pinch it.

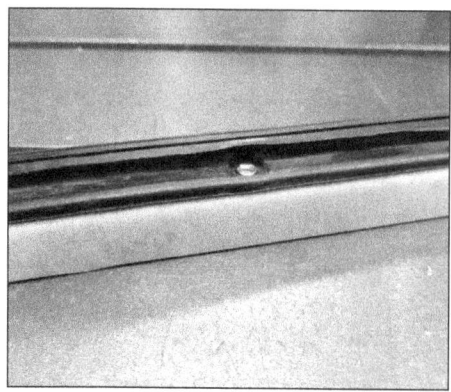

You want a nice, flat, squashed rivet so it does not interfere with the glass in any way.

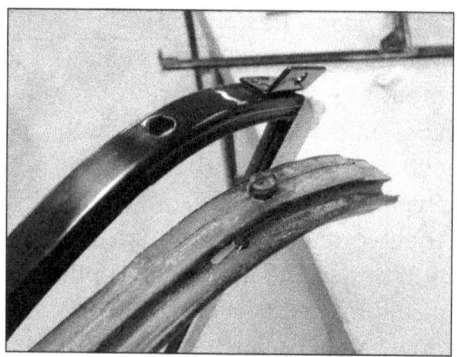

Use the rubber tab to line up the rubber in the channel. I used soapy water to help slide the rubber into place. The rubber fits snugly but very nicely too.

To replace the rivets, I used my bench vise and a 3/8-inch-thick chunk of steel as an anvil to press against the rivet head. The vise opens big enough to use the rivet tool as is; however, if you have a vise with a shorter throw, cut off the tool to meet your needs. Line up the holes with a punch on one end, then put a rivet in one of the center holes to ensure everything lines up good enough to get the next rivet in the hole. I use hemostats to hold the rivet head to start it from the inside.

As it turned out for me, my vise jaw has a hole that happens to fit the tool perfectly, so I didn't have to do any juggling. If that is not the case for you, you can always tape the 3/8-inch anvil to the assembly temporarily to give you enough hands. Press firmly and stop before doing any damage to the rubber.

Next, I put the main rubber in place. The rubber has a tab that goes in its hole, helping keep the rubber from moving. Do not put the bottom part of this rubber all the way down yet. If you removed the latch plate from the vent window, you need to rerivet that back in place first. The rivets in the kit are long enough to work just fine.

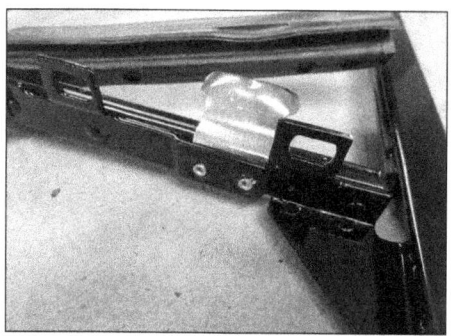

Use the same technique you used on the small rubber to rivet the latch plate in place.

Press the rivets down evenly and firmly so the latch stays in place. Be sure you know which way the latch goes in before attempting this step. With the latch in place, notice there is a slit in the rubber that coincides with the latch. Be careful not to tear it when pushing the rubber in place.

Next comes the felt channel liner that runs up the entire assembly. This will go in tight but not so much as to do damage. Start it at the top, even with the channel top, and use a rubber mallet to push it clear down into the channel. It is not necessary to glue it down since it's tight already and the window will keep it in place.

With the frames mostly out of the way, we can move on to the

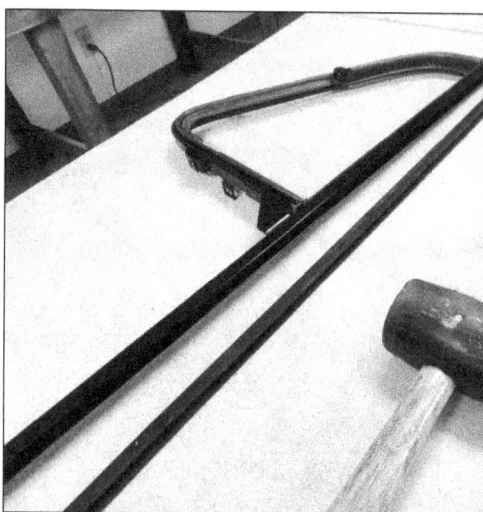

Line up the channel with the top of the assembly, then use a rubber mallet to tap it home.

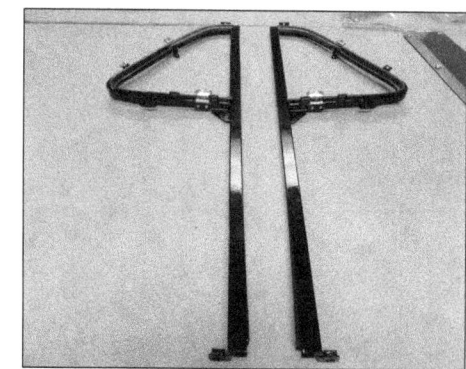

Here are the completed vent window frames. All areas that are visible need to be painted to a pristine level, then care must be taken during installation to keep them that way.

FENDERS, HOOD, DOORS, ETC.

actual glass frame. This is held in place with a roll of vent window setting tape. The tape is pinched all the way around the glass and then the glass is pressed firmly into the channel. If done right, it will hold itself in place forever. Be sure to get the correct 3/64-inch tape made especially for this (Classic Parts part number 70-751). It is made of cork with a fabric backing and the thickness matters a great deal in your success.

Once the tape is in place, set the frame upside down on the table and carefully use a rubber mallet to drive the glass as far into the channel as it will go. Once in place, it will not come out easily. Be careful not to break the glass and use painter's masking tape on all surfaces that are painted. I even put a few diapers over it before whacking it with the mallet. Even pressure is all that is needed.

The latch lever goes on the glass frame with a spring clip, then the latch lever, and is then held in place with a spring pin. You may need to remove paint from the frame's nub so the lever slides on smoothly and rotates as needed. These chrome levers are readily available (Bow-tie Bits part AD-515-VWH-LH or AD-515-VWH-RH).

The entire glass frame assembly then goes into the main vent window frame by sliding the threaded stud into the bottom of the channel through the provided hole. A special washer that slides up the shaft is used first to anchor the spring, then the spring, then another special washer, then the nut. Adjust the fit so the vent window requires a little pressure to open and close. This will make it tight enough that the wind won't affect it.

With the frames together, now we can install the final rivet. There are two rivets in the rivet kit that are different from the others. Those are for riveting the pivot point together. For that rivet, I used the same technique as the other rivets to get it tight.

That completes the vent window assembly. Now for the fun part: the installation!

Window Regulator Repair

The 1952–1955 window regulator is quite a bit different from previous years but still had the same wear point: the roller. I will take you through this step by step, so the old regulator works just like a brand-new one. Of course, do a visual inspection to make sure the spring is not broken and all the spot welds are intact prior to starting.

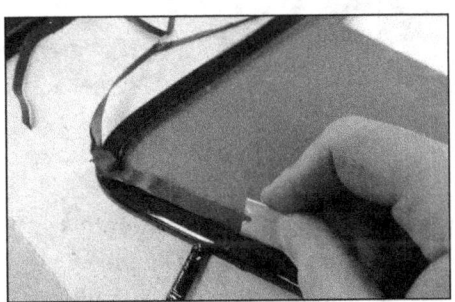

Once the glass is in place, trim the excess tape carefully so as not to ruin the paint.

Push the assembly down through the hole in the vent window frame. Be sure to do it straight and watch the pivot area to make sure you don't scratch the paint!

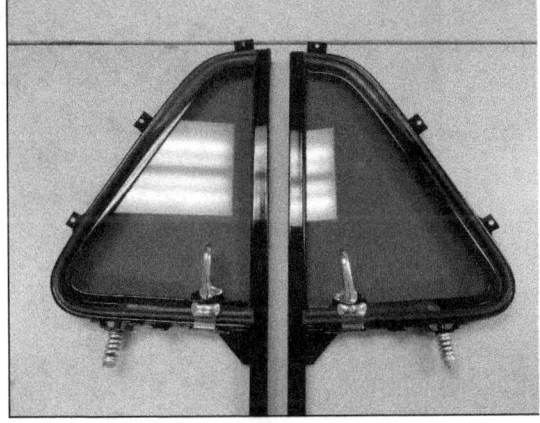

The completed assemblies are ready for installation in the doors.

The latch assembly goes in with a spring clip and a spring pin. It may be necessary to scrape some paint off the nub so the latch moves smoothly.

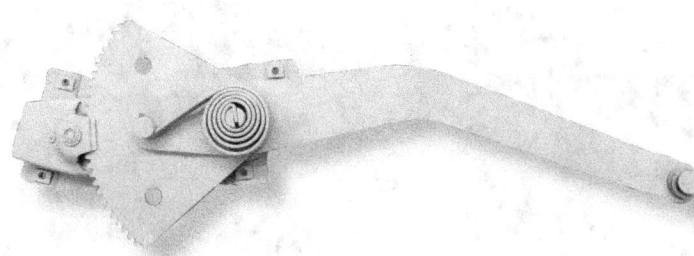

The window regulators generally require new rollers, so I will remove them and then replace the old ones.

Regulator Repair

1 This roller is completely worn out and will cause rattling and inefficient window movement. With a grinder, grind off the back side of the large rivet that holds the roller assembly on. Remember that is not the roller side; it is the opposite side.

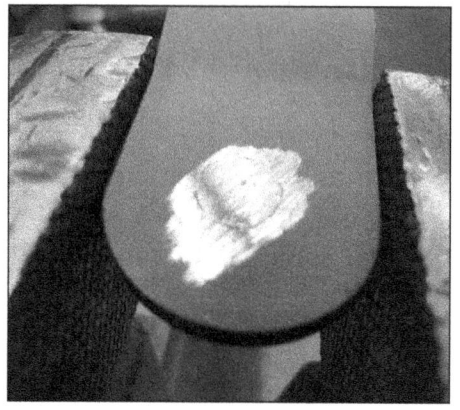

2 Grind smooth the back side of the roller assembly. Be sure you can see the outline of the old press-fit roller.

3 Place the regulator in a vise as shown and use a 3/8-inch punch to knock out the old roller rivet. Clean up that area of the regulator as needed.

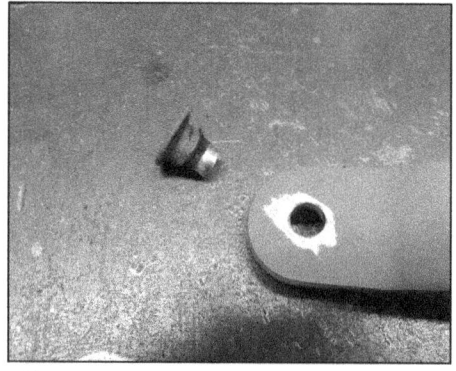

4 Shown here is the separated old roller rivet. Be sure to pay attention to which side the roller goes on!

5 Place the new roller assembly into the hole. With the hole open, set the regulator on a solid table (as shown) and use something to build up the regulator arm so it is solid on both ends.

6 The idea is to create three grooves in the back of this roller assembly that go all the way across the rivet. The first indention should run north to south all the way across, and the next indention runs east to west all the way across. Finally, create two more exactly between the other indentions. Use a sharp 1/2-inch chisel to pound the indentions as far as necessary to allow the rivet to spread in the hole.

7 These indentions allow the rivet to squash down in the vise. With the regulator and new roller assembly in the vise as shown, crank the vice hard. Check the level of squash and try it again until the rivet is tight and the roller rolls smoothly.

FENDERS, HOOD, DOORS, ETC.

8 The grooves spread out to make the rivet tight in the hole. With the shaft tight but the roller rolling smoothly, you now have a renewed window regulator!

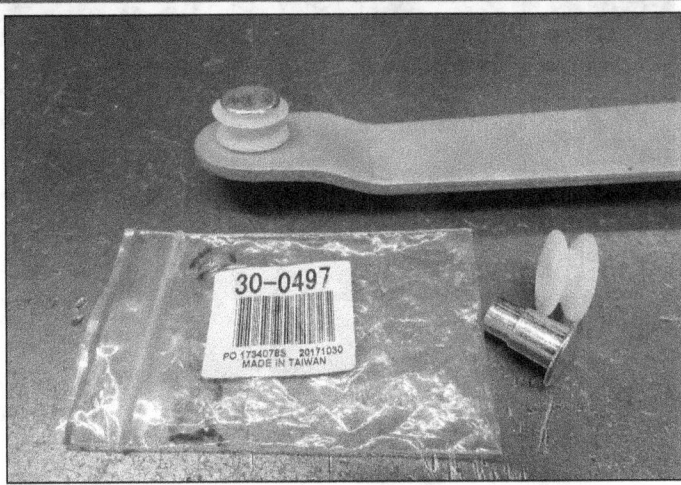

9 Here is the regulator complete with part number for the roller. The roller assembly is available at LMCTruck.com (part number 30-0497).

With the doors' parts assembled and the doors mounted on the truck, I have the best access to the interior of the door and the most stability. The steps for mounting the doors and making adjustments on the cab are in chapter 11.

Door Weatherstripping

Next, I install the door weatherstrip to protect the paint. Cut the inside bottom corner at a 45-degree angle so the bottom strip will neatly meet in the corners. Leave it long by about 1/4 inch. Weatherstrip adhesive is like rubber cement. Put a light coat on the weatherstrip and the door, and let both dry a few minutes before attaching the strip.

With the weatherstrip in one piece all the way around the door, cut the end at a 45-degree angle and about 1/4 inch longer than is needed. There are good YouTube videos on how to do this. Do a Google search for 1947–1955 Chevy Truck Door Weatherstrip Installation.

When the strip is in place around the door, cut the remaining weatherstrip for the bottom of the door. Start with a 45-degree angle meeting in the corner and glue in place without cutting the other end. Once in place, add the door bottom weatherstrip retainer and screw it down with eight #10 sheet metal screws. With everything cinched down, we can make the final cut at a 45-degree angle to meet the top weatherstrip. If you have to make cutting adjustments, you can since you made everything just a tad longer than was necessary. Use a sharp razorblade to make the final cuts.

The door weatherstrip is installed using weatherstrip adhesive on both surfaces in two pieces: the bottom of the door is cut to fit, and the retainer holds it in place.

This is the correct orientation of the door weatherstrip. The longest wing points out.

Because you added 1/4 inch to each side, you don't have to worry about shrinkage later. Cut the bottom piece at a 45-degree angle so they meet perfectly.

HOW TO RESTORE YOUR CHEVY TRUCK: 1947–1955

CHAPTER 9

Screw the bottom weatherstrip retainer in place before cutting the final end at a 45-degree angle.

Door Latch Assembly

Install the door latch inside the door and secure it with four 1/4-inch screws. They only go in one way, and if you painted them, be sure to remove paint anywhere near the moving parts. I also spray lithium grease into the mechanism.

The inside handle latch assembly goes in next. Start the long extension at 90 degrees so it goes into the latch, then bring it around and secure it with three 1/4-inch screws. Yes, the inside assembly goes on the outside of the door. It will be hidden once the cover is installed. Also, the end of the spring points toward the back of the door. This should help you differentiate between driver- and passenger-side assemblies.

Keys

I like all the keyed items to use the same key, including the ignition, the door locks, and glove box. You can purchase kits that have all those locks together and keyed the very same. Also, in GM's infinite wisdom, it decided you must get out of your vehicle on the passenger's side for safety. So, they only provided an external lock for the passenger's side. The driver's side never came with an external door lock! The good news is, with 1952–1955 push-button-style external latches, we can simply add a lock on the driver's side. More good news is that two external push-button locks come in the deluxe locking kit. To change them out or install new ones, you will need a retaining clip pliers, but they are very easy to install.

With the latch plate on the cab and the doors mounted properly (see chapter 11) now you can close and latch the door. To open it, you can push the lever that is inside the hole from the outside or temporarily install the door handle.

At this point, I color sanded the doors while they were on the truck. We do this now because we will be adding the outside door lock and paint protector as well as the stainless steel outside window trim. Sand using 1000 grit, then 2000 grit, then Meguiar's Ultra-Cut Compound.

I purchased the entire truck's lock assemblies together as a kit so one key works with all the locks. This just seemed more logical to me. It happens to also include a driver-side external lock, which was not available from General Motors when the truck was new.

Once the outside door handles are on, the inside mechanism is connected to the latch assembly, and the doors are properly aligned, it is the moment of truth! Time to test the door. I do this before adding the door weatherstrip because it gives me a baseline. When the weatherstrip is installed, it will be harder to close the door. I want to take that out of the equation to begin with. Knowing that it closed properly before the weatherstrip may come in handy later.

The inside door latch does not require any adjusting. It bolts in one way only.

The inside latch extension for the door handle goes on the outside of the door and bolts together with three 1/4-inch screws.

The external door handle pushes a pin against the latch assembly to open the door. This design makes it easy to add a driver-side door lock. I also purchased the paint protectors. When asking the experts, it was unanimous consensus that I should put them on this truck.

Check very carefully that no paint is disturbed anywhere. The *only* place paint should be disturbed is where the latch meets the latch plate. Everything else all the way around the entire door should be left undamaged. Use masking tape in areas you think might scrape the paint. See chapter 11 on how to align the doors properly. Spend time on that step. Getting that right is essential.

Outer Trim and Drip Rail

The stainless steel external trim is next. This is carefully installed before the small drip rail goes in. The holes in the stainless trim do not line up, so carefully drill a few holes in the door with a #36 drill bit to screw them into place. It is a good idea to temporarily set in the vent window to check for clearance for screw heads.

With the drip rail nicely in place, do not redrill the holes for the rest of the stainless trim yet. The felt window channel will require fastening down, and we don't want screw heads behind it. To find out where those holes need to be drilled, we must first install the vent windows.

Insulating Inside the Door

Before we clutter the inside of the doors, it's important to take the time to insulate the area. I used the same Kill-Mat as with the cab and was able to get it nice and stuck to the outer shell of the inside door.

Be sure to clean the insides of the doors thoroughly with metal prep and then a cleaner similar to Simple Green. This will help ensure that the insides are clean enough so this mat sticks to the sides for all time.

Installing the vent windows is relatively straightforward and done after installing the regulator and together with the door glass. The hard part is getting the bolt way inside the door started. You want to leave that bolt out for now so we can adjust the vent window after the door glass is installed.

Interior Trim

In 1950, the Deluxe Cab came with internal stainless steel trim. I have a nice set of these, but I have not been able to find a set for vent windows. To make these work, some cutting is required to accommodate the vent windows. I used a set of painted trim from a 1953 model to mark where I wanted to cut them, then I used a Dremel with a thin cut-off disc to make the cuts.

Also, we must add the shorter felt strip that is affixed to the internal trim via staples. The felt kit comes with new staples, but the original holes are not in the right place for them. To be sure the felt doesn't go anywhere, I used the old trusty JB Weld. Side Cleco fasteners also work great for this.

The stainless steel external window trim is next. You want to put this in before installing the drip rail.

The holes for the stainless may not line up for the drip rail. Be careful to redrill them through the double-walled area using a #36 drill bit.

I could get my arm clear inside to where there was no place I couldn't push down inside the door. If your arms are too big, get someone to help you!

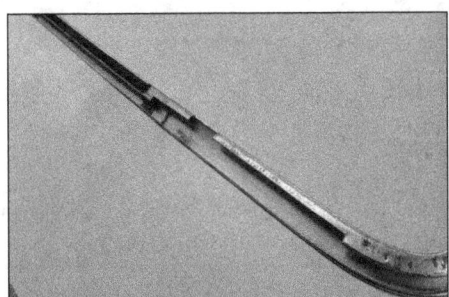

The cuts are necessary to accommodate the vent windows and must be very precise. I used a painted version of the trim and outlined the cut area then trimmed using a Dremel tool.

CHAPTER 9

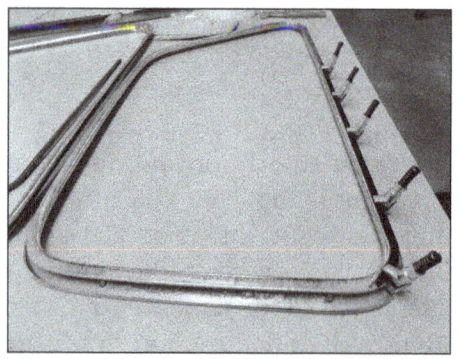

Side Cleco fasteners work great for holding down the felt when using JB Weld to hold it down. The staples that come with the kit have the wrong side-to-side length and I felt it just wasn't worth it.

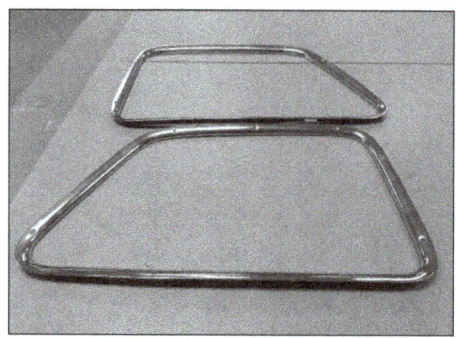

Stainless steel trim will not discolor or chip over time, so a pair of these was prudent. However, it was very hard to find since they are not an aftermarket item.

Window Regulator

The window regulator goes in next with four 1/4-inch round-head bolts. Put the regulator in before adding the vent windows. The door glass will go in easiest with the regulator cranked all the way up. Also, the vent window goes in at the same time as the door glass because there is a little bit of jockeying necessary to get the glass to go in both the side channel of the vent assembly and the door glass channel.

Door Glass

To install the door glass, we must first install the door glass retainer. McMaster-Carr makes sheet metal screws that are called #10/12. I think of them as oversized #10, which works really nicely with old vintage parts that are slightly worn. Sand or grind the heads down just a little so they do not scrape on the cab's door opening when the door is closed.

With the two screws in place, look near the top of this retainer for an elongated and recessed hole. This hole is for another #10 sheet metal screw to fasten the top of the retainer to the inside door channel. For that you need one to affix a #10 slip-over clip to the cab.

Reassembly

The next thing I installed was the outside stainless steel window trim and the drip rail. You must install these prior to the door channel. The new stainless trim does not have the holes in the right place, so expect to do a little drilling with a #40 drill bit. This bit makes a smaller hole than is necessary, so tighten a little, loosen a little, tighten some more, etc., so you do not break off the screw.

For the drip rail, the only drilling necessary right now is to add the three holes through the trim. The holes will be properly drilled in the door, so you only need to mark them and drill through the trim.

The reason we are not fastening down the outside trim is because we will do that when we install the felt door window channel. Using special flat-head sheet metal screws, we are going to fasten down the felt/rubber/metal channel to the double-walled portion of the doors, thus also fastening down the exterior trim.

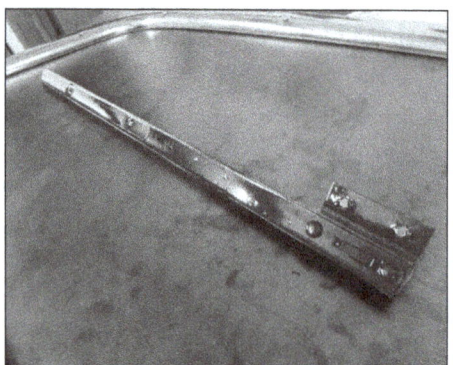

The door glass retainer is held in by two #10/12 round-head sheet metal screws. The heads of those screws should be sanded down to provide a low profile to keep the paint intact when closing the door.

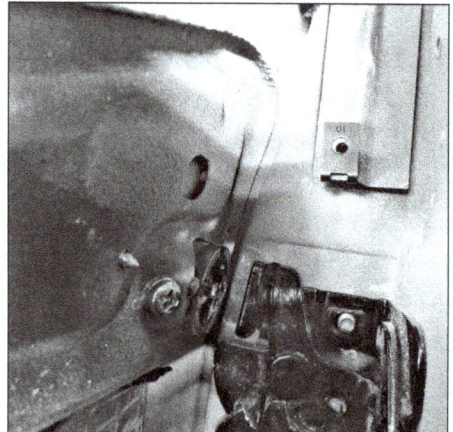

This clip is necessary to hold the top of the door retainer in place. This is inside the door just above the side door latch.

First install the stainless trim, then add the drip rail. Just screw in the three screws for the drip rail for now.

HOW TO RESTORE YOUR CHEVY TRUCK: 1947–1955

FENDERS, HOOD, DOORS, ETC.

Start the channel into the door retainer near the bottom. There is a clip designed to hold the bottom of the channel into the retainer. Slide the channel nicely into the retainer and bring it on up through the window slot and up tight against the exterior trim. Drill a hole through the felt channel into the double-walled portion of the door so the channel is tight against the exterior trim. Then, put a flat-head #8 sheet metal screw near the bottom of the window a few inches above the door glass retainer.

Add screws every 5 to 6 inches, depending on where the exterior trim tabs are located. Keep the channel tight against the exterior trim and be sure to make the channel very tight in the corner where you finesse/bend it to go across the top. Do not drill through the double wall! There should not be a hole on the outside of the door skin when you are done!

Test Fit the Vent Window Assembly

Next, test fit the vent window. Put it in place and screw it down using the three #10 round-head sheet metal screws inside the door opening and the two 1/4-inch round-head screws at the sill. Once it is solidly in place, you can cut the felt channel to meet it. Be sure it is long enough to fit hard against the vent channel. Do not put the last screw in place in the channel yet. Leave about 8 inches without any screw.

Using flat-head #8 sheet metal screws every so often up the door glass opening holds the exterior trim and the channel in place very tightly without any interference. Stop about 8 inches from where the vent window would go. The last screw will go in after the vent window assembly is in place.

Now, slide the vent window forward. The vent window needs to be very loose and moveable to get the glass in. This may require bending the channel inward a little to get it out of the way, just be very delicate about it and it will all go back into place.

With the vent window out and the window regulator cranked all the way up, we can attempt to install the door glass. Tuck the rubber track out of the way and slide the door glass into the regulator's track, tilting the glass downward at the front of the door. It should slide right into place. Roll the window all the way down and hold on to the unsupported side.

Now it's just a matter of juggling. With the door glass all the way down and even on both sides, put the vent assembly into place at an angle to catch the corner of the door glass. Finesse the vent into place, pushing it

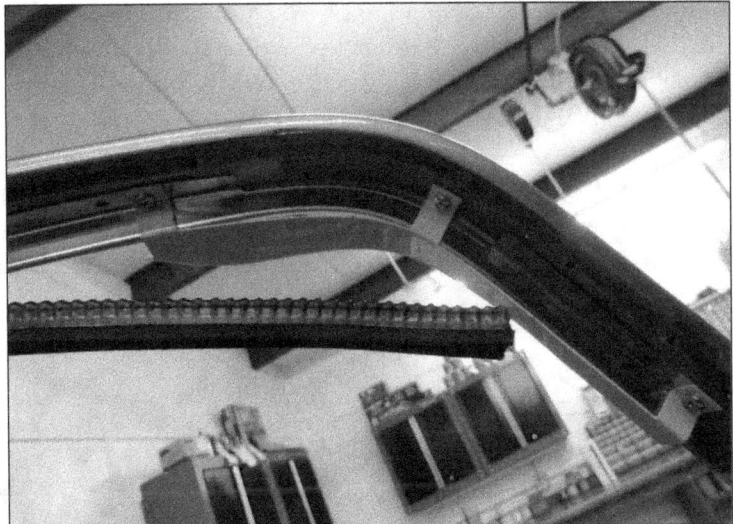

Don't screw down the channel anywhere near the vent window just yet. It keeps the vent window assembly from moving, and we need to do some juggling to get the door glass in!

Test fit the vent window to make sure everything fits nicely. Cut the door channel at the vent window flush after screwing down the vent assembly completely.

With the window crank all the way up and no vent window assembly in place yet, we can slide the main door glass into place.

HOW TO RESTORE YOUR CHEVY TRUCK: 1947–1955 107

down and keeping an eye on that vent channel. You want to always keep the door glass inside the channel.

Roll up the door glass slowly as you get it in, making sure the vent window goes nicely into place. I performed this procedure on a truck prior to this one, so I have done this procedure three times in all. This is the best way I found to do it.

Like the vent window glass, the door glass is held in place with setting tape. This tape must be tight enough to hold the window very well. Once the tape is wrapped at the bottom of the window, it should be hard to get it into place with a rubber mallet. Take it slow and easy so as not to break the glass or bend the sash. A lot of the success will depend on using the correct setting tape. The tape I used is 3/64 inch.

If the door glass is not tight, put the channel piece in a vise and very carefully bend the channel so it is just slightly narrower than before. Be very gentle doing this and it will be tighter when you try again. Also, banging hard with a rubber mallet to set the channel into place may bend the channel, so look carefully at your end result.

I ended up using channel locks to bend the channel straight again. I also used a cloth under the window prior to any hammering with the mallet. I like to tape up the door glass on both sides, keeping the tape away from the edges by at least 1/2 inch. This is to prevent scratches or shattering if something crazy happens.

With the door glass rolled up all the way and in the channel nice and straight, secure the vent window with the three sheet metal screws and three 1/4-inch screws at the sill. Now, roll the window back down (and up) a few times to check fitment. If everything goes right, you are almost done. Put a flat-head screw (or two) in the channel near the vent window to secure it, then put that very-hard-to-get-to 5/16-inch bolt in the very bottom of the vent window post deep inside the door. This bolt is used to ensure the channel doesn't spread and make the window movement sloppy. This hole is elongated to make it tighter or looser as needed.

All that is left for the doors at this point is adding the cardboard interior cover, the handles with the sponge gaskets tightened down with a set screw on each one, the armrests, the

With the door glass rolled all the way down, angle in the vent assembly, catching the corner of the door glass in the vent's channel. Then, push the vent window into place carefully. Once the vent assembly is most of the way in, you can slowly roll up the door glass until everything fits perfectly.

The 1947–1953 doors had #10-24 threaded holes in the door for fastening the interior cover while the 1954–1955 doors just had holes for button clips. Either way, the cover, handles, and armrests are installed pretty easily.

FENDERS, HOOD, DOORS, ETC.

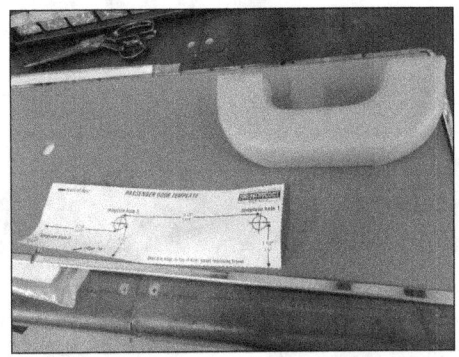

The armrests come with a template for determining where to make the holes in the cardboard. With stainless trim, I had to custom cut the cardboard a little to get everything to fit.

The outside of the door is shown after installation of the vents and door glass. With the glass cut appropriately, the windows slide up and down perfectly.

bottom access cover, and the stainless inside trim that I salvaged and customized for vent windows. Now that wasn't so hard, was it?

My Experience with Window Glass

I had an expensive and time-consuming setback in trying to sort out the door glass. The vendor-supplied vent window channel for the door glass was too narrow and held the glass too tightly. The vendor promptly replaced them with wider channels. Then, the door glass was also made too wide, making it impossible to roll the windows up or down. This was frustrating for the vendor, not to mention me!

Be sure your door glass moves smoothly through the vent channel before total installation. If you get it all together and find it impossible or too hard to roll the window up or down, stop. Do not ruin your regulator. Instead, take the glass to a glass shop and have them trim no more than 1/8 inch off the straightest edge of the glass (left to right). Taking too much off will result in the door cocking sideways as you roll it up, or worse, so be sure to take this situation seriously and patiently if you run into problems. Slightly too small could be fixed with shims on the door channel side, but too big is just an issue that will take time to remedy.

Before you make that determination, be sure the vent window is completely installed and adjusted (even the bolt that is hard to get to inside the door). This problem is due to the inexactness of the door sizes in the 1950s' manufacturing process. In my case, through three different door openings, all the glass purchased needed to be cut 1/8 inch shorter side to side to fit properly.

The Cab Floor

Most vendors sell a nice rubber mat for the floor that looks very original and very nice in the truck. There will never be a good solution for the floor because of the battery door opening and the master cylinder access. I have tried several different solutions, and none of them pass the test of people getting in and out of the cab without messing something up. The rubber mat is the best way to go in my opinion.

Another reason I did not use carpet is because of the drawer system. I needed the clearance the mat provides in its lower profile. Keeping the mat clean is as simple as just spraying on a cleaner such as Simple Green and wiping it off. Any product that does not leave soap residue will work.

The floor mat is tucked under the stainless door trim so it does not flop around. However, that also makes it harder to get to the battery and master cylinder for maintenance.

CHAPTER 10

Heater System Restoration

The heater system in this build will be stock with some very important improvements. The Harrison recirculating heater I found was really a very deluxe system for its day. The system consists of a motor, heater core, fan, housing, Ranco heater control valve that allows you to control the amount of heat produced, and custom (or modified stock) heater switch.

A cable allows us to switch from floor heat to defrost mode. I am not putting air-conditioning in this truck right away, and I want the heater to reflect the same pristine quality as the rest of the build, so let's get started!

Here is the heater just taken out of the truck. Where to start? We have a few issues to consider. The two main issues are making it look like new and making it work like new. In this case it will be better than new since we will also use a 12-volt motor to run it. In addition, the unit must look 100-percent original.

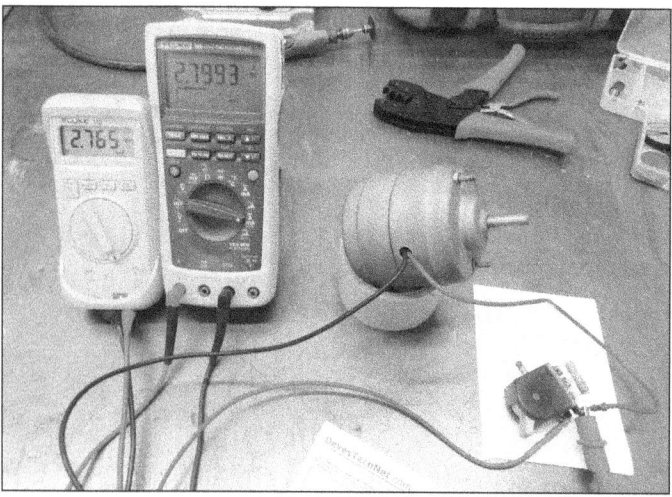

Testing different configurations and combinations of resistors using a car battery and enough wiring we can ensure that we do not create a fire hazard under the dash!

Note not only how the ducts are arranged but also how much play in the defroster cable is normal. This will help during reassembly.

The negative lead of the motor was originally grounded on the outside of the case.

HEATER SYSTEM RESTORATION

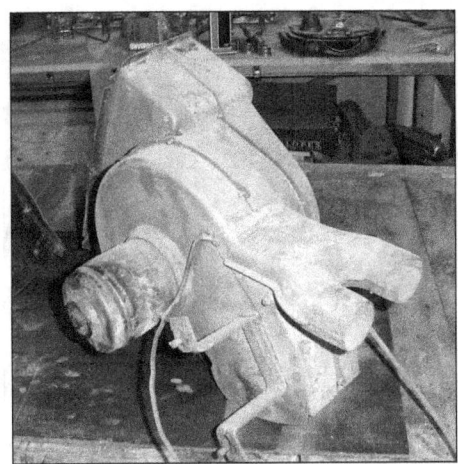

This photo will help us figure out the relationship of the parts during reassembly. Once you have it apart, it becomes apparent how important the before pictures can be.

The heater core and how it is installed in the housing is shown here. This is a 1947–1952 Harrison. The 1953–1955 models had a fresh-air diversion panel that changed the mounting just a little.

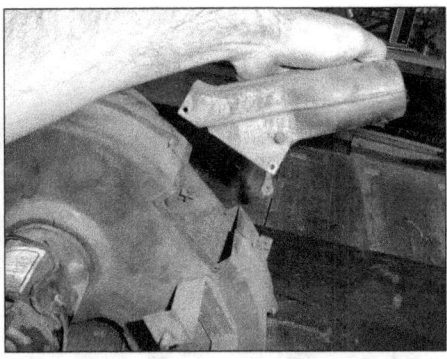

This image shows how the small duct housing is attached to the motor housing. Inside the main housing is a small rubber bumper.

The two halves of the core housing are assembled. Just about everything involved in this project is fastened with #6 x 3/8-inch Phillips Pan Sheet Metal Screws. Buy new ones; they are cheap. I go the extra mile with hardware. I get stainless steel screws for this through McMaster-Carr.

The rest of the core housing has been removed from the motor housing. There are no gaskets between the two.

When the two shells of the fan assembly are apart, a set screw holds in the hamster wheel.

Disassembly

It is a good idea to take plenty of pictures of everything you are unfamiliar with. Nowadays, you can just pull out your smartphone; it's not like back when we had to get the film processed first! After taking photos, you can begin to take everything apart. Be sure to set things on the worktable in a logical order.

Next, check the heater core. They tend to go bad, and we need to make sure we have one that will not leak all over the interior. To check the core for leaks, lower the pressure on your air compressor to 10 psi, plug one end, and put 8 to 10 psi into the core. This vintage vehicle has a 4-psi radiator, which is more than enough but not too much more. Submerge the core completely in a sink or a container and check for leaks. Any bubbles or telltale signs of leakage means it's time to take it to the local radiator shop for repair.

The small duct has two rubber bumpers that are normally either gone completely or too brittle to reuse. You can order new ones from Marshall's Hardware (part number 0505510) for about 70 cents each. Another source is Steele Rubber Products (part number 33-0127-41) for about $1 each. It's best to just replace them since everything else will be like new.

Removing the fan is easy. There is a slotted screw on the side of the shaft that needs to be loosened, and then with a little persuasion with a punch, the fan will come right off. Be careful not to beat on things too hard; it is very possible to bend the fan cage.

CHAPTER 10

The entire heater is disassembled here. There isn't a lot to it, but these photos should help in getting it all back together correctly.

Shown are the Harrison faceplate, the motor-to-housing gasket, and the placement of the aforementioned rubber bumper. There are two of the pesky rubber bumpers.

With the entire heater disassembled, take all the metal parts to the blast cabinet. I cannot impress enough the importance of blasting all sheet metal parts on these old trucks.

After sandblasting, you will find damage that otherwise would have been hidden. In this case, I have rust holes to contend with. Follow the usual procedure of squaring up the hole, finding a suitable scrap of sheet metal, cutting it to size, and butt welding it in.

If we weld this in right, nobody will be able to tell it was ever rusted through. This is what happens when a core leaks and creates rust problems. In addition, we have to make a few metal repairs here and there.

The two rubber bumpers go here. The idea is to dampen the sound of opening and closing the gate.

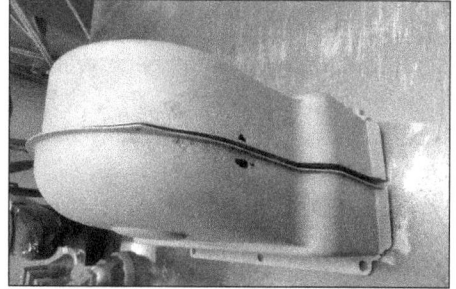

This reveals rust holes that we couldn't see prior to blasting. Rather than painting over them and calling it a day, let's address these problems further.

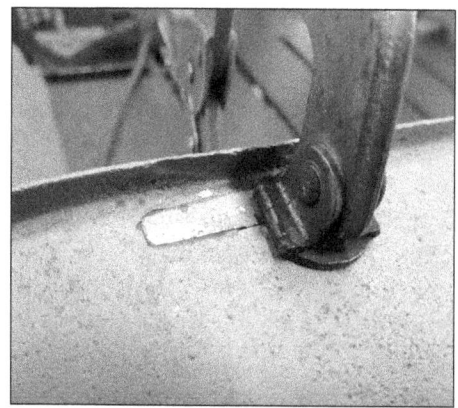

This was just a matter of making the hole more rectangular, putting a small piece of 14-gauge metal in place, and welding it in. Be sure to set your MIG welder to a low temperature setting that is appropriate for thin sheet metal; otherwise, you will have more holes instead of fewer!

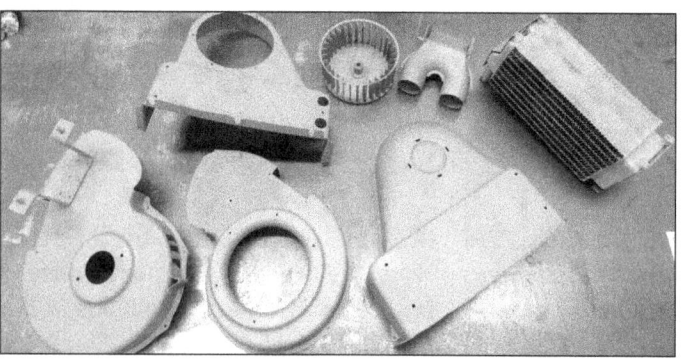

All of the metal parts are fresh out of the blast cabinet. Go easy on the heater core. The idea is to get the cobwebs blasted out. Now we can take care of any damage.

HOW TO RESTORE YOUR CHEVY TRUCK: 1947–1955

HEATER SYSTEM RESTORATION

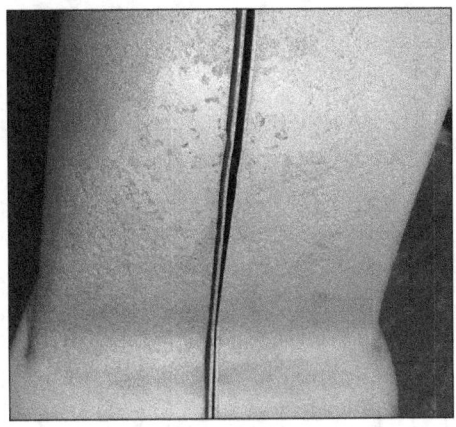

This butt weld looks like it isn't even there on both sides of the work.

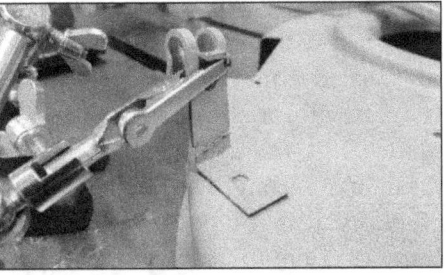

Repairs also included adding the defroster cable clamp that had broken off. This is the exact same one that is used on a carburetor. I fashioned this piece so it could be welded onto the old broken mount.

I use a premium quality filler and then sand everything down. This is a painstaking process, but when completed, the metal will look just like it came out of the factory.

One of the repairs I needed to make was fix the bracket that holds the defroster cable in place. Then I had to pound out the dents and smooth out the sheet metal by sparingly using Rage Gold Filler. After that was sanding and more sanding! When done, it looked just as good or better than factory.

With a missing screen, I found that General Motors used 1/4-inch hardware cloth, and I was able to source that at the local hardware store. I cut out a small piece and used JB Weld to hold it down. The reason for JB Weld is because the hardware cloth is galvanized and will not weld easily. It worked perfectly.

Motor

The motor is another challenge. The original 6-volt motor has a larger diameter and the cab happens to be cut out exactly to accommodate that size of motor sticking out on the firewall. If we used a smaller-diameter motor, it would be obvious and cause fitment issues.

To resolve this, gut the 6-volt motor housing completely, removing the spot-welded retainer on one half of the housing so there is nothing left to remove. Then we can install the 12-volt motor right inside the 6-volt housing.

I'm not finished yet. There is a small retaining hub inside the housing that is spot welded in. It has to go!

Here is the properly gutted housing. No turning back now! The good news is, this is a value-added procedure.

My heater had a missing screen. Fortunately, General Motors used 1/4-inch hardware cloth that is available at most hardware stores.

The motor on the left is the 6-volt original; the one on the right is a 12-volt replacement.

Disassembling the 6-volt motor is pretty straightforward. Remember, all we care about is the case. Remove everything, including any riveted plates you may encounter. We have to make room for the 12-volt motor.

CHAPTER 10

I am often asked how I went about doing this swap. The key thing is to get all the guts out of the 6-volt case. On each end, there is a round molded metal piece that is spot welded into the case. With a Dremel tool or whatever you have to remove spot welds, carefully remove the spot welds, taking care to not go through both pieces of metal. I have a hard time getting these out too, but once one of the spot welds is loose, you can use a pair of pliers to get the piece out.

The 6-volt motor disassembles pretty easily. I use a 1/8-inch drill bit to drill out the rivets holding the brush block to the case, then I tap the outside core out with a screwdriver, lightly tapping all the way around until it pops out. We will use no packing or anything to keep our 12-volt motor centered, nor will we remove anything from the 12-volt motor. The motor just like it comes out of the box will go right into our new case.

I sandblast the case parts inside and out, then clean everything with a Dremel tool with a light wire brush. This shines up the brass and metal quite nicely. Once everything is complete, I will take it apart for the last time and clean the case inside and out with PPG's SX330, then primer and paint inside and out to prevent rust. Don't forget, this is just a shell. The motor inside is 100-percent protected against any damage or anything since it is sealed from the factory.

The motor shown here is a standard 12-volt replacement motor available through any of our truck vendors. It is the best motor for this project. Siemens began making the PM354 awhile back, now the company has been purchased by VDO. Both the 6-volt and 12-volt motors had a maximum of 3,500 rpm, which is perfect for our application.

The only modification we have to do for this setup is to elongate six holes. Four in the motor casing and two in the Harrison housing assembly to attach the motor. Elongating the holes will not change anything, and it will be a nice snug fit. I use a Dremel tool for this process.

The motor shaft is centered in the case's shaft hole, and nothing can move around because it is bolted in from the bottom and from the top. Aligning the top and bottom halves are no problem whatsoever. After this step, I will put a piece of 1/4-inch shrink tubing about 10 inches long over the wires inside the case as far as possible. Then, I added an 8-32 round terminal to the negative (orange in this case) lead for grounding to the case and a splice on the positive lead for adding more length later.

TECH TIP: Swapping Wires

The original 6-volt motor is a counterclockwise motor, but the replacement 12-volt motor (PM354) is a clockwise motor. Fortunately, I can just switch the wires and we are good to go. Using the two wires coming out of the motor, orange goes to ground and black goes to the positive line. Don't forget to do this or you will be very disappointed in the performance of your heater!

Here is what the 6 volt (left) and 12 volt (right) look like side by side.

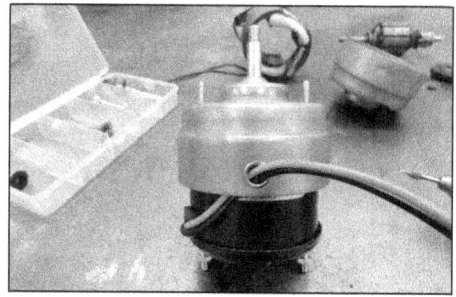
See how the wiring fits through the 6-volt housing hole.

Use a 1/8-inch drill bit to drill out the rivets to remove the brush block. You will notice the spot welds in the pictures.

Test fit the shaft end inside the housing. It fits like it belongs there!

The completed motor. Now is a good time to put 12 volts on it and listen to how quiet it is!

HEATER SYSTEM RESTORATION

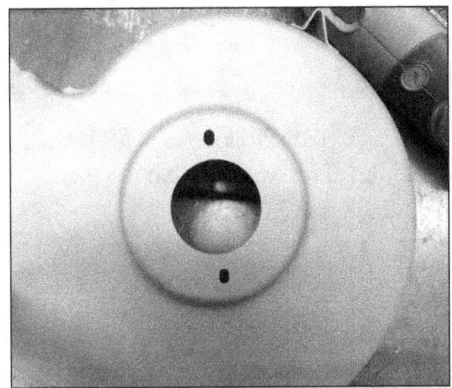

Elongate the two existing holes as shown. This allows for the motor to drop right in.

Here is the new 12-volt motor test fit. Looks good! As you can see, the two mounting studs require a little bit of elongating on the case holes.

The completed motor was painted semi-gloss black. With the 12-volt motor solidly inside the 6-volt housing, there is nothing out of place when installed into the truck's firewall.

I used a length of heat shrink to keep the wire bundle tidy.

This is the box label, but a standard VDO PM354 motor is in the box.

The only modification needed for the Harrison heater is to elongate the two mounting holes for the motor to accommodate the narrower bolt pattern. This is easily done with a Dremel tool with a carbide bit. The nice part about this modification is that if you wanted to put another 6-volt motor back in, there is no reason you can't. I have done this modification many times and I am amazed each time at how easy it is to upgrade your heater in this way. The other major advantage is, you are not doing what everyone else does. You are not converting power to heat in order to reduce the voltage of your motor!

I opted to close the four rivet holes on the bottom of the motor that were there to hold in the brush block. I filled the holes with Permatex Black Gasket Maker. By using masking tape to form a mold around the holes, I was able to make it look like the contour belongs that way. Other than the stainless nuts and washers, this motor looks like it's factory new.

Sadly, the original heater switch is not suitable for 12 volts. We can't use it because the resistors at the back of the switch cannot carry double the wattage of the 6-volt system. There are a few different configurations for switching the new heater. My favorite is the DC motor controller with a rotary potentiometer. With this setup, instead of having low, medium, and high settings, you get infinite motor control from low to high smoothly by simply turning a knob. That is what I am going with in this build. To get the skinny on everything concerning heater motor control, go to devestechnet.com/Home/Native12VUpgrade.

The new motor is a common part number used in many applications. Search for Siemens PM354 or VDO PM354 to find a wide range of places that sell them. The dimensions of the new 12-volt PM354 motor are as follows:

- Diameter: 2.940 inches
- Total Length: 3.560 inches (not including the shaft)
- Shaft Length: 1.450 inches
- Shaft Diameter: 0.314 inch with included adapter
- Shaft Diameter without Adapter: 0.250 inch
- Motor Hardware (nuts, washers; need 6): 8-32

These dimensions are perfect for fitting inside the old 6-volt case to give it that vintage look that modern motors do not have.

CHAPTER 10

The Finish Work

You can get heater paint from any of the vendors, but this product is a name brand and is a perfect factory-fresh match. The best part is that it is in aerosol cans so it's very easy to use. Use a swirling motion and be sure to shake the can extra well. Two cans are more than enough to do an entire heater. The paint is made by the Kilz corporation and its called Hammerite Rust Cap.

> **TECH TIP**
>
> ### Heater Assembly Hardware
>
> The heater assembly hardware consists of 30 pan head Phillips #6 x 3/8-inch sheet metal screws and two motor hold-down nuts and washers that are 8-32. The Allen wrench you need to tighten the fan cage is 3-32 inch. ■

The color and finish are amazing. I painted the inside of each piece first so that I could test my technique on an area that wouldn't be seen. I let the first side dry overnight and then came in the next day and painted the outside. I then let the job set for three days before reassembly.

The perfect paint for this project is Hammerite Rust Cap. There is some argument among enthusiasts as to whether the color should be bronze or silver, so get whichever one turns you on!

Here are the parts all laid out and painted. They came out absolutely perfect. I used three coats for this result.

This is a close-up of the work, so you can see the hammered finish. It looks so original. The colors in these pictures don't do the work justice. My digital camera and the color of the fluorescent lights in the shop change its appearance.

Here is the front view after installing the decal plate. I opted for the more expensive medallion rather than the simple decal.

I will install the DC motor controller on the housing for one very nice, working package.

HEATER SYSTEM RESTORATION

Ranco Heater Control Valve

The heater control valve is very problematic but worth the time to restore. The Ranco Heater Control Valve was very popular and used on many makes and models in the 1950s and early 1960s. This heater control valve is designed to add a passive thermostatic control feature to the system. By turning the warmer knob, you are signaling you want more flow of water into the heater core and you want to maintain that level of temperature. Truthfully, it is antiquated and does not regulate the temperature like modern vehicles, but that was what we had back in the day.

There were two slightly different styles of the Ranco Type HF Heater Control Valve. I will point out the differences as we get to them. The first thing I did was sandblast the entire unit. To properly sandblast this unit without doing any damage, use #1 silica sand or equivalent, set the air pressure in the blast cabinet to 40 psi, and just dust it off for now. This one had cobwebs and lots of dirt and crud all caked inside, making it impossible to see the internals. Always be very careful around the copper tube and bellows. If you do not have a blast cabinet, clean it like you would anything else, being very careful around the copper tube and bellows.

Ranco Valve Disassembly

Begin the disassembly by removing the spring. I used a pair of needle-nose pliers. This is the only part that needs to be removed before we separate the case. With the spring removed, turn it over to the control side and remove the clip that holds the knob control lever on. This lever is indexed and should be put back exactly where you found it.

Remove the clip and the lever and blast or clean everything in that area. Then, put it all back together before moving on. If you choose to put it together later, mark the placement of the lever by turning the control to the stop so you know exactly where it was or mark the metal on the hub-to-lever contact area so that you have a mark across them. This will help you orient the parts later.

There are several reasons for not putting it back right away, including the painting process. I chose to do it later because I sandblast everything thoroughly, run a wire brush attachment on my Dremel tool across the metal to shine things up, and then clear coat each piece separately. The unit originally was zinc or cad

Copper Tubing and Bellows

The copper tube and bellows is central to this unit working perfectly once you have completed the restoration. Inside of the copper tube and bellows is an unknown type of gaseous refrigerant that allows it to work as advertised. It does *not* have the same type of chemical used in the water temperature gauge. These Ranco valves are not rechargeable, and once the copper is broken the entire unit is useless. Be sure to inspect your copper tubing and bellows carefully to make sure they have not been compromised. Take extreme care when working on them to ensure nothing happens to them during the restoration. ■

Set the sandblast cabinet to 40 psi max and blast the entire valve. Stay away from the brass donut inside. We will do further blasting once it's all apart.

Use a pair of needle-nose pliers to remove the spring.

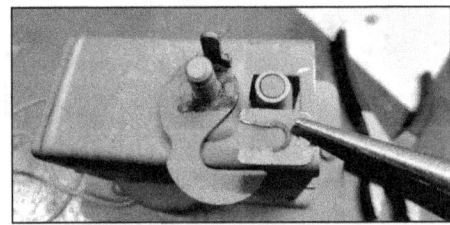

With the spring removed, turn it over to the control side and remove the clip that holds the knob control lever on.

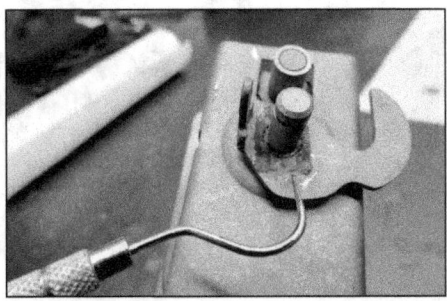

Be sure to mark the metal so you can put this piece back in the very same place you found it.

HOW TO RESTORE YOUR CHEVY TRUCK: 1947–1955

plated. I feel having them replated is going a bit too far, so clear coat is the next best thing.

Next, separate the plate from the rest of the assembly. This needs to be done very carefully, and extra patience is needed. You do not want to break off these tabs much less make them weaker. There is quite a bit of force on these tabs and you will want them to be strong when you bend them back down later. Start with the easy ones: the three brass tabs holding the bellows in place. Very carefully wedge an X-Acto knife in under the tab and carefully lift it enough to insert the next thicker putty knife blade, very small screwdriver, or whatever you need to use to slowly and carefully bend them up just enough to get the bellows loose.

Move on to the four corner tabs and do the same thing. The corner ones are under pressure and will want to pop out once they are sufficiently free. Once free, the parts can be disassembled. The larger spring and wire clip hold the warmer knob on. Some models only have a bellows compressor and no spring, which is normal too. If you have that kind, make note of the orientation for reassembly.

With most of the valve apart, we need to remove the large copper tube from the faceplate. This is necessary to replace the rubber washer, which is the only disposable part of this valve. This is getting to be a rather rare part, so be careful with your new repair kit. The rubber washer with the steel ring around (Balkamp 6601000) is available at NAPA and most of our vendors.

Very carefully bend the tabs up on the plate enough for the tube to come out. You want to take special care not to bend this assembly because it will cause the seal to leak. Put pressure only on the tabs. I find that a small screwdriver jabbed into the slot keeps the copper underneath from bending away and causing damage. The rubber seal is not serviceable and commonly what you see when taking these things apart.

Remove the clip with the slots in it by using a very thin blade to pry it apart enough to get the shaft to come loose. This is not an easy task, but if you take it slow, you can do it. Remove the small copper bell and set it aside. Clean the remaining rubber seal out of its place. Depending on the model of your valve, there may or may not be another copper cap that comes out

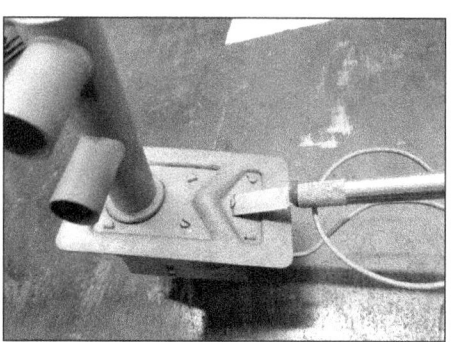

Very carefully separate the plate from the back housing. Slowly bend the tines out, being as delicate as possible.

More tines to bend upward. Who knew we would be repairing these 60-plus years later?

There used to be a rubber seal here! All this rust and corrosion will be dealt with before it's over.

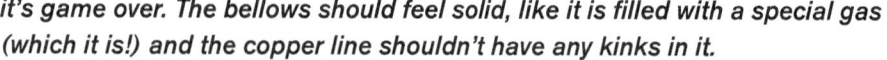

Once free, the parts (to the left) should be what you have as well. The larger spring and wire clip hold the warmer knob on. Your bellows compressor spring and plate may look different, depending on your model. If the bellows or the copper tube has any holes in it, it's game over. The bellows should feel solid, like it is filled with a special gas (which it is!) and the copper line shouldn't have any kinks in it.

Pry this clip (slot on left of clip) apart enough to remove it from the internal shaft.

HEATER SYSTEM RESTORATION

Some models have this type of ledge for the rubber boot.

after this. Some valves came with this piece soldered on.

If you have a valve with a ledge for the rubber boot, you will be able to remove the cap and clean out the inside of the tube better. Also, it's nice to ensure the small tines on the far end of the shaft are straight and the far end cap on the shaft seats properly. If you can't get inside the tube and it really bothers you, the end cap is soldered on with regular solder used for plumbing copper pipes. Heat the solder with a propane torch until it comes loose. I didn't find it necessary because the model I am working on has the removable closure.

Here is the whole Ranco valve disassembled and ready for putting back together. You are halfway there!

Installing the New Seal

Before installing the seal, we need to ensure the shaft and shaft end on the inside travels up and down nicely while staying centered on the hole. Inside, where you can't see very well, is an end cap (on the shaft) with four tines on it that face toward the seal. They must all be on the inside of the hole, centering the shaft at that end. They are only about 1/8-inch deep, so move the shaft around in the hole until everything feels centered and aligned properly. If any of the four tines are bent, they must be straightened to go inside. Once you do this, take a pair of hemostats and hold the shaft as tight to the rubber seal end as possible while the shaft is perfectly centered.

With the shaft clamped in place, install the large copper cap if

The new rubber fits nicely inside the cavity. This valve will work just like new!

Now you can install the large copper cap (if you have one), rubber seal, copper bell, and fork.

you have one, and then install the rubber seal. I put a little lithium grease inside the rubber hole to slide it in easier. Once it is down below the groove for the crimp-on slotted clip, install the small copper bell over the seal, then crimp on the slotted clip. You can remove the hemostats now. You want to make sure the tabs on the copper assembly are nicely bent. What I mean by this is, there is no stress placed on the base of the tabs and you can easily slide the copper tube assembly in place.

Ranco Valve Reassembly

Be sure to get the tube inlets pointed in the proper direction. Once you have it placed by hand and it seats completely all the way around, insert a thin screwdriver into the slot you are working on. Bend back the tabs by hitting them gently with a small brass hammer. This keeps the base from distorting and causing a leak. Don't jam the screwdriver into the rubber seal you just replaced! It is merely there to keep the tabs from distorting the underside of the copper assembly. Be slow and deliberate and finesse those tabs into place. Once you are 90 percent there, you can be just a tad more aggressive with the hammer to set them.

Be careful when getting these tines back down. We are trying hard not to weaken them.

CHAPTER 10

This is where the bellows goes, and you want to ensure you do not kink the copper tube or damage the bellows during reassembly.

Pull the assembly tight before bending down the tines. You want it to be very tight in the end.

Set the bellows plunger in the very center of the bellows.

Now is a good time to test your new seal assembly for leaks. Since the radiator and cooling system is only pressured to 4 to 7 psi, it is not hard to go over to the nearest water faucet and run water through the two outlets with a little pressure. No water should seep through the seal. If you did the above right, you are good to go on to the next step, which is installing the copper tube and bellows. Orientation is important, so look closely at the pictures.

To bend the tabs on this assembly, I used two hemostats to clamp the assembly to the frame and then a needle-nose pliers right at the tab I was bending. The hemostats hold everything straight while the needle-nose pliers do the work. If the needle-nose pliers do not give you the reach needed due to the contour, use the edge of a screwdriver tip or something else to give the pliers the depth needed to crimp the tabs. Be careful when working with this assembly! It is easy to damage the copper bellows.

Now for the tricky part. Place the slotted clip and insert the spring in between the slots. Bend the slots just a bit to hold the spring in place. If the spring falls out during the next part, don't sweat it, you can install it last if you want.

To assemble the faceplate to the rest of the assembly, two things have to happen at the same time: the bellows plunger needs to sit

Use a woodworking clamp or whatever works for you to clamp the two assemblies together tightly prior to bending the tines back down.

Install the adjuster in the proper orientation then install the clip. This shows how the warmer shaft is placed on the end of the assembly.

HOW TO RESTORE YOUR CHEVY TRUCK: 1947–1955

HEATER SYSTEM RESTORATION

This is what the completed adjuster looks like. The clip, the spring, and all of the small parts are cleaned and repainted prior to installation.

The linear switch is so smooth it feels like it's off a high-end stereo system!

perfectly centered on the bellows while on the front part of the assembly and the two slots have to be aligned to go into its holder. To keep the bellows plunger and spring from moving, you can always tape it in place. Tape it where you can retrieve all of the tape when done.

Some of you do not have this type of plunger. You have one that doesn't use a spring. Install that in the correct orientation and no taping is necessary! That one requires that you keep the tabs aligned with the main body so everything fits together properly.

Finish up by putting the adjuster assembly back on in the correct orientation, which you marked earlier, then install the clip. The clear coat will keep it from rusting and the assembly is ready for action.

To test the system, you can get a can of freeze spray from your favorite vendor. Do a search for freeze spray on the internet and you will have no problems purchasing it. Spray the freeze spray over the bellows while looking at the rubber seal assembly.

With the controller on the back of the heater, it's simple to connect the wires.

If it works as intended, the plunger will go down magically all by itself! Do not freeze it too much. Just hit it with a few short shots. This mission is complete!

The last thing to do is decide which switch will be used to control the heater. The problem with the stock switch is, it is only rated for 6 volts and many of the very low wattage resistors attached to the switch are either completely gone or completely ruined. The stock switch, while nice for the purist out there, is inferior to a linear switch and controller. The best way is to have full linear control from 0 to 12 volts (from the slowest motor RPM smoothly through to the highest) with no low/med/high restrictions. To make that happen, check out devestechnet.com/Home/Native12VUpgrade. There you will find how to restore your original switch for 12-volt power.

CHAPTER 11

Front Clip, Hood, and Door Installation

I do not treat the front sheet metal as a "front clip" on these trucks, per se. I do this task a bit differently than most. I use a method that will allow me to install the wiring harness before installing the fenders. This is for superior accessibility.

Start with the inner fenders. Each has three holes that bolt to the toe board of the cab. The passenger's side requires three 5/16-inch bolts, washers, and nuts while the driver's side just requires 5/16-inch bolts that thread into the parking brake assembly bracket. The front of the inner fenders bolt to the radiator support. The front fender support brace bolts to the inner fender and radiator support as well. The grille skirt bolts to the radiator support and the inner fenders at the bottom. Lastly, the fenders are bolted on over the top of everything else. Doing it this way gives me the ability to walk right up to the engine and firewall, allowing for much easier wiring installation.

Front Assembly

The first order of business is to install the radiator support to the front of the frame. You want to leave this *very* loose. Leave about 1 inch of play on those two long bolts. Assuming you have the radiator hoses connected to the engine, it will not go anywhere and there is a lot of alignment to do that will require those bolts stay very loose. Be sure to use the vendor-supplied radiator

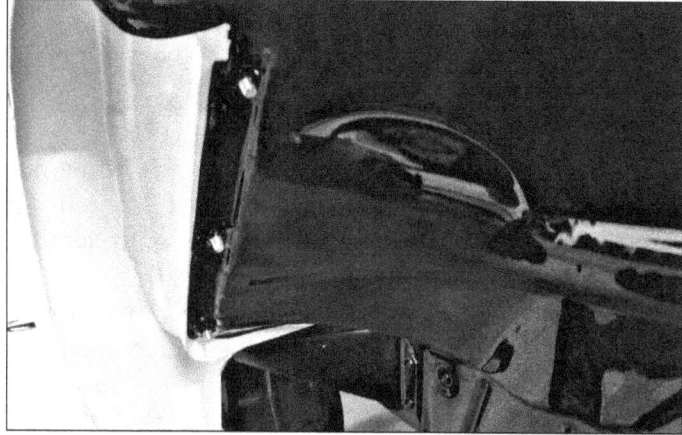

The inner fenders are populated with the terminal strip and inner fender grommet for the headlight buckets and are attached at the cab with three 5/16-18 x 1-inch bolts. The passenger's side requires nuts.

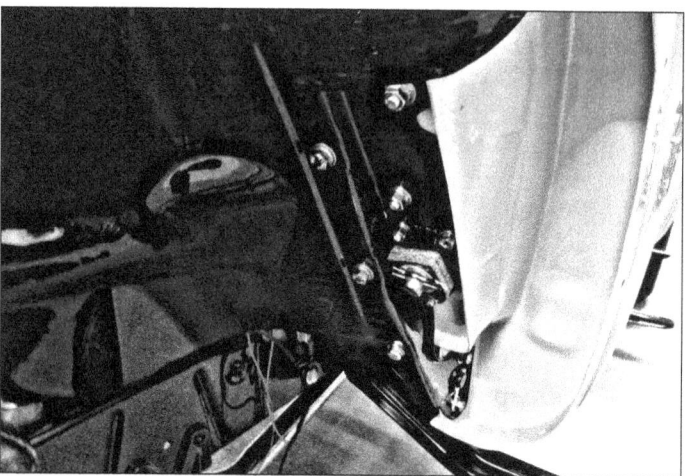

The driver's side has a bracket for the parking brake assembly that has the nuts built in for the three 5/16-18 x 1-inch bolts.

Loosely fasten the large fender brace (for the underside of the inner fender) to the radiator support, using only the inside top screw. The outside one will need to remain open for the fender to go under.

Protecting Paint

If keeping your paint intact throughout this exercise is important to you, use masking tape prior to installing anything. Tape the areas that will see the most potential damage. I also like to use one flat washer on each side of the painted surfaces to minimize paint damage. I am using stainless steel hardware throughout this process. ∎

mounting pads between the frame and the radiator support.

Next, we will install the inner fenders. Use three 5/16-18 x 1-inch bolts and nuts on the passenger's side and just the bolts on the driver's side. This is because the driver's side has weld nuts on the parking brake assembly for that purpose. The inner fender will go right under the two holes in the radiator support. With the large fender brace in hand, I like to install the inside top bolt (radiator support to inner fender) just to hold the three pieces together. Then with more 5/16-inch bolts, turn them into the two radiator support weld nuts to fasten the fender support brace and inner fender in three places for now.

The grille skirt is next. It is what the grille will sit on when it is ready for installation. It has a wing on each side of it with two holes on each side. They bolt into the radiator support between it and the inner fender. Temporarily tighten all bolts securely. This helps with grille skirt alignment. With both sides secure, use three #10/12 3/4-inch sheet metal screws to bring the grille skirt and the inner fender together at the bottom of the inner fender. Tighten them securely. You will not need to loosen those again.

Pay Attention to Detail

With both sides having the inner fenders, radiator support, front fender braces, and grille skirt installed, you can see that setting the fender over the inner fender is almost completely unimpeded. "Almost" because the outer fender needs to slip under the radiator support bracket near the front.

This is easily accomplished by removing the three bolts holding the fender brace and the two bolts holding the grille skirt from the radiator support. With those bolts removed, the radiator support moves freely up and down quite a bit, depending on how loose you have the two support bolts (to frame). We needed to temporarily install everything to get good alignment for the grille skirt. Since

The grille skirt has two bolts on each side to the radiator support then three sheet metal screws on each side to the front part of the inner fender.

This shows the stainless steel cab-to-fender braces. They will have to be removed from the inner fender end when it is time to install the fenders.

HOW TO RESTORE YOUR CHEVY TRUCK: 1947–1955

CHAPTER 11

This is the only area that keeps the fender from dropping right onto the inner fender. By loosening the bottom radiator support mount bolts, we can raise it sufficiently to tuck the fender under it.

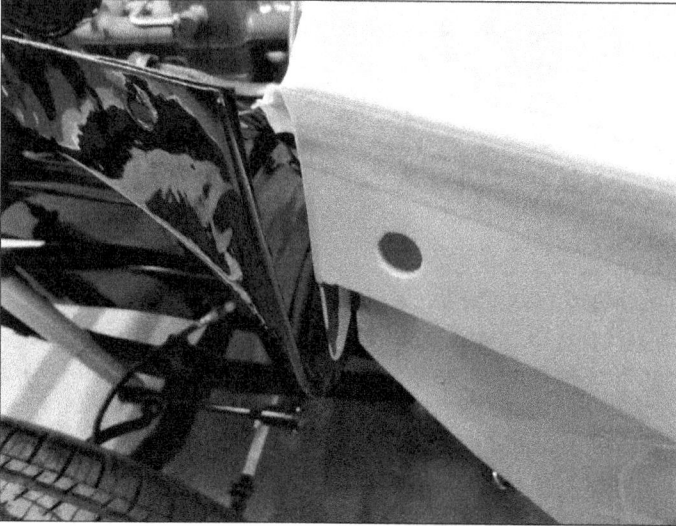

There is even a nice slot for the fender to drop down between the inner fender and the cab. This makes installing the fender easy.

everything has been bolted up once, it will go together much easier.

With the fender brace and upper grille skirt bolts removed, you can now pull up on the radiator support to slip the inner fender under it and bolt it into place. Keep everything loose for now. The two reasons for doing this front clip install this way are:

1. It is much easier to get to the wiring of the engine compartment, inner fender wiring, etc., with the fender out of the way.
2. This method doesn't require two people.

You can get those beautiful stainless steel cab-to-fender rods and braces from Classic Parts (part number 37-877S).

The Fender Welt

I decided to go with fender welt that matched the chrome and stainless trim that is present, so I purchased the fender welt in chrome finish from Bowtie Bits (part number AD-475-CFW). The installation is not difficult, but it requires patience.

Spread weatherstrip adhesive on the fender in only the areas required. Spread it on the welt as well. Let both dry for a few minutes, then push the welt into place.

To properly follow the contour of the fender, make small slits to within about 1/4 inch of the cord. Cut off the slits' excess as required for the welt to lie smooth without any double layers. You want the welt to be pushed as far into the corner or to the edge as possible. Think through what happens when the fender meets the cab and place the cord accordingly. You can remove excess weatherstrip adhesive later with mineral spirits. The welt only needs to go to the end of the cab, so not a lot of welt is used on the front fenders.

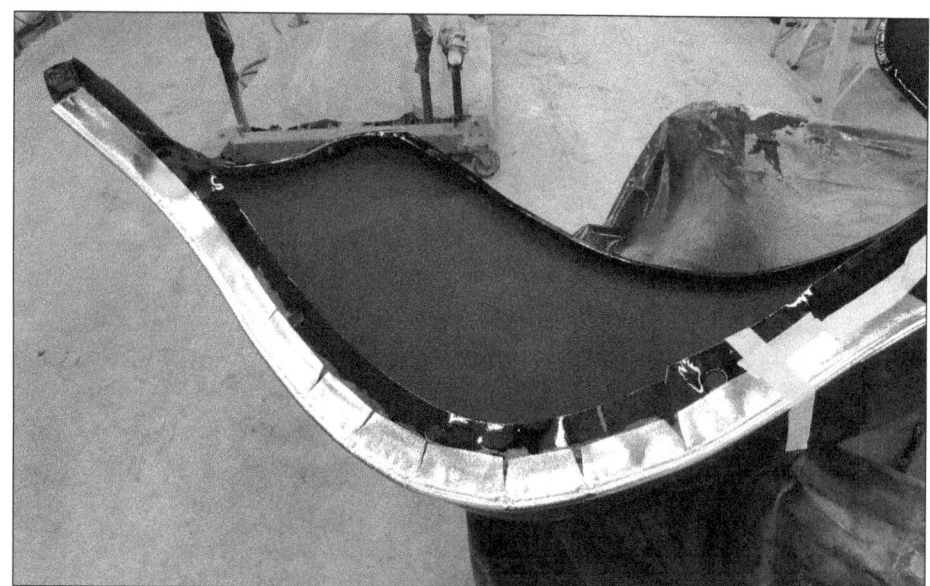

To keep the fender welt in place, use masking tape as you glue it down with weatherstrip adhesive.

FRONT CLIP, HOOD, AND DOOR INSTALLATION

Front Fender Installation

We can now install the fenders. Protect all edges with masking tape prior to installation. Pull up on the radiator support so there is about 1/2 inch exposed, carefully slip the fender's lip under the radiator support so the holes line up, and carefully drop the fender down onto the inner fender. Since you installed the inner fender gasket set in chapter 9, we can be assured everything is properly cushioned prior to bolting it down.

Start to bolt up the fenders loosely. You do not want anything tight at this point. It will be somewhat of a challenge getting the bolt holes to line up, but I did it myself without help. Start at the cab and go around from there. Once the bottom cab bolts are in, the fender has a pretty good idea about where it belongs, then it gets easier from there. When I talk about easy, remember that word is relative to other things on the truck!

Grille Installation

The grille is set onto the lower grille support and bolted on the bottom, then bolted to each fender. The new grille comes with all the necessary hardware minus the sheet metal screws required to bolt it to the underside of the grille skirt. Place the #10 clips in all the holes first before installing. Of course, all of the zinc-plated bolts had to go in favor of stainless steel for this build.

There are three bolts on each side that bolt onto the inner fender/fender from the wheel well, eight sheet metal screws and one 5/16-inch bolt on the underside of the grille skirt, and two sheet metal screws that are on the top side of the fender accessed from under the top grille bar. They are not that hard to get to with a 1/4-inch drive socket with a Phillips head attached. Lastly, there are two 5/16-inch bolts with nuts for the grille skirt to center grille support brace.

Simply tuck the fender into the radiator support bracket and then set it down over the top of everything involved. Be sure to use tape to defend against paint chipping.

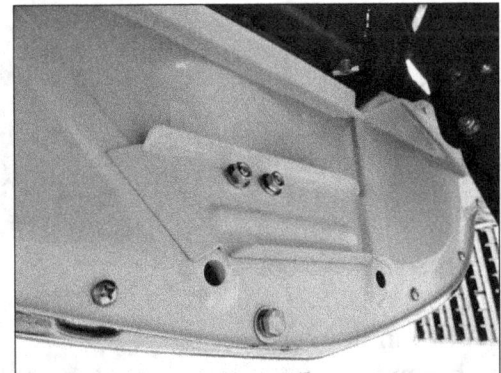

The underside bolt locations for the grille installation are shown. All nuts, bolts, and washers are stainless steel for this build.

The new aftermarket grilles are triple chrome plated and put together very well. It was just easier to purchase a new one.

If you did it right, the holes will be lined up and ready for the radiator support cover.

CHAPTER 11

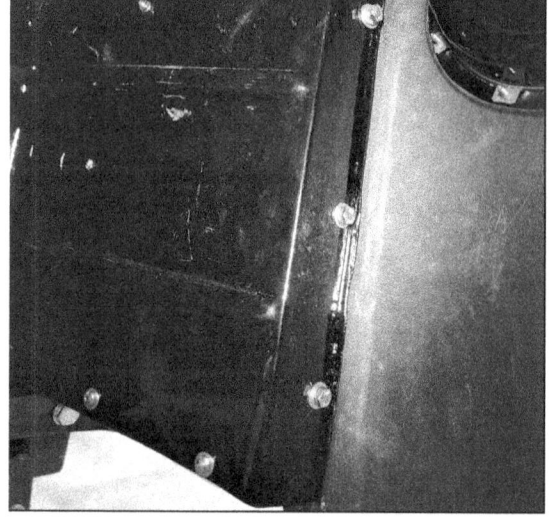

The difficult part was aligning the three holes on each side accessible from the wheel well. But in the end, everything came out great!

> ### 🔧 TECH TIP
> ### Parking Lights
>
> It's a good idea to square away the parking lights before installing the grille. They go in from behind the grille, and they are not easy to get into place without removing the top grille bar (or at least loosening it). It's also not a bad idea to extend the lights wiring so you can get to it easily. I used male and female spade connections for this, then used heat shrink for weatherproofing. ■

Hood Installation

The hood was not as difficult as it has been made out to be. Many say it is difficult because the geometry General Motors used was a little hard to interpret. Let's start at the beginning.

Mount the hinge brackets (the two arms with the plate) on the cab loosely. Fasteners are forward of the hinges. Don't tighten those bolts. Mount the spring hinge to the front of the firewall. They can be snugged down in about the middle of their travel. The only place the hood is attached is at the cab itself. So before doing any adjustments, simply mount the hood. This is best done with two people.

I start at the spring hinge with the smaller shoulder bolt. Tighten the shoulder bolt on both sides. Then, have a partner hold the hood forward and connect the other two arms using the larger shoulder bolts.

With the hood supporting itself in the up position, we can now very carefully make our adjustments. If you just painted your truck (as I have), then you know to use blankets, tape, and whatever else you can to protect the paint.

The hood hinge brackets are mounted with the fasteners forward of the hinges. Each arm is only long enough to meet its appropriate hole in the hood.

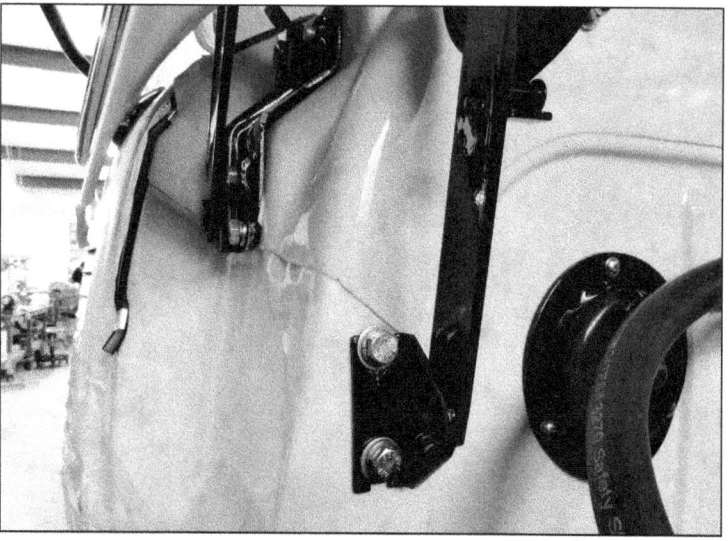

The spring bracket can be mounted in the center of its travel and tightened to start with.

Remove the hood lever assembly from the front top grille cover for now. There is no point in having the latch assembly trying to latch on to anything just yet. Tighten the grille cover bolts all the way around, and tighten everything associated with the front end. This is assuming your grille is in place and everything is assembled.

126 HOW TO RESTORE YOUR CHEVY TRUCK: 1947–1955

FRONT CLIP, HOOD, AND DOOR INSTALLATION

Hood Alignment

At this point, and contrary to everything else I read on this subject, you want one monolithic front clip. The fender-to-radiator supports, grille bolts, and everything associated with the front end should be tightened down with two exceptions: the bolts holding the fenders to the cab (four of them on each side) and the two bolts that hold the radiator support to the frame in front. By leaving those loose, we can tip the front clip side to side or up and down or any combination thereof by adding shims to raise the radiator support (thus the entire front clip) either evenly or not, depending on the need. Then, we have two rods on the front fenders that are mounted to the firewall. Those two long, threaded rods push the fenders away or bring them closer, depending on your needs.

Keeping all bolts loose is a bad idea because it adds ambiguity to your adjustments. If you did that, tightening everything down when you got to where you think is perfect will change the picture. There is no need for cab mount shims as far as adjusting the hood because the hood itself moves

Remove the center latch plate so there are no obstructions in the very front of the hood for now.

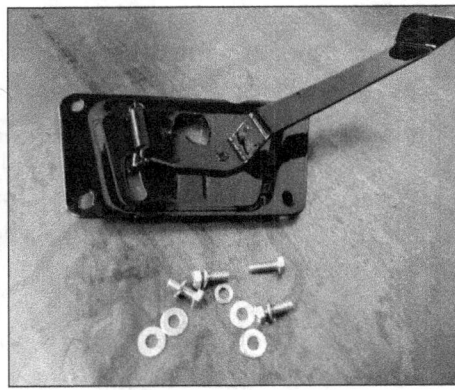
Four 1/4-inch screws hold in the latch plate. Be sure to use some lithium grease on the mechanism.

Even though a 2x4 is only 3 1/2 inches, it's close enough. Wrapping it will keep it from marring the paint.

In this position, we can more accurately adjust the cowl fitment issues.

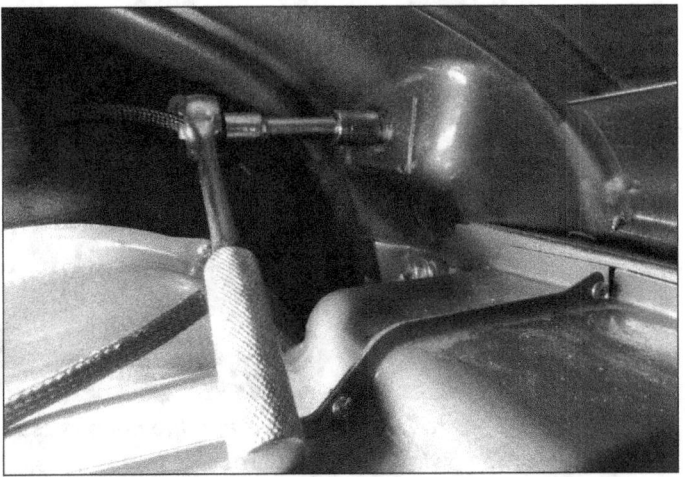
To get to these two bolts, you have to remove the glove box if you have a deluxe heater. But this is where the magic happens!

with the cab, so this is merely an exercise in adjusting the front clip.

Get a 2x4 that is about 1 foot long and place it on the top grille cover where the latch would meet. This is the position necessary to make the following adjustments. I grabbed a 3-foot 2x4 and wrapped it in a blanket to protect the paint.

Now carefully try to close the hood. On my project, the back of the hood (cowl end nearest the firewall) was about 1 inch too high! *Way* out! Also, the hood was crowding the passenger-side fender. So, you would think when something is 1 inch too high and there is only 1/4 inch of adjustment, you have a real problem. You don't. No need to sweat the small stuff.

Let's address the "too high at the cowl" issue first. Chances are the hood is too far forward too. Loosen the two bolts that hold the hinge frames to the cab. They are located inside the cab in the front corners. The bolt that comes in from the outside is the lockdown bolt. Leave that loose for now. Be sure to put that 2x4 in place!

With the hinge frame loose, push down on the side you are working on, and pull the hood toward the firewall as far as it will go on that side only. Don't cave the sheet metal; rather, push down where the supports are located. Have a friend tighten the two inside hinge bracket bolts. With one side tight, go around to the other side and do the same thing again. Watch that large gap disappear! And yes, you must remove the glove box to do it!

Now that you have done that once, you may need to do it a few more times to get the hood positioned nicely at the firewall (cowl) end evenly on both sides.

With that adjustment out of the way, let's bring the hood down to

It doesn't take much turning of those adjustment nuts to enlarge or reduce the distance between the fenders. Adjusting on one side spreads only that fender, so we can use it to adjust the gap when the hood is completely down.

The fender-to-cowl rods are adjusted and the hood is resting nicely on the cowl and gapped properly. In this case, we have about a 3/8-inch even gap between the hood and the fenders. This means we need to raise the front clip to meet the hood by shimming the radiator support.

With a very nice gap at the cab's cowl and fitting snugly, we can raise the front clip to meet the hood.

FRONT CLIP, HOOD, AND DOOR INSTALLATION

The finished hood alignment looks good. I feel it could be better with some hinge modification, but this is the very best with the adjustments that are available.

The gap should be even, and the doors should perfectly fit the contour of the cab. If using donor doors, be sure this is the case prior to paint!

see if the gap between each side of the hood and each fender is correct. Chances are it won't be. In my case, the hood was over too far to the passenger's side. But with the hood nicely adjusted to the front of the cab, we know it's not the cab's or the hood's fault this is happening. We need to adjust those long support rods that go from the cab to the front of the fender. Using the (two) nuts that are on each side of the fender's bracket, push the fender away just a few turns of the nut. It doesn't take much. Rinse and repeat until you have both fenders spread just right.

Next, try setting the hood down on the fenders. Make sure there are new rubber bumpers on the sides of the hood so they do not make metal-to-metal contact. If there is a gap, then we need to do another adjustment. This would be to raise the front clip by adding shims (big washers will do) to the radiator support brackets where it meets the frame to raise the front end.

This procedure worked quite well, but I was still not very happy with the hood alignment. This is just the nature of the beast. The Advance Design era hoods did not fit perfectly, and no two are the same. If I took a lot of extra time to make the holes larger in the cab for the hinges, hammered down a ledge on each side (prior to paint of course), and finessed it a little more, fitment would be perfect.

Door Fitment

I fit the doors without installing the weatherstrip first, knowing I would be removing the doors again. I made sure my doors were aligned perfectly, then I took them off again, leaving the hinges properly adjusted to the cab for adding the weatherstrip.

First, install the hinges on the cab. Leave the bolts loose but mostly threaded in. The bolt heads must be flat to the hinge for the door to close properly.

Open the top spring hinge all the way out and pull the bottom one all the way out to set the door in place. This is best done with two people, especially when fresh paint is involved. Slide the hinges into the door's hinge pockets and use a tapered punch to get the holes aligned for bolts. Put in all six 3/8-inch fine thread bolts and leave them loose.

The idea is to watch the cab's belt line to line up the doors so they meet that belt line perfectly. A lot of care must be taken here with fresh paint. With all the bolts in place, tighten the ones going into the cab first. If you need more upward or downward travel, adjust accordingly. This is a most important adjustment; time and patience are essential.

You will find that with practice this is a pretty easy task. One thing that I am very glad I did was install the doors prior to paint to make sure they would fit. It is an essential part of restoration to dry fit each part prior to paint. You never know what you are going to find. In this case, the doors were from another year, and even though that should not make a difference, it sure did! The doors were 1/4-inch

It's a matter of taste, but I think running boards look really good with the protection.

The chrome frame with rubber and the Chevrolet logo in the center was what sold me on this idea.

too wide for the cab opening. To get them to fit, I had to slice all the way down the cab opening, pull the metal back accordingly, and weld everything in place. Be sure to not skip the step of fitment prior to paint or it could ruin your day!

Running Boards

Lastly for this chapter, I want to briefly mention the running boards. As with everything else on this truck, they were badly rusted out, so after doing the standard sheet metal repair and proper base/clear paint combination in Gloss Black, I decided there just wasn't any way to protect the paint without putting protectors on them. It is still futile, but it should help.

Chevs of the 40s sells very nice protectors with rubber, a chrome frame, and the Chevrolet logo in the center. Other ways to resolve this would be to powder coat the running boards or spray them with bedliner.

The running boards can be installed before the bed and side aprons, but leave the bolts slightly loose so you can move them around a little to fit to the rear fenders. That unexplained square hole on the surface of the running board is for the apron support brace.

If the running board-to-frame bracket holes do not properly line up, do not get excited and start hammering them into place before really examining the issue. If two of the brackets line up, it's the single third bracket that is out of whack.

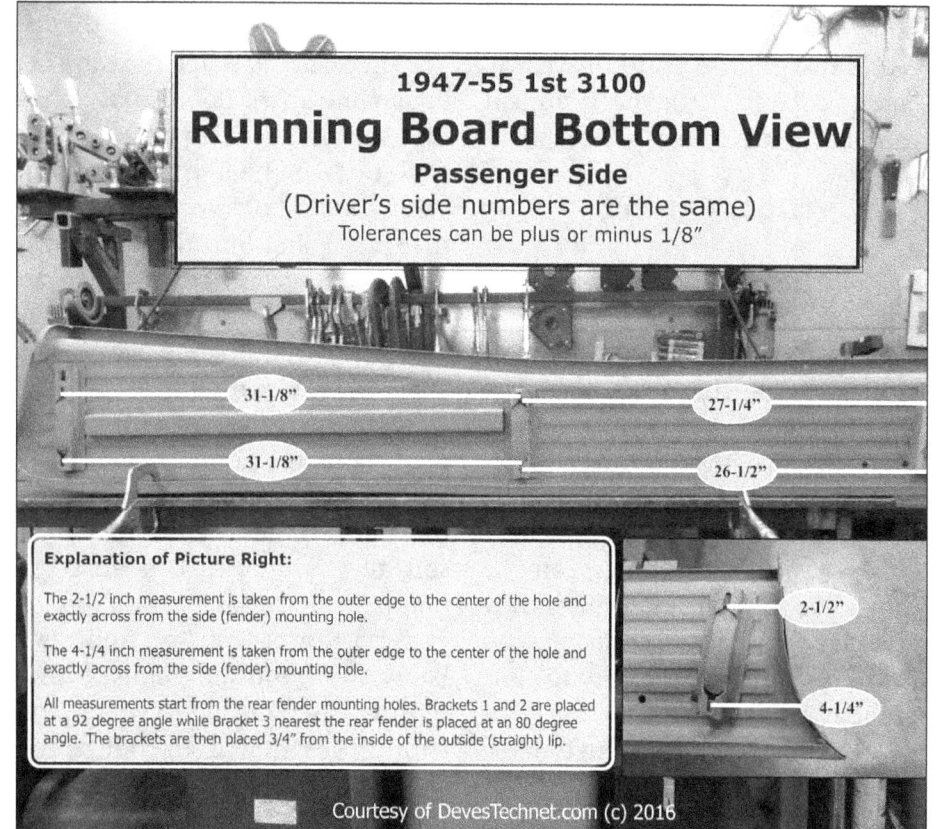

If the frame-to-running board brackets are bent or even nonexistent, new ones are available. This photo should help with bolt hole alignment.

CHAPTER 12

THE BED, REAR FENDERS, AND APRONS

The bed on these trucks get a lot of abuse. While it is possible to repair the bed parts, it is very difficult to get these long panels without support straight and true. Since the ones that came on the truck were so bad off, I felt for the investment of about $2,400 I could get brand-new bed parts and just start off with a new bed. This is a complete bed with all underbed supports, tailgate, and all metal parts needed to complete the bed.

Another reason I went with all new parts is because I wanted a custom configuration. I do not personally like the angled side rails of the pre-1954 beds. Flat side rails look so much better to me, but it's a personal choice. If you go with your current bed, follow the dent removal, paint prep, etc. process outlined in chapter 7. The idea of going with flat rails complicates matters in a few significant ways. Disregard the following if you go with a stock bed for your year truck.

Custom Bed Configuration

The 1954–1955 bed was made a little differently, causing a few complications:

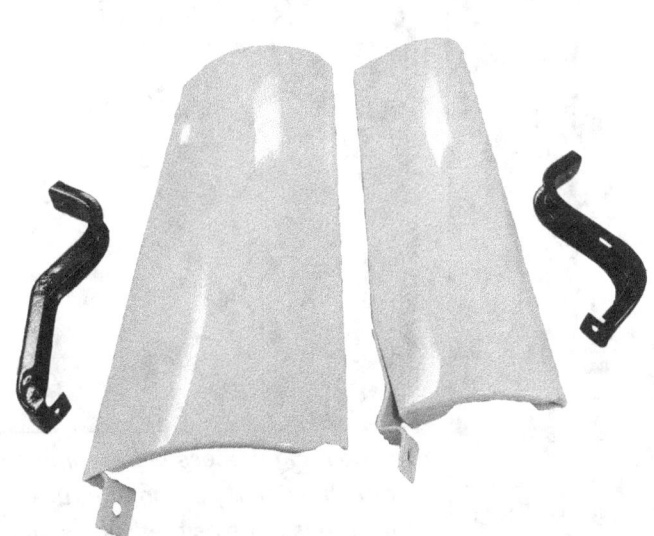

Here you can see the difference in thickness of the side aprons. The 1947–1953 is on the left, and the 1954–1955 is on the right.

A few 1-inch polished spacers to get around that vertical ledge solved the issue nicely. If I had discovered this problem before painting, I may have cut that support out a little to accommodate the taillight assembly, but I have no complaints about this solution either.

HOW TO RESTORE YOUR CHEVY TRUCK: 1947–1955

CHAPTER 12

1 The 1954–1955 bed requires 1954–1955 side aprons. The original aprons from 1947–1953 are too wide and will not properly bolt up. The side aprons bolt to the rear of the running boards, then a bracket (also different than earlier years) holds the apron firmly with a carriage bolt on the running board surface. These side aprons are the last thing I installed on the truck. They fit very nicely in place after everything else has been firmly bolted together.

2 The tailgate and rear cross sill are made differently than the 1947–1953 version. In 1954–1955, the rear side rail design had a vertical ledge for support right were the taillight assemblies are mounted in 1947–1953. This means that you cannot use the stock 1947–1953 taillight assemblies without modification.

Bed Sheet Metal Preparation

This build represents all years from 1947–1955 and the best of the best options. In this case, I wanted flat bed rails that only became available in 1954. The best place to get these bed parts is Mar-K Products out of Oklahoma City, Oklahoma. The gauge of metal they use is the same as from the GM factory, the quality is second to none, and the customer service is exceptional. And it wasn't easy because I have to be different! You can purchase Mar-K beds from our vendors as well. Just ask if they are getting them from Mar-K!

The problem is, the 1950 half-ton frame does not fit a full 1954 bed properly because of the higher hump near the back of the frame rails just above the rear end. Mar-K engineers came up with a bolt-on solution that did not require any welding or much modification. This solution was the perfect thing for this build. The only downside is losing 2 inches or so of the depth of the bed, but I can live with that. If you desire flat rails on your 1947–1953 pickup, Mar-K has a solution for you. Just tell them to use Deve's order as a guide.

Upon receiving the parts, start by removing all the labels and looking for any bumps or bruises that would be unsightly after paint. A few machine scratches here and there is all I could find. Nothing some light sanding won't take care of. They are true professionals in their understanding of how nitpicky a customer can be!

I handled this job like every other painted part of the truck: first epoxy primer and then urethane sealer, base coat, and clear coat. I used Simple Green followed by SX330 wax and grease remover (or equivalent) and scuffing all surfaces with a Scotch-Brite red pad. This is essential for getting the paint to stick. The Simple Green is recommended for taking pitch off sawblades, and it is very good at removing the coating from the factory. Using lacquer thinner at the seams prior to the SX330 ensures there is no oil from the machines is trapped and ready to ruin the paint.

The only modification needed for this special bed is to add a cross sill exactly $12^{13}/_{16}$-inch from the frame rail hole that bolts up the #1 cross

Right out of the box everything is very clean and ready for paint prep.

The painting process is the same for each painted part on the truck. The idea is to be as meticulous and methodical as possible. Sand all parts by hand using a red Scotch-Brite pad to get a uniform finish.

THE BED, REAR FENDERS, AND APRONS

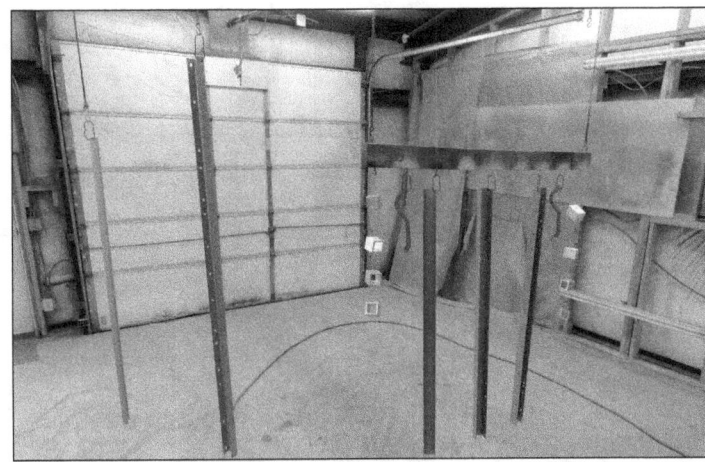

I find that using shower hooks, bungy cords, and safety wire makes the painting process easier. I can get the entire job done at once as opposed to taping and masking half of the work. Shown here are the four cross sills, aluminum blocks, fender skirt supports, and intermediate support.

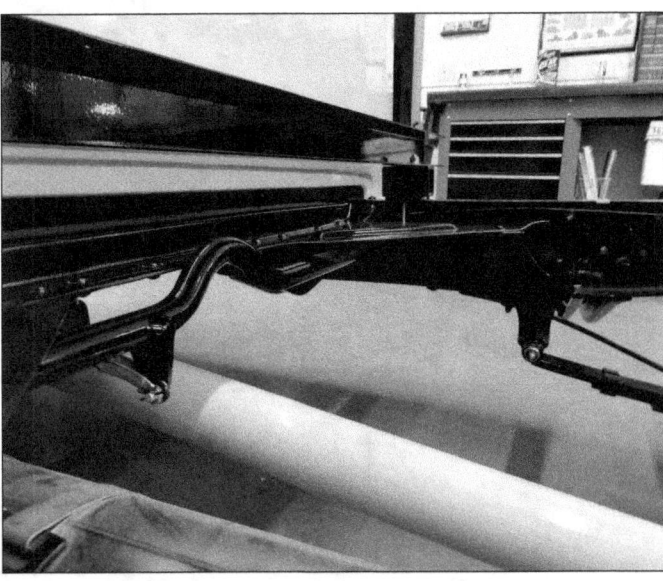

The #1 cross sill is mounted correctly here. Stainless steel hardware is used throughout this process.

sill. A good way to get this hole in the perfect place is to get one of the steel skid strips out of the kit, put the two holes that are close to each other at the front near the cab and measure from the second of those two holes (through that first hole in the frame rail) to the next hole down the line. Measured, it should be exactly $12^{13}/_{16}$ inches. Then measure half the distance of the width of the frame rail (dead center) and X marks the spot. Do this on both sides and you have marked exactly where the #2 cross sill will go. Use masking tape to make this mark and drill carefully in an attempt to protect your paint!

Cross Sill Installation

The kit comes with two $3^1/_4$-inch long 2x2-inch aluminum blocks with 3/8-inch holes offset by 3/4 inch. This is for the cross sill that is closest to the cab (referred to from now on as #1 cross sill). It is mounted with a $3^1/_4$-inch bolt that comes up from under the frame crossmember. A flat washer, lock, and nut go on inside the block. A $1^1/_4$-inch 3/8x16 bolt is then inserted inside the block and bolts down the #1 cross sill.

The #2 cross sill looks nearly the same as others in the kit, but it is a little different. It has two elongated holes that bolt it up in the #2 position. The #2 and #3 cross sills face the opposite direction from the #1.

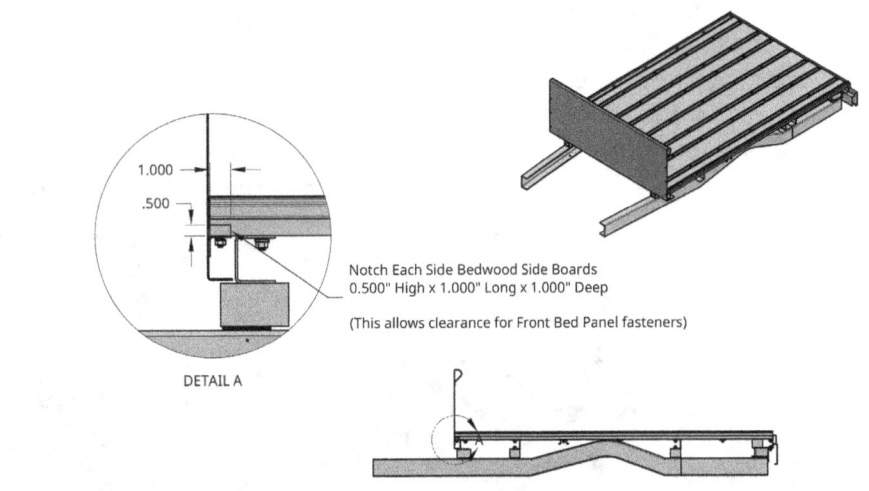

This drawing will help explain the front cross sill mounting procedure. Mar-K was kind enough to share these drawings to help us understand the installation better. (Drawings Courtesy Kevin of Mar-K)

CHAPTER 12

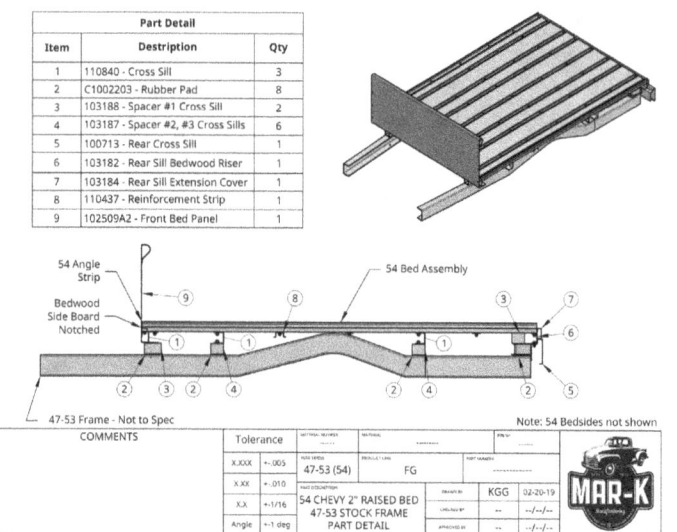

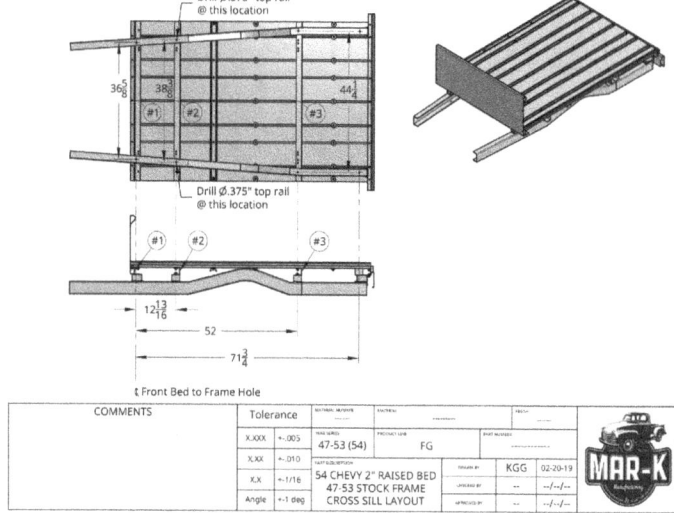

This illustration brings the front wall and rear cross sill into better detail. It is apparent that Mar-K knows exactly what it is doing! (Drawings Courtesy Kevin of Mar-K)

More of the measurements needed are shown here. Mar-K did an excellent job in providing all the necessary drawings. (Drawings Courtesy Kevin of Mar-K)

With the #2 cross sill hole drilled in the frame, insert a rubber pad over each hole, then one of the six 2$\frac{1}{2}$-inch aluminum blocks on each side, then the cross sill. Do the same for the #3 cross sill. The #4 cross sill is totally different and is used as additional support for the rear of the bed. It is narrower than the other three, so it is easy to spot.

The rear of the bed consists of a wide and long cross sill that has two ears for mounting to the last two holes in the frame. Because we need an additional 2 inches in height for this bed, we also need a rear sill extension cover. Between these two parts we will reinforce this assembly with a C-channel "cross sill" (within the cross sill assembly), and then on top of it all, an aluminum block will go through the bed wood.

The first three cross sills are bolted to the frame as advertised, but the rear is more of an assembly. This assembly bolts down through the bed wood and is held in place by two 3/8x6-inch polished stainless bolts and a polished stainless offset washer that is set into the wood to keep it from turning.

This is how the rear cross sill parts are assembled. Under it, a rubber pad goes against the truck's frame.

All of the cross sills are now properly installed. The rear cross sill provides an anchoring for the side rails. Everything comes together very smoothly.

THE BED, REAR FENDERS, AND APRONS

What I will do temporarily is install the two bolts without involving the bed wood so I can confirm that holes will line up, sort of dry fitting everything together. This also will allow a single person to install the bed's side rails without help. Once the side rails are installed, the rear assembly will stay in place for squaring up.

Installing the Bed Sides

To install the bed sides, slide the back of them into the rear cross sill channel, prop the front of the box against the back of the cab (using a cover of some sort to protect the paint), then put a bolt into the top corner to hold them together. The front slides in front of the sides in between the bed's wood rail so the threaded holes in the front piece pull the side rail together with it. It is best to get help with this if you can, especially if there is fresh paint on everything. The box will dip down a little low in the front until the bed wood is installed. This is normal.

It is a good idea to get some help for this step. This is how the front and side panels meet. The top two holes are threaded in the front panel. Be sure to run a tap through the holes after painting.

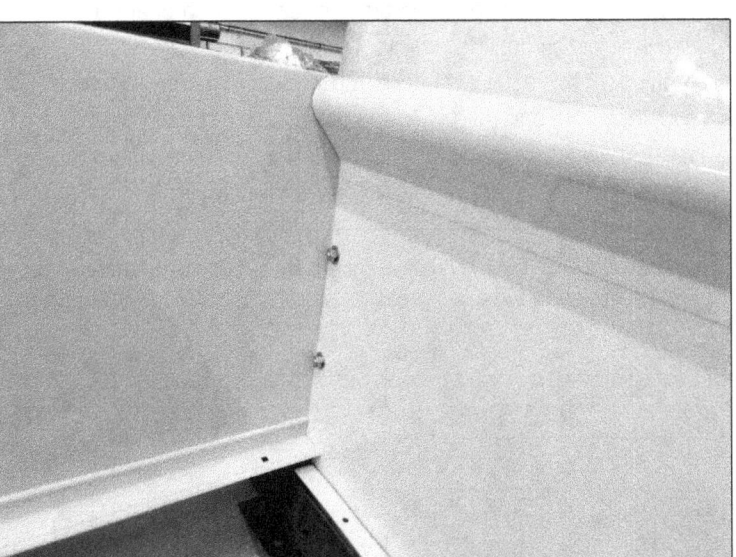

The front and side panels are bolted together. It is normal for the front of the box to dip down a little until the side boards are installed.

Check for square before bolting things tight by using a tape measure from the driver-side front pocket to the passenger-side rear pocket and vice versa. Once you have it square, tighten everything down.

HOW TO RESTORE YOUR CHEVY TRUCK: 1947–1955

CHAPTER 12

The Bed Wood

For this build, I used a half-ton short bed for a 1955 First Series Advance Design Truck. This puts the length of the boards for the bed at 77 1/8 inches. This is an eight-board configuration, and the width of the boards are as follows in order from each bed side: 4 7/16, 6 15/16, 4 15/16, 6 15/16, 6 15/16, 4 15/16, 6 15/16, 4 7/16 inches in width.

The thickness of each board should be 25/32 inch. Of course, there is a special profile needed for each board. Only one side of the outside boards (the 4 7/16 inches) are specially profiled. In this case, I wanted to showcase Mar-K's bed wood, so the profiles and the mounting holes have been cut already. This is new for me because normally when I am not under the pressure of time, I make these boards myself.

At about $4 a board foot (30 board feet or so is necessary), you can save a little money doing it yourself, but there is a lot of woodworking involved. You will notice some measurement anomalies between my numbers and Mar-K's. This is because the router bit profile I use is slightly different, and I like the boards to be 1/16-inch longer for a little tighter fit. Boards 77 1/4 inches would be too long when you add in the varied thickness of the paint. This truck looks amazing using Mar-K's specs!

The Woodworking

To make the slots and special profile, I use a Makita 3.25-hp M12V router and router table and run them through twice. The special router bit is available from Ridge Carbide Tool Company. The diagram is different from the Mar-K instructions because the router profile is a little different. If you adhere to the instructions, it all turns out the same. The diagram and the router profile are something I came up with before doing this particular restoration, and it works perfectly.

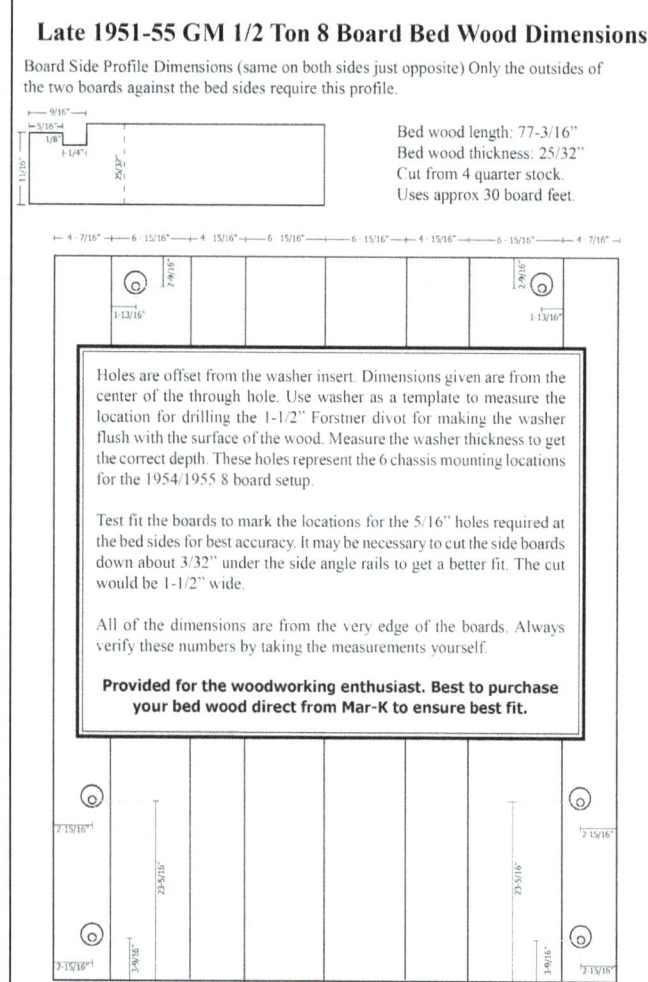

If you are a woodworking enthusiast and would like more information how to make your own bed, this diagram should help.

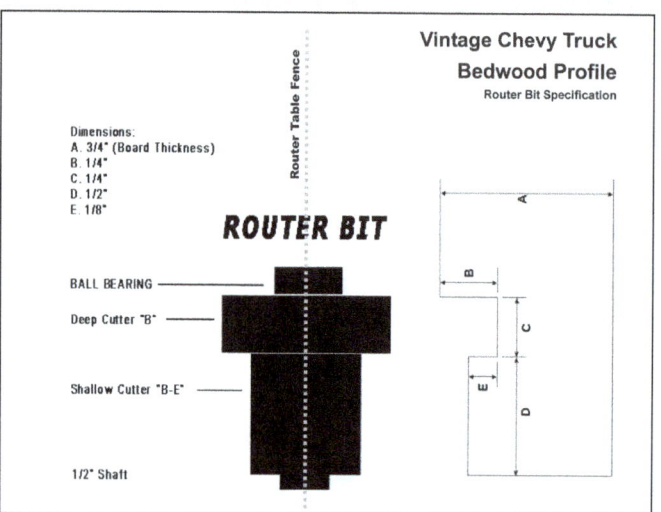

Here is the diagram of this special router bit. A larger-horsepower router with a 1/2-inch shank is important for hardwood.

Here is what the profile looks like and the router bit used. When the router bit spins at high RPM, the profile is cut into the wood.

136   HOW TO RESTORE YOUR CHEVY TRUCK: 1947–1955

THE BED, REAR FENDERS, AND APRONS

The bed wood is red oak, kiln-dried stock. Although expensive, it will be naturally rot resistant and cup resistant in a very hard surface. For one bed, it is probably cheapest to purchase your bed wood from Mar-K. The router bit was $225 a few years ago. It was good for me because I do this quite a bit.

The bed wood also requires four 1½-inch Forstner bit holes for the offset washers and some drilling of standard holes. The Mar-K bed wood packages are exacting and almost ready to paint and install. There is also an option for hidden mounting holes that make for a cleaner look.

The board thickness is 25/32 inch or slightly taller than 3/4 inch. The side rail that the board fits under is tighter and makes it hard to fit up against the bed sides. You want it tight, but I discovered this was too tight after painting the bed sides. Too tight means scraping all the paint off the part that slides under the side rails. To prevent this, tweak the side angle rails upward a little so the boards fit nicely before you paint the bed sides, or do it the hard way like me. I decided to carve a 1/16 inch off the 1½ inches that slides under the rail.

Next, I cut out the bottom corners of the front side boards to accommodate the hardware that is in the way from mounting the front of the box. A 1x1x1/2-inch cutout is sufficient for this. I use the same 1/4-inch router bit as above for this. I mounted a stop 1 inch from the outside of the bit and set the bit 1/2 inch high and the fence 1 inch away from the outside of the bit for this purpose. Then, I carefully pushed the board into the bit slowly until the work was done.

A router bit shaves off 1/16 inch. Several passes with a 1/4-inch bit will make for a nice flush surface.

The router table and a good router make the work go much smoother. Featherboards are used to hold everything tight to the bit and the fence.

The goal is to get past the hardware that is protruding in the way of the side boards in the front.

The cut is made with a flush-cut router bit. I use a 1/4-inch bit so I can take it slower to keep from chipping the wood. The full 1/2-inch depth can be made if you take it slow and have a nice sharp carbide bit.

The Bed Wood (Continued)

The stop makes sure you do not go too far. Set up this way, it makes it impossible to ruin the board by going too far.

Drilling the Holes

The last thing we must do to finish the woodworking on the side boards is to drill the 5/16-inch holes for bolting it down. Mar-K doesn't do this because each bed side is unique enough that it just makes more sense for the end user to do it. With the cutout completed, the side boards should fit right under the angle rail nicely.

With everything very hard against the bed side, mark the holes for drilling by marking around the square holes with a pencil. I use a brad point 5/16-inch drill for this purpose. The brad point makes it easier to locate the center of the hole and makes for a cleaner hole. Drill through to some scrap under the board so the drill exits cleanly.

I set up the drill press for making the holes. They are approximately 3/4 inch from the fence and placed so the bolt will go through both holes.

With all the drilling and cutting out of the way, I like to sand the bare wood with 320 grit by hand, then use a small electric sander with 600 grit before the first coat of paint. This ensures the paint will stick well and give a very nice shiny look to the finished product.

Painting the Boards

After discussing the bed wood painting process with Mar-K, I came to the conclusion that the longest lasting and most durable finish is a product called POR-15. This product is much more durable than stain and polyurethane clear. I purchased two quarts of POR-15 Chassis Gloss Black.

Use a brad point 5/16-inch bit for the through holes that mount the side boards to the bed sides' angle.

The POR-15 sticks very well and seals the wood so a good base/clear combination has a chance of lasting a very long time.

THE BED, REAR FENDERS, AND APRONS

The color sanding is only needed on the top side of each board and really brings out a glossy finish. Of course, we won't be tossing engine parts, or anything else really, into the bed without careful consideration!

Doing this right means less maintenance. The standard staining/poly finish lasts about two years in direct sunlight. Doing it this way means a much longer time between refinishing, if at all.

I applied three coats to each board with my HVLP gun with the 1.8 tip, then used 400-grit paper to smooth things before the base coat. I then applied two coats of DBC-9000 Black Base Coat, then five coats of DCU2021 Clear using a 1.4 tip, then color sanded the clear coat for a very glass-like finish.

The reason for the base/clear combo after the POR-15 is because right on the POR-15 can it states that it is sensitive to UV and will break down in direct sunlight. Why use it then? Because it acts as the best barrier for rain and weather there is!

It is easiest to install one board at a time, keeping the bolts/nuts loose before going on to the next board. Leaving everything loose is necessary so the angle strips can set into their places properly. If you find something not fitting correctly, make sure everything is loose so you can slide things around to fix it easier.

You also want to check the bed for square throughout this process. Measure across the bed at an angle each way to ensure the bed is square. This will make installing the wood much easier. ∎

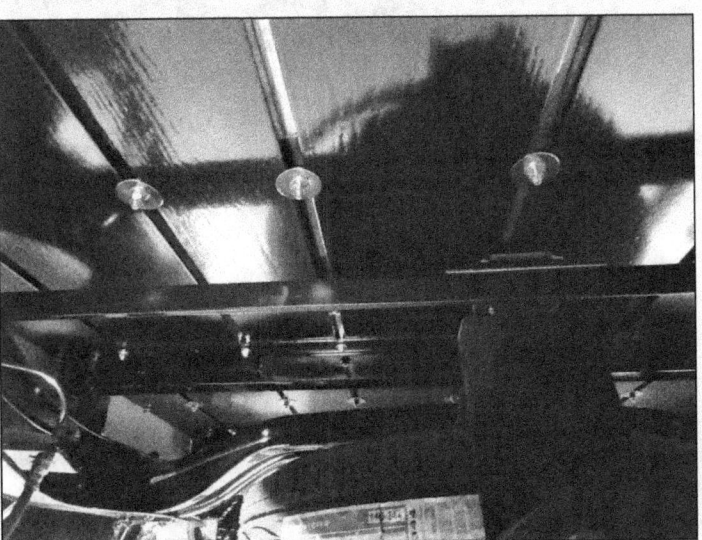

The hardest part of doing this without a lift is crawling under the bed to attach all the screws and large fender washers that firm things up. Be sure to slide the boards and angle strips around until everything looks aesthetically pleasing before tightening these bolts.

The best way to put this box together is on the floor or a low table, then get three friends to help pick it up and set it on the chassis. I am a little short on available friends, so I am telling you how to do all this the hard way!

Rear Fenders, Aprons, and Taillight Assemblies

The reason for doing the bed wood first is because when properly installed the bed wood will put the entire box at the correct height for installing the rear fenders, running board gaskets, the running board-to-bed aprons, and the taillight assemblies. It is also easier to get to those pesky gravity-stricken bed wood nuts as much out of the way as possible. Since I am using a stainless steel angle cover on the bed sides, the fenders are installed next.

This is a two-person process if you want to protect the paint. I like to hang the rear fenders with two bolts to start with. One near the front, one near the back but leave the very top hole for last. This is because of the under-fender brace that is installed in that top hole and goes to the center of the fender's top wheel well.

This brace is normally riveted to the fender, but I wanted to sandblast and paint the back side of it, so I will use two #10 stainless screws with nuts to mount it. I like the look of stainless and feel it will be aesthetically more pleasing than just painting over them.

The rear fenders are attached to the rear of the running boards with three 5/16-inch bolts using a rubber gasket between them. These holes line up pretty well if the bed is installed and the running boards are tight.

The rear fenders also have a support rod that goes from the rear wheel well to the frame. Once everything is properly fastened and tight, you can sit back and enjoy the view! I have to say that if I could have lived with angled bed sides this would have been easier, but I think the flat rails give it a unique appearance yet looks exactly like it belongs on the truck. That is a hard balance to strike.

Thanks again to the folks at Mar-K for taking my sometimes tedious and annoying phone calls. My hope is this chapter will help answer your questions so they don't have to. As with everything else in this book, no special consideration was given by Mar-K or any of the other vendors in price breaks or anything. I wanted to use their services as anyone else would as a matter of principle.

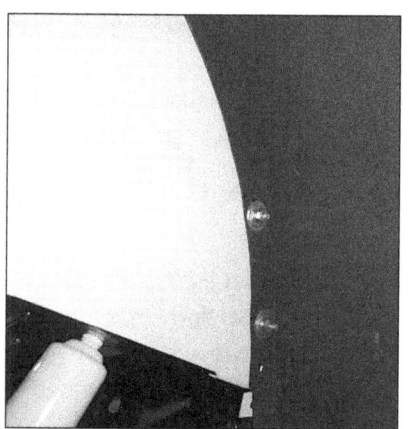

I found some stainless 5/16-inch bolts that I liked from McMaster-Carr and used fender washers on the inside. Everything that goes against paint gets a flat washer without exception. The Allen heads come very close to the clutch head originals.

These two screws are where the rivets used to be. It makes sense to color sand the fenders before placing them.

The connection at the running board rear to rear fenders has a very clean look when using the rubber gasket.

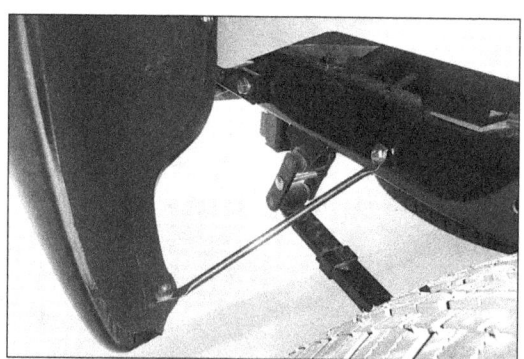

The rear support rod placement is shown here. I got these in stainless steel from one of our vendors.

Bed Rail Dimensions

The dimensions of the wood are:
- Side Boards: $78\frac{1}{2} \times 2\frac{3}{4} \times 1$
- Four Vertical Posts: $15\frac{3}{4} \times 2 \times 1\frac{1}{2}$
  (measure your bed side post holes to confirm)
- Front Rails: $50\frac{1}{2} \times 2\frac{3}{4} \times 1$
- Front Rail Vertical Supports: $9\frac{3}{8} \times 2 \times 1$
- Rear Rails: $54\frac{1}{2} \times 2\frac{3}{4} \times 1$
- Rear Vertical Supports: $9\frac{3}{8} \times 2 \times 1$

Bed Side Rails

No self-respecting farmer would do without bed side rails, so to honor our forefathers, I won't be any different. I used the same red oak that was used for the bed wood. A lot of these measurements are arbitrarily based on what looks good to me. For example, the $1\frac{1}{2}$-inch spacing between the two horizontal rails looked about right to my thinking.

There was some careful planning and measuring that went into this. I wanted the front rail system to set inside the two side rails while the rear rail system is to the outside. Then there is the question of what hardware to use. I purchased zinc-plated utility trailer corner latch brackets and had them chromed because they do not make them in stainless steel (go figure). These brackets drop into each other so when mounted the rack is very stable.

The top brackets are perfect for the four corners on the top rail, but you don't want the bottom of the front and rear rails to flap around. To hold everything together, the spring-loaded latch barrel bolt hardware locks everything down. The barrel goes into a drilled hole in the sides of the side rails and, since it is spring loaded, everything is very secure. They even lock in the open position for easy removal.

The horizontal spacing between the two rails is $1\frac{1}{2}$ inches for the wood dimensions to work out. To make the connections between the vertical and horizontal rails, I used oak dowels to make pins, then pinned those connections, glued the pegs into place, and then began the work of installing the hardware. Doing that first allows you to clearly see where the hardware will be best installed.

More photos of this entire project can be found at devestechnet.com/Home/Morepix. This archive should help you if something is unclear.

These vintage pickups would not look complete without bed side rails. With a black bed, it follows that I used the same red oak to make these black rails.

The hardware allows for simply unlatching and pulling up on the rear tailgate rail for easy removal. These pieces had to be specially chromed because they are not available in stainless steel.

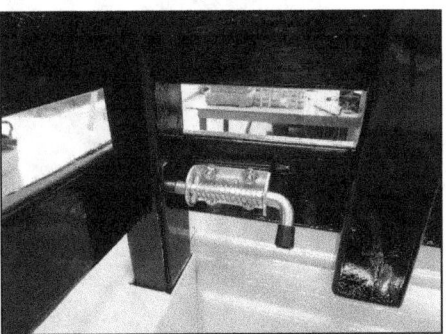

Shown are the spring-loaded inside latches used to pull everything together. The top pieces set inside of each other when dropped down while the bottom hardware pulls the rails toward each other.

CHAPTER 13

ELECTRICAL

In order to make the chores under the dash less maddening, they need to be done very methodically. Start with installing the new electric wiper system. Once you have the gauges and everything else installed, it's a lot harder.

I am installing an Optima 12V D35 Yellow Top Battery. I hear good things about them, and so it's time to find out myself. I am also running a cutoff switch (on the positive side) from the starter to an underseat pedestal switch then to the battery. This is the best way to kill power in an emergency or just for security.

Electric Wiper System

Electric wiper installation is relatively straightforward if you have a completely vacated dash to start with. I installed the best electric wiper system out there: the NewPort Engineering system (part number NE4753CCT), which is the version that clears the choke cable in the stock position.

Let's look at what we have to deal with under the dash. The bracket this new wiper motor will mount to is the steering column support bracket that runs from the firewall down to the steering column support. The small black bracket that comes with the kit will be mounted there. This is strictly to reinforce the motor and give it more support. The motor itself mounts across the bracket system that is spot welded under the dash.

Mount the included bracket to the steering column support and the motor support that is spot welded under the dash. Now, we are ready to install the motor with two #10-32x1 screws. No nuts are required because the motor's mount is threaded.

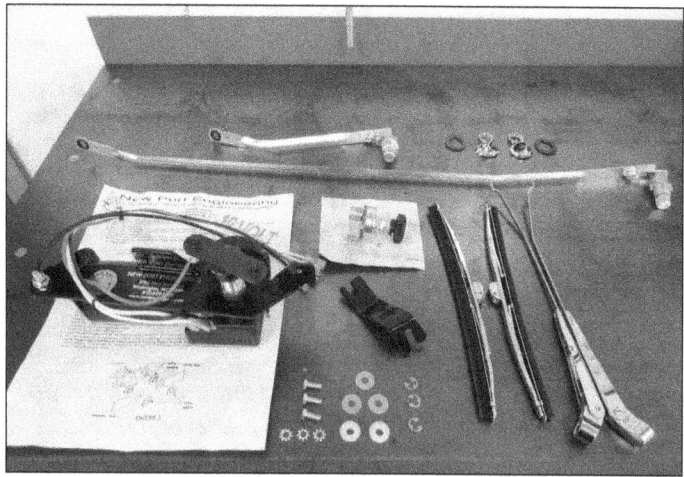

The Newport wiper motor, modern replacement wiper arms/blades, new linkages, and chrome nuts/bezels are included in the kit. This is the entire wiper system.

This spot-welded bracket mounts both ends of the wiper motor.

ELECTRICAL

The included bracket mounts from the steering column support to reach the underdash support, giving the motor added reinforcement.

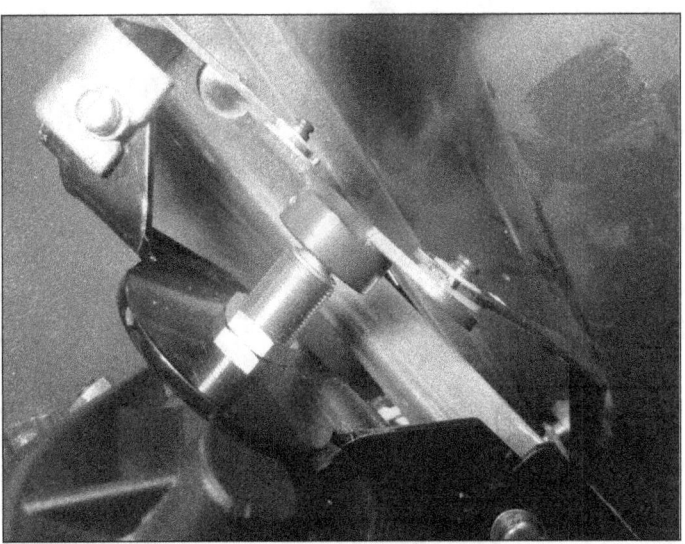

This shows how the motor is mounted across the two brackets. The passenger-side linkage goes to the rotator assembly that is closest to the passenger's side.

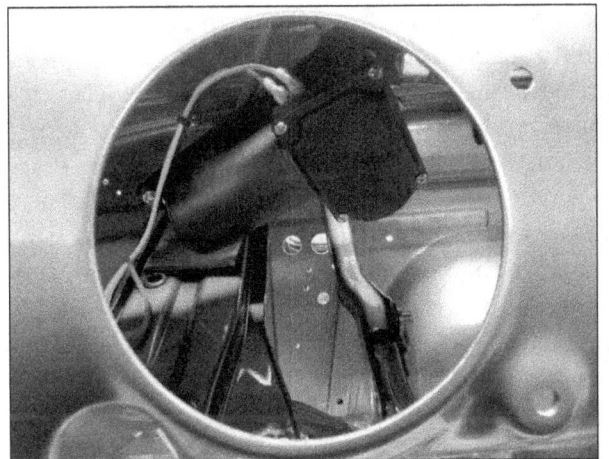

Here is a shot taken from the speedometer gauge hole, which is exactly where the motor sits. The speedometer gauge hole perfectly frames the installation. The motor just barely allows for enough clearance for the speedometer cable and the choke.

The motor (just barely) touches the steering column support bracket, so I added a piece of rubber between the two to avoid vibration and excessive noise.

Situate the motor so that the wiper control arm and the twin rotator arm that moves the linkages are facing toward the front of the truck and the rotator arm is nearest the passenger's side of the vehicle. Take two 10-32 screws (included) and mount the motor across the underdash bracket.

With the motor securely mounted across the main bracket and reinforced by the bracket that comes up from the steering column support, I moved on to mounting the two main wiper transmission linkages. I ordered new ones from Bowtie Bits (part number AD-473-WTL). I also purchased new chrome bezels (AD-473-WB), chrome nuts (AD-475-WBN), bezel gaskets (AD-WW-473), and the modern-style wiper arms and blades (AD-473-WBSM). Since the switch comes with the motor, we now have everything that pertains to an electrical wiper conversion. Let's install the transmission linkages next.

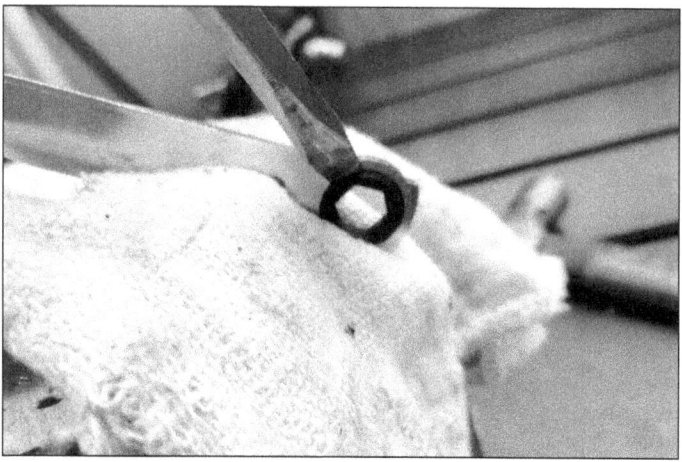

The new transmission linkages come with hex-shaped plastic inserts. They are not needed for this installation, so remove them. I just used a screwdriver.

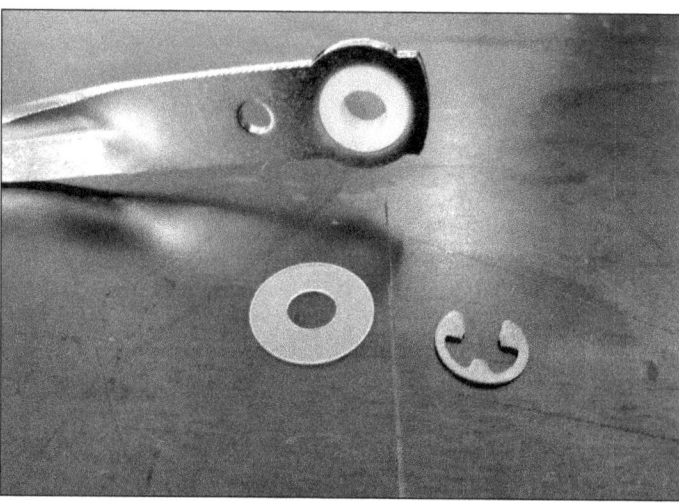

We need a round hole because the wiper motor comes with the appropriate plastic inserts for smooth movement.

The motor kit comes with the round inserts that fit nicely into the new transmission linkage ends. The plastic insert is installed from the rear and the plastic washer is added on the front side, then the keeper clip secures the linkage to the motor.

Installing the linkages, bezel gasket, bezel, and bezel nut is very straightforward. The long transmission linkage is the one for the passenger's side.

This particular job of installing an electric wiper conversion is not my favorite task because it *is* hard to get under the dash to do this, but it can be done even with a populated dash and you will be glad you have modern wipers in your precious truck!

The Newport kit has a wiring diagram for the switch. Use the ground wire on the motor and attach it to the nut on the steering column support for a good ground. The lone red wire goes to the accessory panel 12-volt positive.

Wiper Switch

The switch on the new electrical wiper system looks too modern. If you can live with that, you are doing better than me. Plus, the idea of tightening two nuts together against a nice, freshly painted dash to hold it down just doesn't sit well with me. So, here is what I did to fix it.

Once the linkage is pressed tight from the inside, the bezel gasket, bezel, and chrome nut all fit together nicely. Do not gorilla the nut. It just needs to be snug.

The wiper arms are pushed onto the outside rotator, so they are about 1/4 to 1/2 inch from the bottom of the windshield.

ELECTRICAL

These old vacuum wiper switch assemblies are hard to find because they are rarely salvaged from scrapyard vehicles. Used parts vendors may still have them, so check around.

Here are all the parts of the switch once it is taken apart. It is a very good idea to take pictures of the orientation of each part and how to put it back together.

As you can see, we need threads into the switch, not out of the switch, so we can use the stock bezel.

Warning! You really must have the desire to go the extra mile for this modification. You are taking the switch completely apart and MIG welding it to the housing. Sadly, I know of no other solution. Take pictures at every step and be sure to be particular about orientation at each step. The instructions for the Park/Low/High Wiper Switch is available from Newport Engineering.

Dig out the old original wiper switch assembly. You will need the threaded chrome bezel that affixes to the dash and the nut that tightens it down from underneath. These are much easier on paint!

Switch Disassembly and Modification

Gently and very carefully take the wiper switch apart, making sure you know how it goes back together. Bend those three tines very slowly and just enough for the switch to come apart. The metal cover is what we are after here. Using a punch, knock out the pressed-in threaded short shaft. Grind out the center threaded post and drill out the resulting hole to accommodate the original bezel's nut.

Make that hole round and just large enough for the bezel to go through.

Add two or three 1/2-inch washers to the top of the housing and place the nut on top. This is so the bezel can screw all the way down to the top surface of the housing. There needs to be space there! Now for the tricky part. Weld this assembly together, being careful to set your MIG to a low setting and be sure everything is centered.

Center everything carefully. I used a 1/2-inch bolt with a nut that I can adjust to get things to center to aid in alignment.

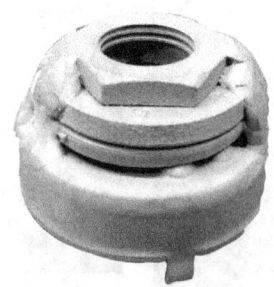

Weld carefully on a low setting so you do not burn through the very thin housing.

The washers you weld to the housing should raise the bezel high enough to not go into the housing, rather just meet it.

HOW TO RESTORE YOUR CHEVY TRUCK: 1947–1955

Once the welding is done, clean up the welds as best you can and check the inside housing for any extra weld that could be there. Use a Dremel with a flat grinding tip to clean up those areas. Reassemble the switch, making sure to orient everything correctly. The shaft goes on first, then the spring, then the wafer with the conductive area facing toward you, then the back two wafers. This is the hard part. Everything must line up.

Check the switch using a multimeter. Screw in the bezel first so it doesn't wobble. The battery terminal is your common to check for continuity for Park (or Off), Low, and High. If everything checks out, tape up the contacts and shoot the switch with some chrome paint to make it look normal again. Also, it is good to shoot some lithium grease into the shaft area to grease the switch for smoother operation as well as longevity since there is no zinc plating on the inside of the housing.

Modifying the Knob

Knob modification is next. There are two methods I found that work for mounting the knob. One is for metal and one is for plastic knobs. This almost concludes the modifications to the switch. The last thing we will do when we are ready is cut the D-shaft down a little so the knob sits nicely on the top of the bezel.

The shaft, then the spring, then the wafer assembly (right), then the back wafer assembly. This combination is shown in correct orientation for installation.

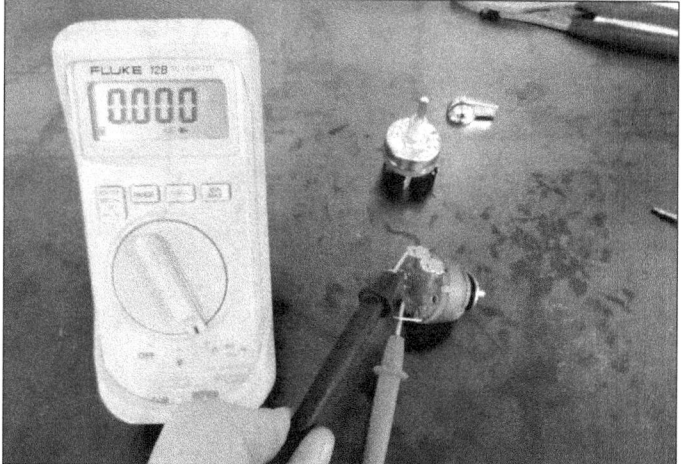

Check the switch using a multimeter. Since it wobbled, I screwed in the bezel for stability in turning the switch. The battery terminal is your common to check continuity for Park (or Off), Low, and High.

This shows the difference so far between the original unmodified switch (left) and the modified version (right).

The switch looks almost normal again after a shot of chrome paint! Since the switch requires it be assembled first, the best we can do is use some sort of paint to protect it.

ELECTRICAL

The original knob is metal, which is a good thing for our purposes. Once you have removed the shaft from the knob, we have one issue to contend with: the D-shaft on the switch's outer diameter (OD) measures 0.187 (3/16 inch) or 4.76 mm. The hole in the metal wiper knob's inner diameter (ID) is 0.240 (31/128 inch) or 6.07 mm. So, leaving it alone, the knob would be too sloppy for mounting properly. A D-shaft adapter is needed to make the shaft larger to accommodate the knob. I ordered these from McMaster-Carr (part number 6391K122).

Clean out the knobs hole thoroughly and press them in using a rag or something to keep from gouging the knob. If you start it straight, it will go right in. I used the vise jaws for that.

Once the brass bushing is down all the way flush with the bottom of the knob, use a #10 drill bit to drill a straight hole all the way through the bushing. This is the size needed for the D-shaft on the switch. This is when you drill the hole for the set screw. Drill through the bushing and then use an 8-32 tap for the 5/16-inch #8-32 set screw.

Lastly, put the knob on and see where it bottoms out. You want the D-shaft to allow for a flush mounting of the bezel. I had to remove about 1/8 inch from mine. Sneak up on it because you want the shaft as long as possible while making it flush with the bezel.

Installation is a matter of setting the bezel through the hole and turning the switch to tighten. If you do not like the orientation of the knob when it's tight, you can add a washer to change it or set screw it down somewhere other than the flat. This is the most solid solution, and from the outside, you can't tell the difference between the stock vacuum switch and the electric one. There is a lot of work involved in this, so you have to *really* want to do it!

Alternative to the Original Metal Knob

Most vendors sell a plastic knob. My truck actually uses one because I was unable to find a metal one in time. The plastic knob method is completely different from the metal knob method. I have tested this method extensively and it seems to work really well, and it's simple.

Using an X-Acto knife, scrape all the paint/chrome off the inside of the plastic knob where the shaft will reside. This is so JB Weld can be used to attach the knob more reliably. Screw the bezel all the way down on

The original knob is made of pot metal but is still strong enough to use a set screw. The problem is the difference in the shaft's and the knob's size. Here is the D-shaft adapter I found to fix this problem.

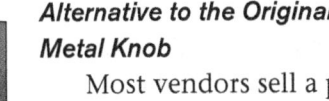

The set screw looks like it belongs there. I like to use stainless steel ones for looks. With the D-shaft adapter oriented properly, there is a very tight fit and the knob can be removed at any time.

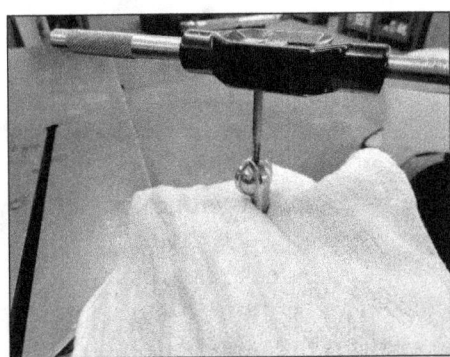

A drill (#29) and tap for an 8-32 set screw are shown.

Modified switch, bezel, and knob are ready for easy install.

Since the JB Weld will not stick to the greased chipboard and the hole is small enough around the shaft, the glue will stay put and dry nicely to the knob.

the switch, then lay the knob on the switch and mark how much of the shaft needs to be cut off for the knob to lay completely flat on the bezel. Cut the shaft accordingly.

Find a piece of chipboard about 3 inches square and punch a small hole in the middle of it. The hole should be just large enough for the shaft to go through. Mount the switch on the dash by setting the bezel on top and in its proper slot so it doesn't move, then turn the switch from underneath until it is as tight as you can get it. You cannot make it tighter later, so be sure it's as tight as you can get it now.

Grease the 3-inch piece of chipboard with axle grease or petroleum jelly on both sides. Soak it good so the JB Weld cannot adhere to it. You can clean the dash later. I like to put masking tape on the paint to protect the dash. Place the chipboard over the protruding D-shaft, mix the JB Weld, and fill the knob's hole about two-thirds full. You do not want it leaking out, so don't overdo it. Use a paperclip to drop the JB in place neatly so it's only on the inside of the knob where the shaft will meet.

Be sure the switch is in the Park position (fully counterclockwise). Place the knob over the shaft and ensure it is in the very center of the bezel so everything is aligned nicely. I like the Park position to follow the contour of the windshield. Kind of up and to the right, so when I go to Low and then High with my right hand, I am pulling it downward. This is just a matter of choice.

With the knob glued down and oriented properly, use a piece of masking tape to hold it down and walk away for at least 24 hours. This worked perfectly for me, and I test it every day to check its durability. It's been holding strong. Keep in mind that if the switch goes bad, we have to break the knob to get it apart again. But I do not anticipate that switch going bad in my lifetime.

Overdrive Electricals

The BorgWarner R10 Overdrive, if installed correctly, has quite a bit of wiring related to it. There is the governor, solenoid, kickdown switch, and overdrive relay to consider. It is imperative that each part works correctly to avoid catastrophic damage to the overdrive's mechanicals. It is not advisable to take shortcuts here.

I made my own wiring harness for the Overdrive and felt it necessary to install that prior to the main harness installation. To understand how to wire it up, another publication is in order. Randy Rundle of Fifth Avenue Garage in Clay Center, Kansas, is the go-to guy for everything R10. He published a book called *The Official Guide to the BorgWarner R10/R11*, and it has a nice wiring diagram in it. I highly recommend this guide to anyone doing this install. In addition, I have the original service manual, operating manual, and electrical tips on my website at devestechnet.com/Home/HowTo.

The harness is made from five different colors of 14-gauge primary wire. The kickdown switch has four terminals on it. The top two *make* (join together) when the gas pedal is pressed all the way down and the bottom two *break* when the gas pedal is pressed all the way down. All the available parts, kickdown switches, overdrive relays, etc. are available at Fifth Avenue Garage.

Here are the routes each wire takes. This is the orientation it is in on the vehicle.

- White goes from the negative side of the ignition coil to either one of the top two terminals on the kickdown switch.
- Blue goes from the solenoid connection on the Overdrive relay to #4 on the Overdrive solenoid.
- Red goes from one of the bottom terminals on the kickdown switch to the SW terminal on the Overdrive relay. Note that top and bottom in this context means the push button on the switch is down, the terminals are up.

Here is the completed switch using the plastic knob method. Understand that the knob is not removeable at this point, so if the switch goes bad, the plastic knob has to be carefully broken off to get the switch out.

ELECTRICAL

- Orange goes from the other terminal at the top of the switch (adjacent to the white wire) then to #6 on the solenoid.
- Yellow goes from the bottom of the kickdown switch (adjacent to the red) to the Overdrive's governor.

Once that is wired correctly, run a power wire from the battery terminal on the relay to the fuse box and 12-volt power.

Electric Fuel Pump

I did a bunch of research into the stock fuel system and exactly how it behaves and decided to add an electric fuel pump behind the stock mechanical one. The reason for this is simple: After the truck sits for several days without starting, the contents of the carb's fuel bowl evaporate, and it takes longer to start. Since the check valve in the stock mechanical pump only checks in one direction (it won't allow the fuel to flow backward), we can add an electric pump behind the stock one, then add a new invention I came up with called AutoPrime to the electrical circuit.

AutoPrime turns the electric pump on for 10 seconds upon activating the ignition switch. This ensures the fuel bowl is always full before starting. Once the 10 seconds are up, ground is transferred to the oil pressure safety switch to ensure fuel does not flow in case of low (or no) oil pressure.

Wiring Harness Electricals

For this build, I installed a brand-new, high-quality wiring harness from Bowtie Bits. I have installed many of these harnesses in trucks before and there is no need to spend $600 or more on wiring that you will never use.

To be clear, this truck has an alternator, a stock (self-canceling) blinker system, and Overdrive electricals. I also left the door open for air-conditioning. This $200 harness will be alternator and blinker ready but will not have wires for some of the other features I want. But that is an easy fix. There are two desired types of 12-volt power you will want: switched power that comes from one side of the ignition switch and unswitched power that is tapped off the headlight switch via battery directly using 10-gauge wire. I am going with the 1953–1955 wiring configuration because of the stock blinker system from 1955.

I found a nice solution for fused power that is neat in the 8-position fuse block. I set one block of six for switched and the other two for unswitched. Each position is fused, is easily accessible, and is every bit as safe as those huge fuse blocks that come with the expensive harnesses. The cost is about $12 each! I will explain how I did this in detail.

Contrary to popular belief, fuse sizes are not based on the item being protected; rather, they are based on the *smallest* size of wire being used in the item's path. Since I am using automobile wiring sizes and the smallest size in any path is 14 gauge, the fuse blocks will be filled with 10-amp fuses.

The stock harness that has been available for these trucks since the beginning of time is just fine, even for a modernized truck. The cost is between $150 and $200, depending on the vendor.

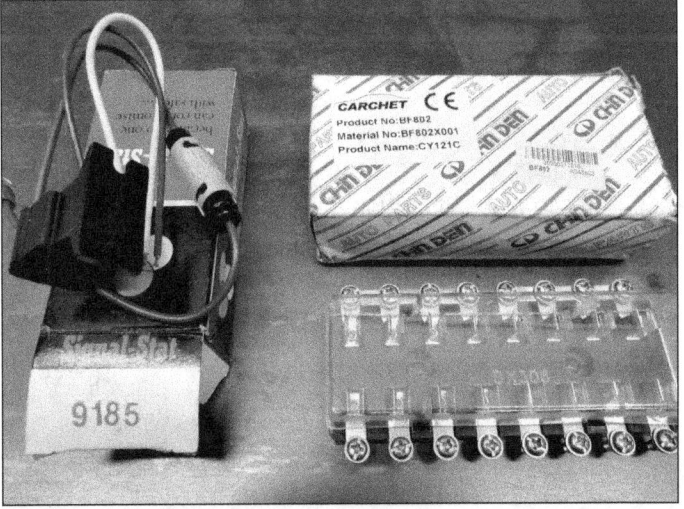

Glass fuse blocks go with this vintage better than the new style of fuses. This one is readily available, inexpensive, and can be fastened anywhere you choose. Also shown is the SignalStat 9185 fused flasher plug and mount.

CHAPTER 13

The Parts List

These part numbers are for a 1950 truck with a stock 1954–1955 blinker system with alternator. I took license to make this a 1953 electrical system because the harness is 1953–1955. Some of these part numbers are not for a 1950 truck, so please research the part numbers you need if they are different.

The 1953–1955 Wiring Harness for an Alternator System

This is a no-nonsense harness that mounts exactly as stock with the very same stock features. The exceptions in this case are I want this harness to plug right into a three-wire, self-regulated alternator. I also want stealth turn signals, meaning there are no extra lights mounted to the vehicle anywhere. The turn signals will work through the existing park lights in front and taillights in back. This very same harness is available through Bowtie Bits (part number AD-535-WHA), Jim Carter (EL-171C), or Classic Parts (52-026).

Park Lamp Double-Contact Conversion Kit

This kit (Classic Parts 47-905) will help you convert a front park lamp socket for use with a dual-filament bulb. This is necessary for use with the turn signal wiring above. For this project, I am going with LED tail and park assemblies, which are already wired for turn signals and this conversion kit is not needed.

12-Volt Bulbs

To replace all the bulbs on your 12-volt truck, you will need:
- 2 each of 6020 Halogen sealed-beam 7-inch headlights
- 1 each of 1073 for dome light
- 2 each of 1034 dual-filament for park lights
- 4 each of 67 for taillights
- 6 each of 57 for gauge (4), high beam (1), and ignition switch (1)

Note: A person might be tempted to replace the dash lights, dome, etc., with LED equivalents. While this is a good idea, be careful to choose dimmable LEDs! Most LED equivalents are not dimmable, so research this before ordering. Otherwise, you get max brightness at any dim setting and then wonder why.

Turn Signal Switch/Flasher

The socket and fused plug/mount for the flasher is a Signal-Stat 9185. For this project, I am going with LED and a stock 1955 six-wire blinker system, which uses a two-prong LED flasher (NAPA part number EL-12L-1).

Firewall Grommet Kit

This is a six-piece grommet kit that has all the grommets necessary to completely replace them on the firewall. This kit (Bowtie Bits AD-505-FG-KIT) comes with a four-hole grommet for use with water temp/oil pressure/choke/throttle, a starter/coil wire grommet (x2), a speedometer cable grommet, a vacuum wiper grommet, and a main harness grommet.

Headlight Grommet Kit

The grommets at the back of the headlight buckets are typically hard and crispy. You will likely need new ones, such as the kit from Bowtie Bits (AD-475-HLBG).

Headlight Gasket

If you remove the buckets, you should replace the gasket (Bowtie Bits AD-475-HLBFS).

Headlight Bezel Kit

Stainless bezels, seals, clips, and screws can be found in the Bowtie Bits kit (AD-475-HLB-KIT).

Headlight Bulb Retainer

This stainless ring holds in the bulb (Bowtie Bits AD-475-HLBR).

Park Lamp Set

The LED park lamp set with clear lenses is sold in pairs (Bowtie Bits AD-473-PL-LED).

Dome Light Assembly

The assembly from Bowtie Bits (AD-475-DLAC) comes in chrome.

Inner Fender Terminal Strips

Purchased from Bowtie Bits (AD-475-IFTB-3), you will need two: one for each inner fender as original.

ELECTRICAL

The Parts List (Continued)

Brake Light Switch

This switch (Bowtie Bits AD-475-SLS) mounts to the firewall between the firewall and the brake pedal.

Headlight Switch

This original-style switch (Bowtie Bits AD-475-HLS-12VFC) uses your old knob and bezel at 12-volt.

Dimmer Switch

A dimmer switch is available from Bowtie Bits (AD-475-DS).

Ignition Switch Housing

This housing from Bowtie Bits (AD-473-IS) is also original style.

Entire Truck Lock Set

The Bowtie Bits (AD-523-CLS) set has all matching keys (1952–1953) for the glove box, ignition, and doors.

Fuse Block

A rebuilt stop/tail fuse block can be purchased from Classic Parts (52-973).

Horn Relay

Bowtie Bits part number AD-475-HR-12 is the horn relay.

Horn

Research this, but I just used two universal ones: one with high note and one with low. Both are 12 volts.

Ground Strap

A ground strap is available from Bowtie Bits (part number AD-475-EFG).

Inner Fender Grommets

Purchase two inner fender grommets for the headlight wiring. I get a grommet kit from Harbor Freight and pick the right size.

12-Volt Gauge Set

I had gauges professionally refurbished by Jeff McCoy at Bowtie Bits. Call them for pricing. ■

Front End Electrical

We will start at the front of the truck and move toward the back to make things as sequential as possible. The advantage of a fresh, new truck with every part in pristine condition already, is there is no guesswork on the condition of the associated parts. We will assume you have repaired, cleaned, and painted your headlight buckets, small parts, etc.

Headlights

The headlight buckets get the same treatment as all other small parts: sandblast, prep, and shot with a good single-stage urethane in Gloss Black. Then, insert the headlight bucket grommets in the buckets and install the inner bucket assembly to the main bucket. Align the two properly so the two adjustment screws and the spring line up properly. Slide the adjustment screw nuts into their slots. Using a needle-nose pliers, pull the spring into position. This is a good time to be sure the adjustment screws and nuts do not have thread issues and move smoothly. I like to use spray lithium grease on threads for adjustable items on the truck.

All of the headlight bucket parts are laid out and ready to put together. The new stainless steel outer bezels really look amazing.

CHAPTER 13

Once the grommet and inner bucket are installed correctly, the headlight bucket is ready to install on the fender.

Once the fender clips are installed (Bowtie Bits AD-475-HLBS-KIT) the bucket assembly is pushed into the fender and screwed down with the kit's sheet metal screws.

This is how the trim ring assembly goes together. Each of the four clips is installed as shown.

To install the buckets, you will need to make sure your fender-to-bucket clips are serviceable. If they are not, it's Bowtie Bits to the rescue with AD-475-HLBS-KIT. The kit contains all the clips and #10 sheet metal screws to do both buckets. I substitute the screws for stainless steel ones. Add the bucket to fender gaskets (Bowtie Bits AD-475-HLBFS) then install the buckets. They only go in one way.

Once you have the buckets installed, put a grommet in the inner fender (Bowtie Bits AD-475-IFWLG). The headlamp harness goes through that hole in the inner fender and connects through the headlight bucket. While we are on the inner fender, add two terminal strips to the upper inner fender. There are two holes made for this.

The terminal strips are held down with two 1/4-20 x 1-inch bolts with nuts and washers. Depending on the

With the completed headlight install, you can see that the inner bezel has to be stainless steel too because it is seen surrounding the headlight.

The inner headlight retainer ring is held down with three screws that come with the kit.

ELECTRICAL

year of your truck, there are two types of terminals. The three-screw type or the four-screw type. Since the inner fenders dictate which one you use, get the appropriate one (either Bowtie Bits part number AD-475-IFTB-3 or AD-475-IFTB-4).

Thread the headlight harness through the inner fender grommet so the terminal ends of the wires go to the terminal strip and through the inner fender grommet. The headlight socket goes through the headlight bucket. Add the 7-inch sealed beam 6020 headlights and connect them. Push them into the bucket and fasten with the inner bucket bulb retainer ring (Bowtie Bits AD-475-HLBR; two required).

Lastly for the headlights, we need to add the trim ring. To do this right you will need a new ring with the bezel seals, springs, and screws. I got the kit because it contains a stainless steel trim ring (Bowtie Bits AD-475-HLB-KIT). Install the clips and seals inside the trim ring, then install on the fender.

Firewall Grommets

Use the diagram to decide which grommet goes where. Once you have them in your hands, it will be apparent as to where each grommet is supposed to go. The diagram represents the stock locations for each of the wires or parts that go through them.

There are two grommets that require modification in order to fit the application. The speedometer cable will not go through the grommet. With a sharp X-Acto knife, cut a straight line between the center and one edge. The four-hole grommet requires the same kind of cut but only to the larger hole for the water temperature copper line.

I used a new oil pressure line kit and added the end once it was through the firewall, so no cut was necessary for the oil line. Do nothing with the gauges yet, assuming they are not yet installed.

The choke and throttle cables can be removed from the carb and then pushed through and reattached without cutting. Once you feed the water temperature gauge copper line back into the four-hole grommet, you can reattach the sender to the engine's head and then refill the cooling system. You can also take this opportunity to attach the oil pressure line back up by putting that copper line through the grommet on the opposite side.

As long as the gauge is still accessible for the wiring part, you are good to go. You can also put the choke/throttle cables through the four-hole grommet, completing this grommet's installation. The same can be said for the speedometer cable. These are two grommets that have little to do with the harness installation, but it's good to replace all of them at the same time.

Since I used a brand-new New Port Engineering Clean Wipe Wiper Drive System (part number NE4753CCT) that clears the choke cable, there is no need for a wiper grommet. However, I will use that hole in the firewall for the overdrive cable.

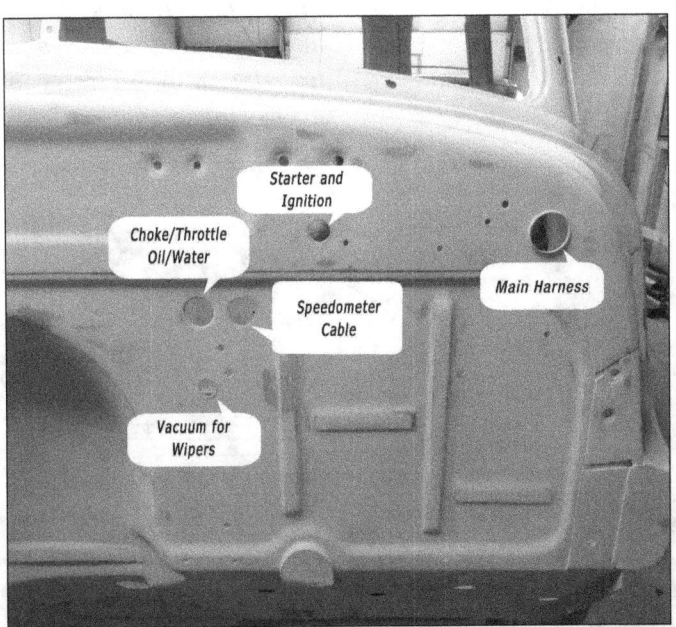

Here are the appropriate holes for the appropriate firewall grommets.

The firewall is shown after completion of the harness install.

HOW TO RESTORE YOUR CHEVY TRUCK: 1947–1955

CHAPTER 13

The Ground Straps

The grounding system on an AD truck is often taken for granted. Then when someone wonders why something isn't working, they spend hours scratching their heads because they didn't understand the designer's intent. There are two ground straps: the negative side of the battery to a bare metal point on the frame and a bellhousing-to-frame ground strap. This gives the engine ground, the frame ground, and then because you mounted the cab via the front mounting bolts to the frame, you should have a completely grounded vehicle.

The problem is, today's very hard paints make it possible that the cab is not grounded even after you bolt it down. It is essential you provide a very solid ground to the cab as well as the frame and engine. Use a multimeter to check this. If you have a problem, scrape some paint off or better yet, add a third ground strap.

Stainless Steel Fasteners

I like to use stainless steel hardware to reattach everything. If you have ever had the pleasure of taking entire trucks apart at the salvage yard for sale to the vendors, you will *fully* understand in technicolor the reason for this. Never again will rust be a problem. You can get button-head stainless bolts that look just like the older cad-plated original clutch head bolts only with an Allen head at McMaster-Carr. Almost every other fastener is also available there in stainless steel. Why put yourself through the joy of grinding off bolt heads, breaking the bolts inside a weld nut, etc. This follows with our preservation philosophy. ■

The Park/Tail/Blinker Lights

Next, we will attack the park lights. Since we are using the turn signal wiring that comes standard with our harness, we need to either modify the original park lamp housings or purchase the LED assemblies that are available. On this truck, I am going with the LED assembly because it is already wired for turn signals and is much brighter than the older incandescent style.

The taillight assembly I chose has a bright, shiny stainless steel housing and LED lighting. Since it is also turn signal ready, there is just a matter of two wires and mounting. This assembly also provides stop lighting. The driver-side taillight assembly has a license plate LED light as well.

I got two aftermarket horns: one high pitch and one low pitch. Each horn has two connections: ground

Be sure the frame has the paint removed under the bolt so there is no doubt about making good contact, then check with a meter to be sure.

The newer-style LED park lamp assembly advantages are longevity and brightness. They are also wired for turn signals.

This little clip is often missing. Having it helps redirect the cable so it does not interfere with the mechanical starter spring. You can always make one.

ELECTRICAL

The LED taillight assemblies also have stock turn signal capability.

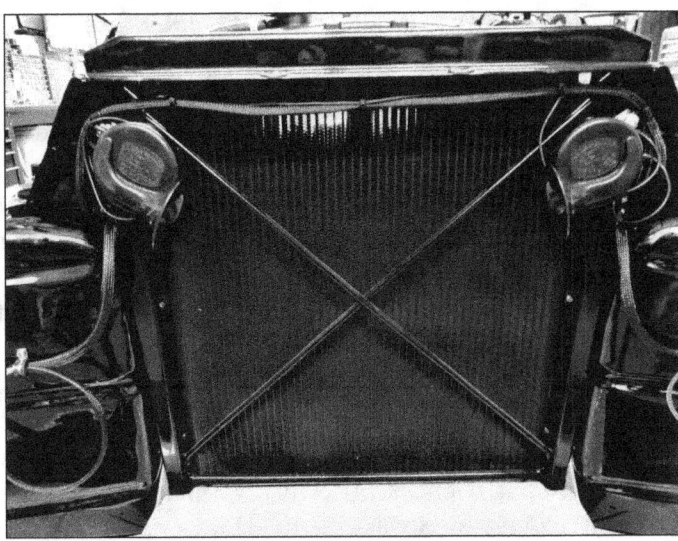

The two horns after installation. They are out of the way here and sound great!

and positive 12 volt. You simply run a short wire on each one to the horn's mounting bracket for the ground and connect the 12 Volt wire to the single horn wire in the harness.

Inner Fender Terminals

I do not trust the old terminals (in my case what was left of them), so I purchased new ones. One might be tempted to get a four-wire terminal, since the vendors sell both, but this is not good because the inner fenders have mounting holes that fit their respective terminal strip. In 1950, AD trucks had three terminal strips.

Mount the new terminal strips using two 1/4-inch bolts/nuts/washers on each inner fender. I might also caution you that when it comes time to tighten the wires to the screws on the terminals, do not gorilla them in! These terminals will strip too easily. Ask me how I know.

Install a new #10 sheet metal screw beside the terminal block. That will be used for a ground from the headlights. The terminal strip is used as follows:
- Front-most terminal screw: high-beam wires
- Middle terminal screw: low-beam wires
- Rear-most terminal screw: parking light wires

I said it that way so that you won't get confused from side to side about what goes where.

The Horn Relay and Fuse Stop/Tail Fuse Block

I didn't want to put parts back on the firewall and then find out they were defective after I have the new harness in, so I removed the horn relay and stop/tail fuse block from the firewall to check them for serviceability. I opened the covers and sprayed them really well with electronic contact spray. I then took a fine wire brush on the end of a Dremel tool to clean the screw terminals thoroughly. I want everything to work!

The fuse block is used only for the brake lights and taillights. Both are 20-amp circuits that use 20-amp fuses. There is a fuse holder in the inside of the cover for spares. As it

Both inner fenders are the same on this year's model, so three position terminal strips on each are necessary.

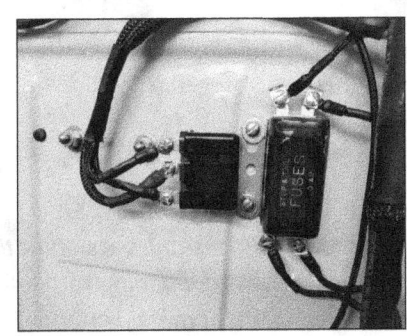

The three-wire horn relay (left) and stop/tail fuse block are mounted in the stock position. Since the stop/tail fuse blocks are not available new and the cover is plastic, I clear coated the outside after a thorough cleaning.

HOW TO RESTORE YOUR CHEVY TRUCK: 1947–1955

is oriented on the firewall, the right side is for the brake lights and the left side is for the taillights. They are marked on the inside deck.

These two parts share the same two screws for mounting to the firewall. To test the relay for proper operation, connect a 12-volt battery positive to the center terminal and the negative to one of the mounting screws or base. Then, take a jumper wire from the mounting screw or base to the bottom terminal temporarily to see if it clicks. After using the contact cleaner, I was able to get mine to reliably click each time.

If you want to take it a step further, connect the horn to the top terminal and a jumper from the base of the horn to the base of the relay and try again. The nice part about the way they made this relay is, if you ever suspect your horn button on your steering wheel, you can jumper that bottom terminal (see below) and the horn should sound off. If it does, it is the switch or wiring on the column.

The Brake Light Switch and Headlight Dimmer Switch

The brake light switch is unique in that it doesn't matter which way you install the wires. What does matter is that it is oriented and mounted to the firewall properly.

Remove the switch from the firewall. Use a multimeter set to ohms or continuity to see if it gets a short or 0 ohms about halfway through the action of the switch. This should happen consistently and in the same place each time. Since this switch is sealed, it is probably best to get a new switch if yours shows any indication of inconsistency. Replace the switch on the firewall in its proper orientation.

The headlight dimmer switch takes a lot of abuse and could very well suffer from too much dirt in the switch. I spray this switch heavily with contact cleaner, then test to see if the switch opens and closes consistently and the springs pops it back up consistently. Using a multimeter, check the switch by putting one lead on the battery terminal and the other on one of the contacts. Press the button to see if you get a

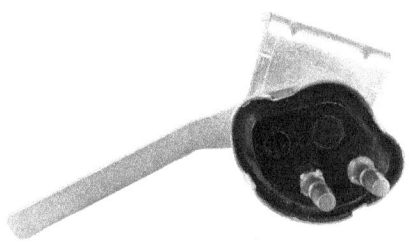

The firewall-mounted brake light (stop) switch has no special wire orientation with the two terminals. Either wire will work at either terminal.

clean 0 ohms reading, then move your lead to the other contact to see if it's working there. If anything isn't adding up, replace the switch. It is not worth it to have a problem with a relatively high amperage switch. The diagram will help you when it comes time to install the harness.

Aftermarket dimmer switches come in two styles: type 1 and type 2. The difference is, the battery terminal is in the center on type 2. There would be no damage from wiring it wrong, but the high beams won't work if you choose the wrong diagram. See the documentation that comes with the harness.

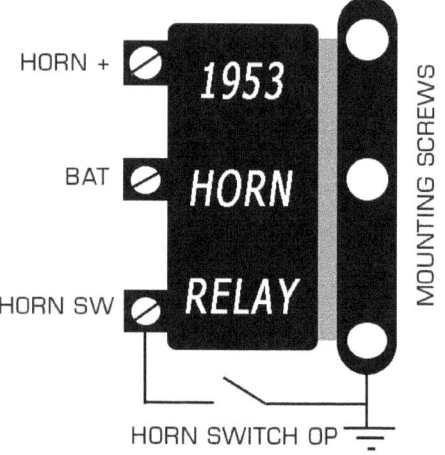

The AD horn relay wiring diagram is shown here. You can test your horn system by grounding the bottom terminal to the mounting screws.

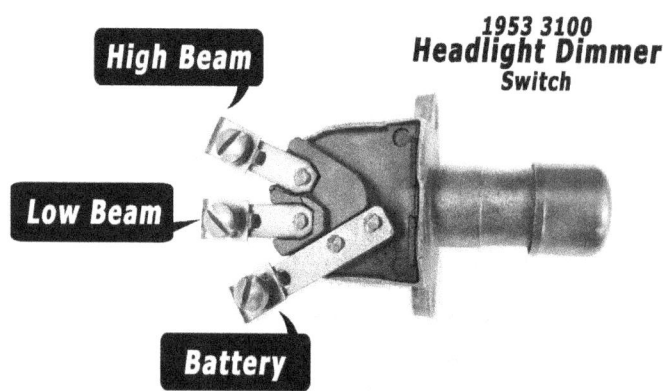

This is one version of the floor-mounted dimmer switch wiring diagram. I mounted mine to the floor with #10 fine-thread screws and nuts instead of sheet metal screws.

ELECTRICAL

The Headlight Switch and Ignition Switch

The headlight switch in this vintage Chevy truck is pretty central to the entire electrical system. In more modern vehicles, we have a fuse/terminal block that serves to provide two types of power: switched and unswitched. Switched power is provided by the ignition switch, and unswitched power is provided by the headlight switch. Remember, these are vintage vehicles and they do not have terminal blocks for that purpose, so it is essential that each accessory you add to your vehicle has an inline fuse.

An accessory is anything that requires power, either switched or unswitched. The turn signals, heater, electric wiper system, etc., are considered accessories and require an inline fuse. Without the fuse, you are exposing your entire electrical system to potentially catastrophic damage.

Always keep safety in mind when addressing electrical system issues. Fuse sizes are not based on the accessory as much as the wire that connects them. Of course, both are kept in mind. An example is the heater. The motor itself draws about 5 amps of current. The wiring for most of the vehicle is 14 gauge. The amp charts available online suggest a max of 15 amps for 14-gauge wire. Personally, I like to know a bit quicker when something that I know should only be putting out 5 amps is putting out 15, so I choose to use a 10-amp fuse. It's a very good idea to know exactly what your turn signals, electric wipers, heater, etc. is rated at and then ensure your wiring is appropriate and you use the correct fuse.

The headlight diagram (below) is your guide to wiring the switch. The far end of the switch is the battery terminals. All three of those end terminals are connected together and used for unswitched power. Since they are all tied together, it is acceptable to piggyback a new accessory if you run out of terminals.

The ignition switch is what you use to connect switched power. The only time switched power allows an accessory to be provided with electrical energy is when the ignition key is turned on. Ammeter negative is the connection to the starter/battery

Aftermarket Switches

Some of the aftermarket switches are made differently. The headlamp terminal is upper left on the diagram, then tail, then park. The way to check this is wire it up per the diagram that comes with the wiring harness, then swap to this diagram if you find something not working as planned.

Another interesting anomaly is the stock wiring system was made so the front park lights do *not* light up with the headlight switch in the headlight position. If you want the park lights illuminated while the headlights are on, make a very short jumper wire and jumper between the park light terminal and the taillight terminal. They are next to each other, thus the very short jumper. ∎

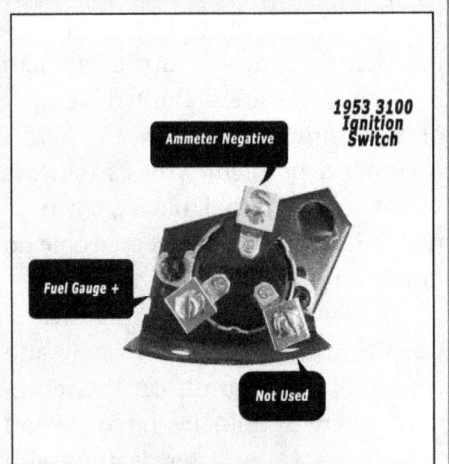

Shown here is the ignition switch diagram. The "not used" terminal can be used the same way the fuel gauge terminal is used: to switch power using the switch.

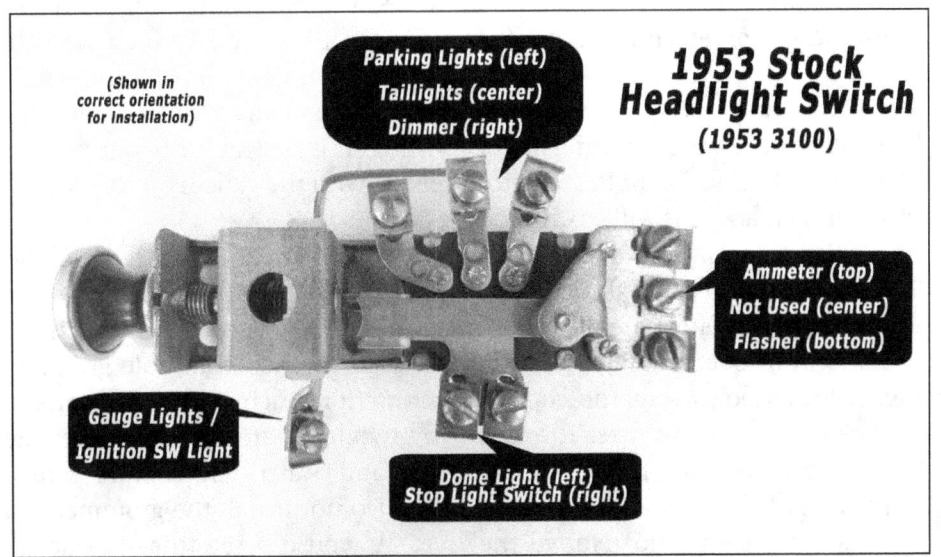

You will need the stock headlight switch diagram to determine where the wires go. Since it goes in this exact orientation, it can be mounted and still accessible.

HOW TO RESTORE YOUR CHEVY TRUCK: 1947–1955

directly. The one labeled fuel gauge is your switched terminal. So, anything that you require to be switched, you must stack onto that one terminal. This is generally not a problem because there are a limited number of accessories to begin with. If this becomes a problem, you can always add a fuse/terminal block. It would not be hard to do, but most people do not find it necessary.

Remove and clean both switches. Use the contact cleaner liberally and then use a wire brush on the terminals. There should be no corrosion present anywhere. After cleaning with the contact spray, the gauge lights will dim smoothly and everything will work much better. Reinstall the headlight switch, making sure the terminals are facing the gauges, giving you great accessibility when it comes time to wire the switch. Leave the ignition switch out for now. It is very hard to wire with it in place, so we will install it after it is properly wired.

The Gauge Clusters

The gauge clusters are held in by four nuts that are screwed onto studs that are placed appropriately for holding the cluster in place. This arrangement can be really difficult; however, the key is to just

The stock gauge cluster has the 0–60-psi oil pressure gauge, which is used when installing the later 1954–1962 engines.

sit on the bench seat, reach under the dash, and feel the studs/nuts. Use a nut driver to feel around to get them out blind. Remove the four #10-32 nuts. There is no real worry about the gauges falling out the back because there are water temp and oil pressure hard lines going to it.

The next step is to remove the water temperature sensor from the engine's head. The sensor is screwed into an adapter that is placed on the driver's side close to the firewall. It has a copper line going to it. Remove this to get the gauge cluster completely out of the truck so you can do some refurbishment to the gauge cluster. New chrome bezel, glass, decals, and even new gauge parts are available if needed. If you do not need any servicing of your gauges, no need to remove the water temperature sensor from the head.

The water temperature sensor is a permanent part of the gauge cluster and is not removable. The copper tube and sensor are filled with a special gas that makes the gauge useless if released. Be careful not to make sharp bends or crush the line.

Carefully remove the old four-hole grommet and remove the sensor from the head. It is advised to lower the water level sufficiently so you do not have water spurting out of your engine's head. Drain the radiator by about half and this will ensure you do not have a gusher on your hands. Thread the sensor back through the grommet hole, being careful to keep the line from overbending or crushing. A loose loop about the circumference of the gauge cluster is a fine way to keep that line from crushing or bending.

The next step is to remove the oil pressure line. This line is simply a piece of copper tubing with the

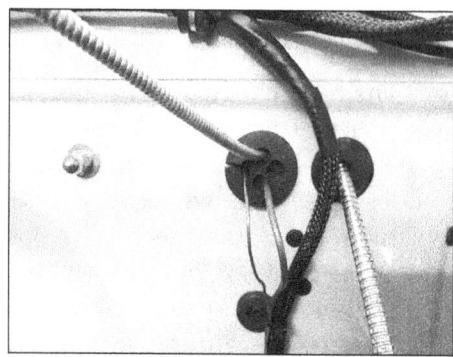

The four-hole grommet is normally populated with choke and throttle cables and water temperature and oil pressure lines. Be careful not to kink the two copper lines! For this build, I will not be installing the throttle cable, so I can use that hole for the defroster cable.

correct ends on them for connection. It is a good idea at this time to remove it and make sure the line is serviceable. Blow through it to ensure there are no obstructions. To do this, remove the line from the engine near the driver-side bottom. Sometimes it is on the end of a 1/8-inch NPT tee connection.

By now, the gauge cluster should be very accessible, so it will be easy to see the oil pressure line and disconnect it with a 5/16-inch wrench. We are removing these hard lines for easier accessibility for connecting the wiring. It is best to start your harness install with the gauges on the floor of the vehicle.

Are the choke and throttle cables in good shape? If so, remove them from the carb end and thread them through the new four-hole grommet across from each other. The remaining two holes are for the oil pressure line and water temperature sensor line. Do not install the grommet just yet. As you can see from the detail, if there is any reason to change out those cables, now is the time.

ELECTRICAL

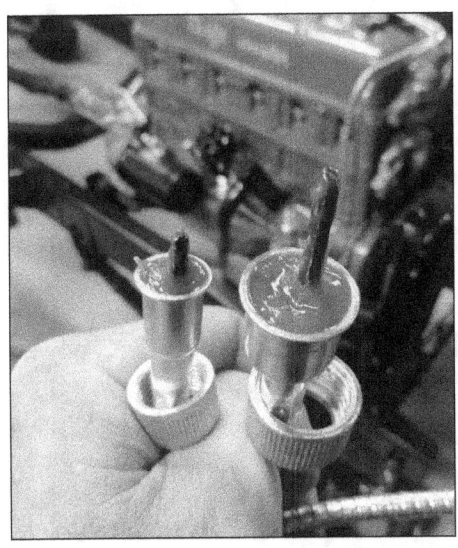

The speedometer cable is installed with the smaller end at the gauge. It is a good idea to grease the ends.

The speedometer cluster is easier to remove. It requires loosening the threaded speedometer cable and then just pulling three bulb fixtures out of the back. Once you have it out, check the cable for serviceability. Remove it at the transmission and spin it by hand. It should move very freely with very little resistance. It is then a good idea to add grease in the grease cavity on each end of the cable.

Install the new speedometer cable firewall grommet by cutting the grommet from the hole to the outer edge with a sharp X-Acto knife to get the cable back in. Do not be tempted to install the speedometer gauge just yet. It is much easier for access to the other cluster if left to be installed last. Just like the other cluster, maybe now is a good time for new gauge parts or any maintenance you may feel is necessary.

Next, remove all the wires and bulb fixtures that are connected. Do not worry about wire placement for the new harness. That will all be taken care of with the documentation you get with the harness. It is also okay to now remove the main harness to this point. All headlight wiring and everything to the gauges can be cut out in any fashion you wish. The only thing to be careful of regarding removal of the old wiring is to note the routing. Especially how the wires go down from the lower firewall and to the back of the truck. Also, read the next section before cutting the dome light wire!

The Dome Light

The dome light is next. The wire from the dome light to the headlight switch is routed through the driver-side A-pillar. This is a particular pain to do unless you know the secret. The secret is to attach the new wire to the old wire and fish it through the pillar.

As it stands now, the headlight switch has nothing on it, so you can locate the wire that is very close to the switch and is routed up. It will be easy to spot. Cut the terminal end off that wire and have it ready so when you get to that point, you can use electrical tape to tape the new wire to the end of the old wire to pull the new wire up the pillar. You want to be very slim about it. Do not make a huge wad of wire and electrical tape because the A-pillar is surprisingly narrow, and you can bind it pretty easily. If you do end up breaking it and fail to get it into place, try again with 0.030 safety wire.

The dome light comes off with a few screws, and it's a good time to look it over carefully. In this case, there was good reason. The original cloth wiring was present and in very dire shape. There is no doubt a shorting hazard exists. The problem is, upon close investigation, the cloth wire goes directly to the bulb. A soldered end fashioned for a bulb contact was all there was to it.

I fixed this by removing the small copper bulb contact from one of the old harness sockets. I pried it open to receive a new wire then crimped it on and threaded the wire through. The switch wires were just as bad, so they were replaced as well. I left a 12-inch lead wire with a barrel connector on the end to attach to the new harness wire. After doing a little maintenance on the dome light, put it back where you found it. It's ready to accept the new harness without surprises. You will also notice along the headliner lip is a few wire clips. You want to set the new wire back into those clips to aid in proper routing.

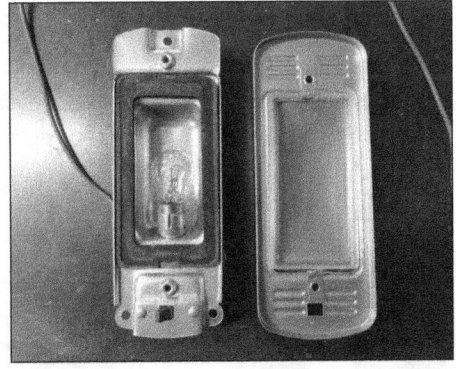

This is the stock dome light assembly. Since most LED assemblies are not dimmable, a regular incandescent bulb is appropriate here.

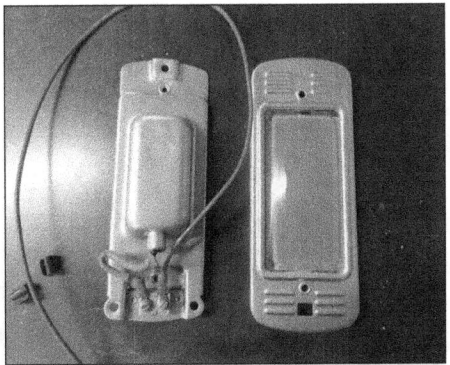

This is the front and back sides of the dome light assembly. As usual, it's a one-wire setup with ground being the light's housing.

HOW TO RESTORE YOUR CHEVY TRUCK: 1947–1955

CHAPTER 13

The Fuel Sending Unit

In keeping with the plan, the fuel sender is next. The wire for the sending unit is routed from the firewall down to the driver-side frame rail and to a grommet near the center of the cab rearward underneath. It follows the same initial path as the taillight wiring. There is only one wire. It is not hard to feed that wire up to the sending unit from underneath when the time comes.

Remove the back of the bench seat to access the sending unit. It is mounted to the top of the gas tank with six screws. Pay attention to how it is oriented in the tank and be sure to put it back the way you found it. The arm needs to freely swing, so a 90-degree turn when installing could be a problem.

The reason we are taking it out is because it should be tested before the new wiring is installed. I know it may have worked before, but a simple test will tell you if it needs a proper cleaning. With it out, put the multimeter on it: one lead to the center terminal and the other to the side of the sender, just to get a good ground. With your multimeter on ohms, move the arm up and down. You should see between 0 and 30 ohms (0=empty, 30=full). The thing is, we do not want any hiccups in the reading. It should smoothly go up and down the scale with no erroneous numbers. If you are getting hiccups, use the electrical contact spray to spray it really good at the resistor array. With it clean, you will notice a much smoother reading. Reinstall it the way you found it awaiting the new harness.

It is a good time to shine a flashlight down the sending unit hole and take a good look at the gas tank. If there is fuel, is debris floating around in it? How about the overall condition of the tank?

The Taillights

The taillight wiring takes a left turn for the passenger's side at the front side of the rear crossmember. I like to use rubber-inserted stainless steel Adel clamps placed about every 2 feet apart wherever I can find a bolt hole that isn't used. I used a total of 12 of them. Five were 3/8-inch Adel clamps and the rest were 1/4 inch. I also used stainless steel 1/4-inch hardware. This keeps the wires safe and provides a nice clean installation. The rear crossmember even has two holes through it at the frame rail for grommets so the wires can reach through it and to the taillights.

The taillights may be fine the way they are, but my project vehicle had none. I ordered new LED ones with stainless steel polished housings. These are already wired and set up for turn signals and 12-volt power.

It is important to know which wire goes to the brake/turn signals and which wire goes to the park/taillights. On the new LED assembly there is a sticker that tells you which is which. You need to know this so when you install the new harness, the most dominant light (the one that is brighter) is the brake/turn signal light. Mark the wires so you know when installing the harness which one is which. Also, the white wire on the taillight assembly is ground, *not* the black wire. This is a new convention used for LED lighting. Always verify these things before applying power.

Turn Signals

Chances are, the turn signal switch you have is not correct for this harness. To find out, check to see how many wires you have

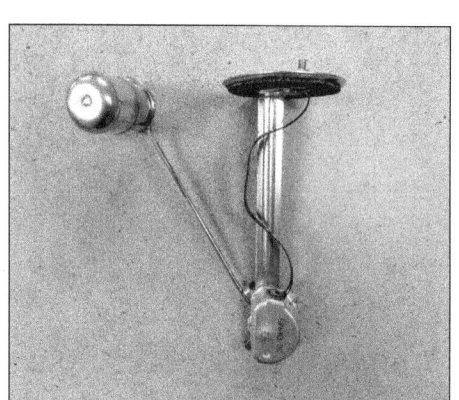

The standard 30-ohm fuel sending unit must be installed with the arm going the long way in the tank!

The rear crossmember junction for the taillight wires is where the driver-side taillight wires separate from the passenger's side.

The LED-style taillight assembly with polished stainless housing has a white license plate LED on the driver's side.

ELECTRICAL

going to the turn signals. My old switch had two. There is the flasher wire and battery and ground, but just two for signaling a turn. This arrangement will not work with our new wiring harness, and we are happy about it! Why? Because with this new harness, there is no need for extra fixtures for turn signals.

Seven-Wire Switch

The park lights are modified for dual-filament bulbs, and the rears are good because they have two bulbs. This, unfortunately, requires a seven-wire turn signal switch. So, if you have a seven-wire switch, you are good to go. If not, there is a very nice switch that is still in production today. They are used for large trucks and vintage vehicles!

Enter the SignalStat 900, which I hear is very popular. I did a search for this switch and found one for $42 on eBay. From the look and feel of the switch, it is very high quality. This switch requires a Number 263 Turn Signal Flasher, which is a special flasher used for this switch. There is also an LED-capable version available. The new harness's instructions will have a nice explanation of where each wire goes and enough wire placed in the proper place for connection. The switch also has wiring and installation instructions. No way to lose!

Six-Wire Switch

I am not going with any of the above but provided the information in case you want to. I am using the stock 1955 turn signal assembly, which is a six-wire arrangement. Now, for the good news: the color coding of the wiring harness turn signal wires and the color coding on the turn signal switch is the same! For this install, I will be using a two-wire LED flasher. This is definitely the way to go because the turn signals are even self-canceling.

1955 Steering Column

If you really want a great turn signal system and feel adamant about it looking stock when you are finished, there is nothing better than the stock (dealer installed as everything else was back then) 1955 turn signal system. This means you need to locate a 1955 steering column. Make sure the wire bezel that covers the wires about halfway down the column comes with it. You also want to make sure you have the blinker cup and all associated parts. Vendors sell the new switches and a lot of the assembly. This also requires you use the 1954–1956 steering wheel because it mates with the blinker cup. With the switch wires being color coded to the wiring harness, installation can't get any easier!

Wiring Harnesses

Let's take a look at the new harness. Opening the bag, there are two sheets of paper. Surprisingly, neither is a wiring diagram! I spent a few days building up the courage to start on this project, wondering why there was no wiring diagram. It just made no sense!

The package has the following contents:

- Two headlight harnesses. Good quality with the headlight sockets connected and ready for installation. These go from the headlight buckets to the terminal strips on the inner fender.
- One two-wire harness for the

This is the stock 1955 blinker system. It requires a 1954/1955 steering column because there are additional bolt holes and wiring cover. The blinker hub is behind the 1954/1955 steering wheel.

This same harness is available from most of our vendors. It is elegant in its simplicity.

starter/battery to ammeter negative (10 gauge) and the other wire is the ignition (top terminal) to coil +. This two-wire harness has its own firewall grommet.

- Headlight switch to ignition switch single wire. This is to convert unswitched power to your switched power. This wire attaches from the back of the headlight switch directly to the lower wire on the ignition switch.
- Dome light single wire. This single wire attaches from the dome light terminal on the headlight switch through the A-pillar to the dome light.
- A bundle of extra wire. Since I never contacted them, I do not have a real explanation as to what they were thinking, but the only thing I can think of is this wire is used to extend the taillights, sending unit, or other things that may be too short. But the color and gauge of the wires did not match the harness, so I am still not sure what they were thinking. The taillights *do* need extending and so does the sending unit. You can use these wires, but do not expect the proper color.

The Main Harness

There is no mistaking this harness, which has three main branches. One branch has the gauge lights and wiring on it, which is easy to identify. One branch goes to the headlights and park lights. The other branch goes down to the dimmer switch, brake switch, sender, and taillights. The demarcation to decide how much of the wiring to stuff through the main harness grommet is the stop/tail fuse block and horn relay wires. For some reason, I was surprised at how well the manufacturers gauged how far apart to make the terminals.

There are four male terminals for plugging in to a special female splice connector. These are used for the horn switch at the column, the brake light switch at the firewall, and the dome light connection.

For the park light wires from the park light to the terminal strip on the inner fender, you can use the extra wire they included. However, if you want the colors to be correct, get some yellow 14-gauge wire and run it from the farthest back terminal on the inner fender to the park lights. The connection from the taillights to the harness will require barrel splices and some length of properly colored wire (or use what is in the harness bag) to get to the taillights.

Another thing that is a good idea is plastic tie straps. In certain places, it's nice to firm up the job by pulling the wires together. This is an economy harness, so the tie wraps were not an expectation. Aside from those two items, a terminal kit and tie wraps, get a roll of electrical tape. We need to extend the taping job they did another 10 inches on the starter/coil wire bundle.

Remember, if you really think you need a diagram, they are available through our vendors for a price. The first page is the one you will find the most important. The second page is helpful for knowledge of the turn signal and extra wires. The back of the first page has good drawings that help in connecting the wires.

Starter/Ignition Wires

Let's clear out everything in the harness package other than the main harness. Start with the starter/battery and ignition bundle, which is two wires with electrical tape

Wiring Harness Tools

Whenever you are installing a new wiring harness, it is understood that you will have to stock new wire end connectors of various sizes, barrel connectors for splicing wires together, etc. This also means having a good crimper and a wire stripper. These things are just standard fare. However, to take this to the next level and do it right, I am going to use shrink tubing around each wire end connector as well as in places where I want to keep certain wires together. This requires a new tool: the heat gun.

You will also need a few different sizes of shrink tubing. The sizes used are 1/8, 1/4, 5/16, 1/2, 7/16, 3/4, and 1 inch. Then, if you want to take this over the top, braided wire loom can be added to make the entire job look like a very expensive cloth wiring job. For that I used 1/8, 1/4, 5/16, 3/8, 7/16, and 3/4 inch. There is some expandability in this braided loom, so not as many sizes were necessary. To keep the loom from excessive fraying, use heat shrink on each end to hold it all together. I also like to have about 10 different colors of 14-gauge wire on hand to extend the wires if they are too short or need to be lengthened for any reason. This harness is very well thought out, but as with any harness install, more tools and supplies are needed.

ELECTRICAL

holding them together. This will go through the starter/ignition grommet on the firewall. Place the wires with the smaller terminals through the grommet and into the firewall. Secure the grommet and route the wires across the firewall.

Connect the thicker red wire to the main battery terminal on the starter. This will provide your entire electrical system with battery positive. Connect the other end to the ammeter's negative terminal. To end the confusion once and for all as to which is negative and which is ammeter positive, use the markings on the face of the gauge. The discharge (-) terminal is your ammeter negative.

The ignition wire that accompanies the above wire goes to the ignition coil (+) side. This wiring harness is for 6 or 12 volts, but the instructions cover 6 or 12 volts with electronic ignition. If you have a stock 12-volt points system and you want a bypass wire with ballast resistor, follow the instructions provided with the harness. In this case, my system is our very own HEI system. I found this bundle could have had another 10 inches or so of electrical tape wrapped, so I just extended it myself. Use Adel clamps with rubber inserts to secure these areas. You will need about 20 of these 3/8-inch clamps to complete the entire harness install.

Before you install this two-wire harness, you might want to consider the idea of having a tachometer. If you want a tachometer, add a third wire to this harness before installation. The tach wire goes from the negative side of the coil to the tachometer, so it really belongs in this segment of wire. Thinking ahead will prevent you from later annoyance.

Headlight Harnesses

Included in the harness kit are two headlight harnesses. Thread the wires through the bucket grommets then install the buckets to the truck with the nine sheet metal screws. Next, install the inner bucket (start by pulling the spring up and fastening it first) then the two adjustment screws followed by the headlight. Finish by adding the headlight retainer. Leave the outer bezel off for now because your headlights will require adjustments. Reach under the fender and thread the headlight harness through each inner fender grommet hole. Replace the grommet as needed before threading it through.

Once you have the wires through, you will notice they are very close to the inner fender headlight terminals. Connect them as follows:

1. Terminal closest to the front of the truck: high beam
2. Terminal in the middle: low beam
3. Terminal closest to the firewall: park lights
4. Black wire from headlight harness: sheet metal screw beside the inner fender terminal block (ground)

Do not tighten the inner fender terminals yet. We need to connect the main harness.

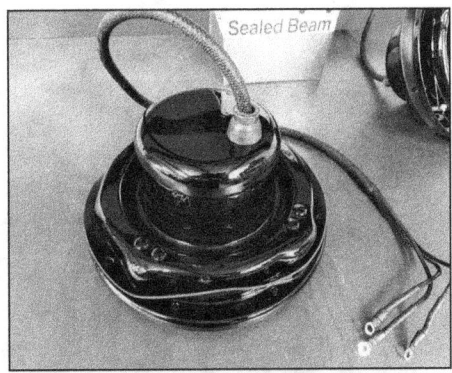
The headlight harness is installed through the headlight bucket grommet.

Park Lights and Horn

This is where you need to cut a piece of extra wire from the provided lengths of the wrong color or find some yellow 14-gauge wire to keep the color coding to the park lights intact. You want to extend one of the wires from the park lamps to the inner fender terminals. The other wire of your new dual filament bulbs or LED assembly goes to the turn signals and will need to be extended as well. Start by removing the hood latch pan from the radiator support and grille so you can easily get to the park lamp and horn wires.

There are two wires coming out of each park lamp. The problem is, we do not know which one is the dominant one to be used for turn signals. You can either test the bulb using 12-volt power or take your chances with the understanding you may be switching the wires around later.

Do both sides the same. Extend the lesser bulb wire to connect to the rearmost terminal on the inner fender. There is a nice little space on the radiator support bracket just where it meets the inner fender that

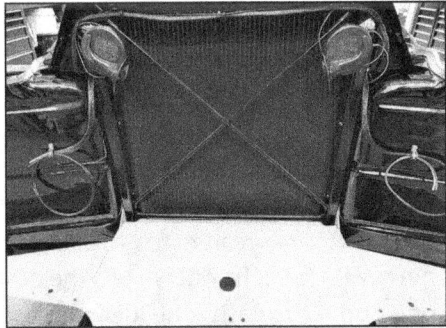
This shows the routing for the park lights and horn forward of the radiator. You want to do this prior to adding the front sheet metal assemblies. The park lights are routed to the inner fender terminal and the horn is routed to the horn relay. Use rubberized stainless clamps and route carefully.

is perfect for threading through to the terminal block. I ran my horn and park lights through that on each side. The turn signal wire on the park light assembly goes through that same hole, then with a barrel splice you can splice to the proper turn signal wire when we install the main harness. So, to be clear, you have three wires on the driver's side going through that hole in the radiator support: horn, turn signal, and park light.

The park light gets screwed down to the firewall end of the terminal block on the inner fender; the other two are left hanging for now. On the passenger's side, two wires are going through the radiator support hole: turn signal and park. If you have two horns, just jumper them together for power. The horns are expected to be mounted in that radiator support cavity since that is where the harness puts them.

Dome Light Wire Revisited

We are putting this here because we want to get rid of everything in the harness kit except for the main harness. This is one wire by itself labeled for installation as the dome light wire. It goes from the headlight switch (see diagram in headlight section) through the A-pillar right beside the switch up and over to the dome light.

This is somewhat a revisit but now we are ready to install the new wire. Tape the old wire to the new one under the dash. The idea is to fish the new wire up through the A-pillar using the old wire. Butt the two wires together and tape them sparingly but securely. Any wad of anything will not go through. Carefully feed the new wire up to the dome light. Once it is threaded through the A-pillar, attach the terminal end to the headlight switch. Using a barrel splice, connect the dome light end to the new wire. Secure the wires using the stock wire clips that are affixed to the lip of the inside roof.

Switched Power Wire

With the goal being to get rid of all the wires in the harness kit other than the main harness and extension wires, we need to connect the last single wire that is marked in the package. The wire needs to extend from the battery terminal on the end of the headlight switch to the bottom terminal of the ignition switch. This single wire is thicker than the others because it will power all your switched items. Leave the included length intact so it is long enough when factoring all the gauge cluster items.

Main Harness Install

So, we have put the main event off long enough! Let's spread this harness out across the fender. You will notice there are three branches, one has the gauge lights dangling from it, one has headlight terminals and the other goes down to connect with the stop light switch, dimmer switch, fuel sender, and taillights. Spread it out so the gauge lights are near the main harness grommet; the center branch that goes down is ready and the headlight ends are about where they would go.

Cut your main harness firewall grommet with an X-Acto knife from the center outward so you can get it around the harness. Feed the gauge lights, terminal wires, etc. on that end through the firewall from the outside. Feed things through until you see where the stop/tail fuse block and horn relay connect. The harness manufacturer did a wonderful job of spacing the wires here, so they connect top and bottom. Go ahead and connect the fuse block and horn relay per the instruction sheet. This is just a matter of looking at the number of the wire and corresponding it to the first page of the instruction. It is very simple.

Next address the headlight terminals, park light connections, and horn connections. Each wire is nicely marked and connects to its appropriate place. The harness loops across the front of the radiator over to the passenger-side headlight. Remember to observe the proper inner fender terminal connections as described earlier.

Remember, automotive electrical systems are basically one-wire systems. Ground is generally relegated to the connection devices nearest a mounting bracket or a chassis ground. This means the wires we are referring to for the most part for power are positive. Also, do a good job! Adding rubber-lined Adel clamps or wire looms will give your truck a much nicer finished look!

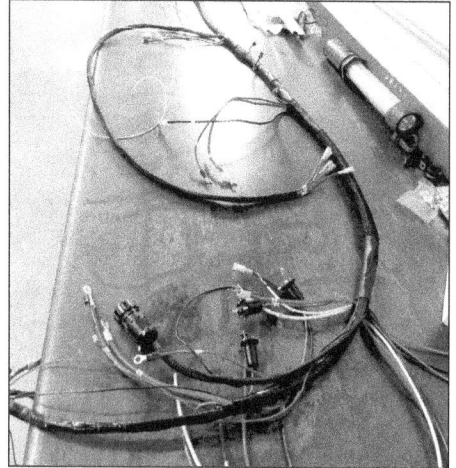

Spread the main harness out and identify what goes into the cab and what stays outside. The numbers on the wires are clearly marked as to where they go.

ELECTRICAL

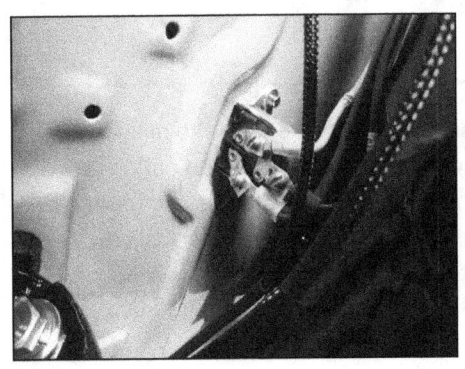

The dimmer switch comes in two varieties, and it's hard to decide which one you have. Type 1 means the battery terminal is in the middle terminal; Type 2 means the battery terminal is on the top as it is installed. Be sure you know which one you have.

 ### A-Pillar Wires

The fuel sending unit wire can also be routed from the sending unit on the gas tank up through the A-pillar and down to the gauge. This eliminates the single wire routing under the cab and makes for a cleaner install. You can also route rear speaker wires through the A-pillars on each side. There is a limited amount of room for wires, but I was able to thread the dome light, sending unit, and two speaker wires through the A-pillar. ■

There is no polarity on the brake light switch, so the two wires can be plugged into either post.

With the headlight, park light, and horn wiring out of the way and the gauge wiring stuffed through the firewall, it's time to address the branch that goes down and back to the fuel sender and taillights. First, you will find terminal ends for connecting the dimmer switch and brake light switch. You will also notice clips on the firewall made for the purpose of holding these wires in place.

Use your wiring instruction to put these wires where they belong. Refer to the dimmer switch diagram earlier. The stop light switch doesn't care which wire goes where, just that they are for that purpose.

Now we have a bundle that needs to find its way down the driver-side (inside) frame rail. Thread the rest of this portion of the harness through to the driver-side inside frame rail in such a way as to prevent problems with moving parts, such as brake pedals, etc. There is a clip on the bottom of the firewall that helps with this. Once the path is correct, install the fuel sending unit wire.

Before you get there, use those Adel clamps to secure the wiring as you go. The sending unit wire will be numbered as such. It goes through the bottom of the cab near the gas tank. You will need to remove the seat so you can fish it out from the floor. Once you have it through, connect it to the center of the fuel sending unit.

At this point, there will be wires with barrel connection splices on them. They will be numbered and ready for continuing to the taillight assemblies. Do the best you can to maintain color coding in adding length to these wires. If you have a seven-wire turn signal switch, one of the wires can just stop and go nowhere. In my case, it was wire number 22. The turn signal switch will control the stop lamp circuit. Follow directly down the driver-side frame rail for the driver-side taillight. Back in the day, you would be finished since they didn't have a passenger-side taillight. I went across the rear frame rail crossmember with my wires to the passenger-side frame rail.

Once at the taillights, there are grommets on the side of each frame rail, or there should be. Install a new grommet and then thread the two wires through it to the taillights. Again, you want the most dominant light, in this case the center bulb, to be your brake light. Open the taillight to determine the color of wire that corresponds to that one and connect accordingly on each side. That concludes the outside part of the harness install!

The alternator connection has a provided plug to make everything very easy. There is the main terminal wire that goes to the ammeter positive and then the two smaller wires. One is jumpered direct to the main terminal on the alternator, the other goes to the ignition switch. The one

This is how to connect the alternator using a one-wire system. The wire going off to the right is for the alternator warning light if you wish to use it.

that goes to the ignition switch is your idiot light function.

Now for the fun part! It is not as big a deal as it looks when you work from the floor of the cab. With the gauges sitting on or near the floor, you can more easily manipulate the wires. Be careful when connecting to ensure you do not route a wire on the wrong side of an obstruction. Be careful and deliberate and you will be fine.

Install light bulbs in each socket per the parts list. Push the sockets into the gauge cluster: two for the left cluster, three for the right, and one for the ignition switch housing. The third one on the speedometer cluster must be numbered to correspond with the high-beam indicator. If the wires are too short to work from the floor, let them dangle wherever they want. Follow instructions on which wire goes to which terminal carefully.

The fuel gauge may need extra attention. If you are going to 12 volts, you will want to add a reducer or order a new 12-volt version of the fuel gauge. The reducer shown in the parts listing will work great. Face the stripe of the diode away from the gauge and use a round terminal on the non-stripe end and a barrel connector on the stripe end, then cover the diode in heat-shrink tubing to prevent a short and install it on the power side of the fuel gauge.

As you can see, it's infinitely easier to make these connections with the gauges and ignition switch out. The headlight switch is the exception because the terminals all face the clusters, making them easy to get to. There is no need to say much more about how to wire the dash items other than just follow the wiring instructions on page one of the harness install document. They did not include a cigarette lighter wire, but that would go from the top terminal (as installed) of the ignition switch to the lighter center terminal for switched or to the back of the headlight switch for unswitched. Remember those two locations so when you add accessories, it is no problem for you.

Button everything up carefully. Once you are sure your terminal connections are solid and your copper tubing is routed properly, reinstall the gauges using the four #10-32 nuts per cluster you removed when taking them out. Install the ignition switch using the two 1/4-inch bolts and nuts. Check over everything physically to make sure everything is tight, well routed, and clean. Once the gauges are installed, it is very difficult to get to connections, so be sure of your work as best you can.

Testing Your Work

If you were careful and meticulous, your installation will be absolutely bulletproof. Apply battery power and watch carefully for any smoke or strange noises. Then here is a list of things to look for.

- Switch on the park lights. Are the dominant ones *not* lit? Flip on the turn signals one at a time. This is where you may need to swap the wires around to get the desired result.
- Check the taillights. Are the dominant ones lit when you depress the brake pedal? Are both sides lit properly? Check the turn signals.
- After the above passes, turn on the headlights. Are they both lit? Hit the dimmer switch. Do you get high beams? In a darkened room, turn the headlight knob. Do the gauge lights change brightness? Does the high-beam indicator light on the speedometer cluster illuminate?
- Does the dome light/switch work?
- Turn the ignition switch to on and look at your fuel gauge. Does it reflect the amount of gas in the tank? If it is not full and you are sure of that, but it reads full, the likely problem is the sending unit at the gas tank needs a short wire from one of the mounting screws to the cab ground somewhere.
- Look at the ammeter. Flip on the headlights. Does the meter bounce a little from about center to discharge? That is a good indicator prior to starting the alternator.
- Hit the horn button. Does the horn sound off?
- With the ignition on, start the truck. Does it run?

Park Lights with Headlights

This vintage truck's wiring had one quirk that didn't make sense to me. When you pull out the headlight switch for headlights, the park lights go out! I want my park lights on *with* the headlights too. To do this on a stock switch, make a small jumper wire and jumper between the topmost back two terminals on the headlight switch. These are the taillight terminal (center) and the park lights (right or rearward). See the diagram earlier in this chapter to confirm. They are right beside each other.

ELECTRICAL

Final Thoughts on the Harness

This is by far the easiest harness install I have run across. If you follow each numbered wire corresponding to the instructions, you simply can't lose. If you do run into issues, you can usually think your way through them. This is because of the intuitive nature of the harness build. This cannot be said for all harnesses.

I was impressed with the ease of the install, the kit contents were above average, and when it's all said and done, the truck is back on the road again with none of the worry about all the old frayed wiring. Of course, small things were criticized, but in my opinion, if you didn't have to run to your local auto parts store for something small more than twice, you have a winner.

Radio Installation

If this were the 1950s or 1960s, I would advocate putting in the original radio. I had the original upgraded using 12-volt filament tubes and it is ready for installation; however, I just couldn't bring myself to do it! The setup weighs 15 pounds and really crowds the area under the dash. For all that trouble, they are AM only and with all the jarring around, how long does a radio last with all those glass vacuum tubes in there? I do not wish to find out for this truck. Enter a much nicer, more updated solution from Retro Manufacturing. It has all the bells and whistles of a modern radio, including AM/FM/Bluetooth with USB input for playing MP3s. It even has hands-free phone capability.

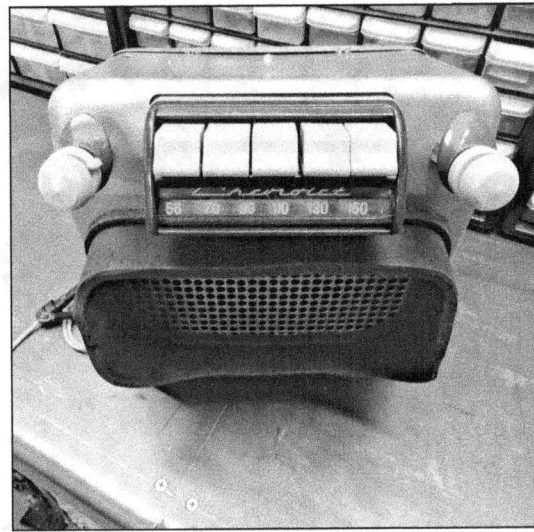

The original radio was a behemoth, weighing in at 15 pounds! It was mono and AM only. It also took up a lot of real estate under the dash. We need a more capable unit for these modern times.

Converting a 6-Volt Vehicle to a 12-Volt the Right Way!

As a trained US Air Force Electronics Technician, I can relate to the dangers of electricity, especially if the job is not done right. Old wiring is very common in these vintage vehicles and can really exacerbate the issues. The good news is, 6-volt systems are required to carry two times the current as its 12-volt counterpart. This means that, generally speaking, your 6-volt wiring (if in good shape) will not require any rewiring work. Earlier in this book, you learned how to address the original heater motor, so now we will address the other aspects: the fuel gauge, the ignition system, and the lighting system.

There are a few ways to handle the fuel gauge. My preferred method is to purchase a replacement gauge that is natively 12 volts from the vendor. If that is not possible or you just want to use your old one, put a Zener Diode (1N5342B) in line with the voltage terminal at the fuel gauge with the stripe on the diode facing away from the gauge. The total cost of doing that is less than a dollar (DigiKey part number CZ5342B CT-ND for about $0.89 each). Another good way is to purchase a Runtz voltage reducer.

The ignition system requires a 2-ohm 50-watt ballast resistor on the firewall. It needs to be hooked up between the ignition switch and the positive side of the coil. These ballast resistors are standard fare at any vendor. You can also go to HEI instead. There are choices here.

The lighting systems has you changing all the 6-volt bulbs to 12-volt equivalents. Here is the breakdown for that.
- 4 each of #57 for the gauge cluster
- 1 each of #57 for the high-beam indicator
- 1 each of #57 for the ignition switch housing
- 4 each of #67 for the taillight assembly
- 2 each of #1034 dual filament for the front park lights
- 1 each of #1073 for the interior dome light
- 2 each of #6020 7-inch sealed beam for the headlights

While I am at it, I like to put dual-filament sockets in the front park light housings, so I can use them for the blinkers as well. That is Classic Parts #47-905 or equivalent.

As of this writing, LED equivalents are available for each socket type for dash, dome, etc. They are simply made to plug into the old sockets. One thing that is important to note, the LED equivalents are *not* normally dimmable. This means that your dash lights will not dim with the headlight switch.

Since I am writing a frame up restoration book, I have the 12-volt gauge, the 12-volt heater motor, the alternator, and all the bulbs, so this particular build was never 6 volts to begin with. ■

CHAPTER 13

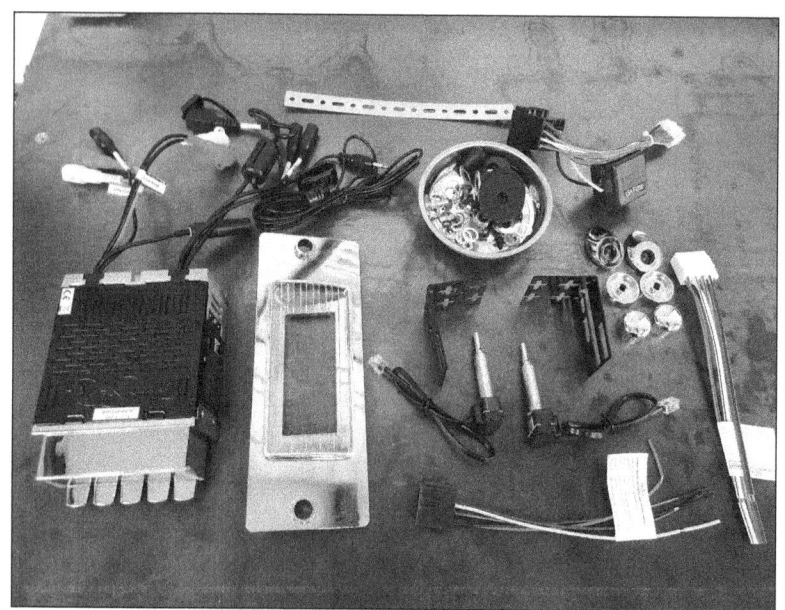

This is the entire Hermosa radio package laid out with all the parts shown.

The angles do not line up, so we need to make a few brackets to overcome this problem. It is relatively easy to do, but know that it is not ready to install right out of the box. Retro Manufacturing is aware of this and is designing a new bezel for the Advance Design era. Check with them for availability.

I purchased the Hermosa Radio (RH4753C) and Electronic Antenna (RA010) from Retro Manufacturing and the Dual Speakers from Custom Autosound (S5020) that are mounted below it in the stock position from Classic Industries.

The RetroSound Hermosa is a very nice radio. I also purchased the dual speaker setup that mounts just below it, so the audio comes through the original dash grille in stereo. I wired the truck for speaker wires through the A-pillar to the back corners that I may get around to later.

Installation requires some patience because this radio fits a very large variety of vintage automobiles and is not made exactly to fit. It so happens I enjoy this sort of challenge, so I will explain in detail how this is done. The main problem I needed to address is the 1947–1955 dash was angled wrong for the stock parts. To see what I mean, place the large chrome bezel behind the dash with one radio control shaft and the exterior knob bezel to the dash. This is enough to see we must overcome an issue with the angle.

The two black brackets that come with the Hermosa are not long enough to work for our purposes. Using a piece of sheet tin, I cut out the exact replica of the included bracket only long enough to accommodate all four mounting holes. To drill the 1/2-inch hole for the radio knobs, put the large chrome bezel on and mark the holes through to the bracket with a permanent marker. The bracket will come out exactly straight with the radio, but the large bezel will not. Drill that 1/2-inch hole about 1/8 inch higher than the center of the bezel's hole.

The large chrome bezel that makes everything look good on the dash has a fitment problem on AD trucks. The hole should not be straight out, rather it should have a lower angle to it. To make it like we need it to be, I used a Dremel with a cutoff disc and just flattened out the plastic on the bottom in the front and on the top in the back.

The brackets are easy to make with thin sheet metal. To find the holes, you can use the shorter bracket that comes with the kit.

168   HOW TO RESTORE YOUR CHEVY TRUCK: 1947–1955

ELECTRICAL

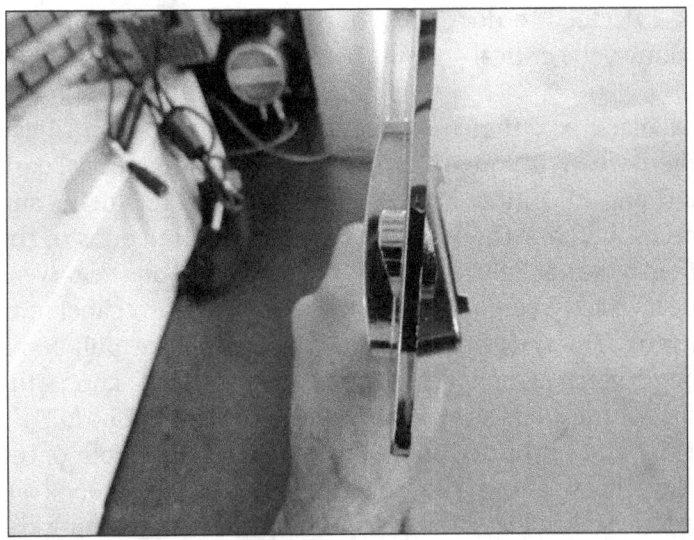

Other than the brackets being too short and this bezel not having the correct contour, the installation is very straightforward. Changing this angle on each radio knob is essential in getting it to fit properly.

As you can see, the bezel has to be angled differently from the radio for a proper installation.

With the bezel's angle changed properly, we can partially assemble the radio. Putting each radio control through the bracket from the inside with a nut and a large washer threaded all the way down first, add the dual-speaker assembly, then two nuts, then the black shroud washer, a thin washer, another nut, then the large bezel as shown.

Some of this is trial and error because you need just exactly enough threads sticking out at this point for the radio knob bezels and knobs to go on properly. The modular design of this radio is wonderful because we can adjust the knobs to go on just about any vehicle.

The radio and speakers go in together as an assembly. I had to bend the speaker bracket outward a little to get it to fit snugly behind the dash grille. Do a test fit to see how much to bend it. With everything bolted together, simply put the assembly behind the dash and install it. There are no nuts or washers digging into the paint; rather, put the radio knob bezels on against the paint, then tighten them with a nut, then the inner knob and outer knob.

The electricals are very straightforward, and the wires are very well marked. I do not have a place for a radio antenna on this truck, so I opted for a RetroSound electronic antenna (RA010) that is hidden under the dash or really anywhere you want. You must plug this electronic antenna into 12-volt, power and the radio provides a power antenna wire just for that.

One of the nice things about this radio is the way you can stick a USB

With everything bolted together, this turned out to be a very elegant solution for a very nice radio.

Although not perfectly stock looking, this radio really looks nice and gives you all the amenities of a modern radio.

I made a slot in the side of the glove box to accommodate that USB cord so I can put my USB memory stick directly into the glove box.

memory stick into the provided USB cord and if the radio finds MP3s on the stick, it will just automatically play them! No external MP3 player is needed. I simply routed that USB cord into the glove box so I can swap memory sticks without any unsightly external cords and equipment. This is my preferred music delivery method because I can also hear audio books this way.

The Critical Information System

So, you have spent a lot of money on a build like this and now you want to protect that investment. Since you live in 2019, most likely every modern car you have ever owned has a warning system for when your oil pressure suddenly drops, your water temperature suddenly rises, or your alternator gives out. Back in the early days, we had to scan the gauges and hope we caught something such as oil pressure tanking in enough time. Most people really do not scan their gauges as often as they should. I am guilty of this, so I decided to do something about it. Enter, the critical information system.

This system is a black box that you install under the dash. With an audible alarm system and LED indicator lights mounted low on the dash, you can not only see a light come on but also hear exactly when the problem is occurring. The system mounts high on the driver-side kick panel and has sensors for the alternator, water temperature, and oil pressure and even has a low fuel warning.

Using more modern technology, we can sense water temperature using an automotive-grade thermistor. An oil pressure safety switch will tell us when oil pressure suddenly drops, the resistance of the sending unit will tell you when you have low fuel, and the alternator's warning light system will tell us when the engine is running and give us a warning light when it malfunctions as well.

I have made everything you need to make this yourself available on my website. It is not a cheap system at upward of $500, but it gives me peace of mind knowing that my precious 261 Stovebolt engine is going to be safe from my stupidity.

Being an Advance Design Chevy pickup fan, I even made a special dash plate to integrate the LED lights and a few of the normal functions of the truck into a nice place on the driver's side of the dash. The dash panel integrates the parking brake pull lever, the Best heater control knob, the overdrive cable, and the four LEDs. I shaped it to match the contour of the lower dash, so it doesn't even look out of place. The plate mounts using the

The underhood wiring is simple to incorporate in the harness install prior to installation or it can be followed and tie wrapped together afterward.

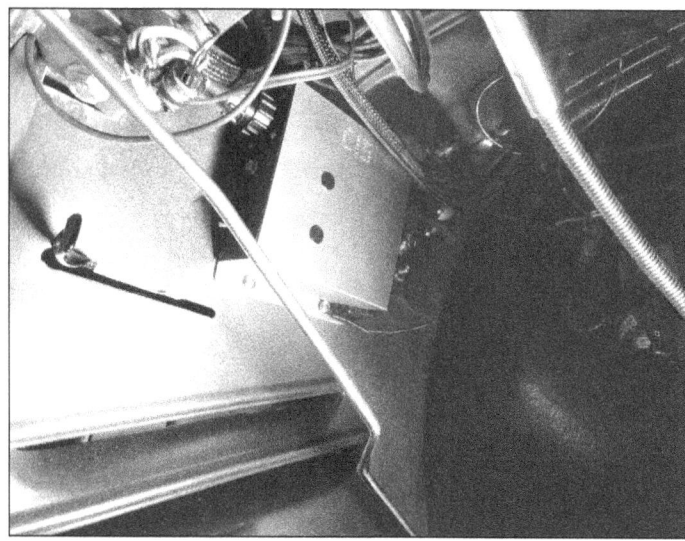

Mounted under the dash on the driver-side upper kick-panel, this box is completely out of the way. It is designed with 1/4-twist cannon plugs for easy removal.

The dash control plate is out of the way and looks like it belongs there.

ELECTRICAL

holes that are already in the dash so there are no mounting issues.

The only thing I had to do was make a different-profile parking brake pull rod bent a little differently. With a little 1/4-inch solid cold rolled rod from the hardware store and a tap for the threads, it was not that hard to make.

All of the particulars would take too much room in this book, so check out devestechnet.com/Home/WarningSystem for how to do it yourself or how to purchase it from the website. The prototype box has changed over the years and now we have a nice box to put it all in with nice connectors and a much more solid solution. There is also a YouTube video.

Small Things Worth Mentioning

So, I have 3-D printers and I like to design things. In this case, if you haven't thought about it, the blinker system is very nice, but the dash didn't have any indicator lights in 1947–1953 models. Since I

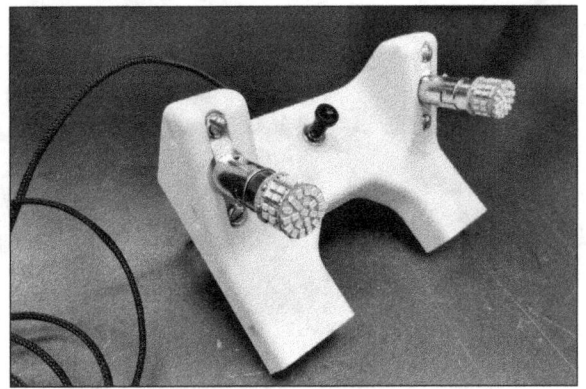

Although fused, there is no protection from weather. This system is still in the testing phase, so we will see if it's needed over time.

was bent on installing a tachometer anyway, my solution for that was two of those retro LED housings and a little design work.

The hood is yellow in this case, but the inner fenders are black. This makes for a very dark place under the hood. I have always thought we needed a hood light kit anyway. This system uses two 1156 (BA15) LEDs to really put out the light. It mounts using two existing holes in the front of the hood that are not being used for anything. The wiring is brought in from the seam down the center of the hood, then connected to a 12-volt unswitched power source. It is equipped with a pull-out switch for operation. I did not go with an automatic switch because I do not want the light to come on every time the hood is up.

I also decided to add an hour meter. Lawn mowers and airplanes have them, and I felt it would be nice to know the hours I have put on the new engine. This is accomplished by wiring the 12-volt positive to the meter and the negative to the three-prong oil pressure switch. The two terminals on the switch that are across from each other are for the CIS, but the lone one works great for an hour meter. Wired this way, the hour meter will not engage until oil pressure is higher than 12 psi.

There were no inside indicator lights for blinkers on our trucks between 1947 and 1953. That would be nice, don't you think?

I 3-D printed a housing for the hour meter so it is easy to read just under the hood beside the radiator.

CHAPTER 14

FINAL THOUGHTS

It has been a real journey. Do not forget that life is all about the journey, not the destination, so above all, have fun! There were a few difficulties along the way, but the really cool thing about all of this is not just the enjoyment this brings but the vast amount of knowledge you accumulate. To have a truck like the one pictured on the cover of this book is very satisfying and knowing what it took to get there even more!

The half-ton pickup that inspired all of this is still in existence and was previously owned by the late John Erb. The significance of this truck is that John got in it one day from Hesston, Kansas, and drove it all the way to Anchorage, Alaska, and back. The 261 engine with the Borg Warner R10 Overdrive proved itself to be a great combination. Special thanks to John and also to Carl and Sharon Weaver for allowing us the privilege to not only get pictures of John's truck but also to let us use their beautiful farm for the cover photo shoot.

Prepping for the Road

The last thing we do before starting up and driving off into the sunset is to go over the truck to ensure all the nuts and bolts are tight; the transmission, brakes, and engine fluids are topped off; the tires have air; and all the electricals are in perfect working order.

This unique 1951 3100 pickup was the start of it all. John Erb installed a 261 with BorgWarner R10 Overdrive and drove it from Hesston, Kansas, to Anchorage, Alaska, and back!

> **WARNING!**
> This fuel contains 10% ethanol.
> It may cause permanent damage to the fuel systems of small engines or to vehicles built prior to 1990.
> Use at your own risk!

Look for a filling station with a pump clearly marked "No Alcohol" and use that one!

FINAL THOUGHTS

The final pictures before pulling it out of its stall and heading for its first photo shoot. What a ride!

Another important thing to consider is the gasoline. Back in the day, gas would last virtually forever sitting in a tank when your truck was parked over long periods of time. Not anymore! Some gas stations have one pump that is marked "No Alcohol." *Always use that one!* The reason we are staying away from ethanol is not because it is inferior in performance or can erode fuel system parts but because it breaks down very quickly.

Every lawn mower manufacturer has a warning in the documentation to drain the gas tank if you leave the mower sitting longer than three months. The very same is true for your precious truck! If you *have* to use ethanol-blended gasoline, use Stabil, a product that stabilizes ethanol with every fill-up. This is not a myth! I have many friends with antique autos who forget or put off adding Stabil and we end up having to remove the gas tank, flush the lines, and rebuild the carburetor for making one mistake. If you let your truck sit except for that very rare Kansas day where it isn't windy, raining, or storming, be sure to drain the gas tank and run the truck out of gas completely. Your upgraded electric fuel pump system will fill everything quickly the next time.

The Advance Design era was a stepping stone for Chevrolet and its manufacturing techniques and processes. The machinery used then was not as precise and fitment of parts was not exactly uniform between the many different manufacturing facilities back in the day. Doors from the St. Louis, Missouri, facility could be 1/4-inch larger than the ones from the Kansas City, Missouri, facility. This was the case for this build. How could that be possible? They churned out several million of these trucks and did it in about eight facility locations, not counting engine facilities. That is a very impressive feat for its time. Hood fitment, door and door glass fitment, and even holes between inner fenders, supports, and grilles were placed "pretty close" by today's standards. This is part of what makes these trucks special. It is also what makes the task of a full restoration more challenging when parts from any facility are expected to work with any other. I enjoyed every minute of it in some way.

With the knowledge learned during this process, there is really

HOW TO RESTORE YOUR CHEVY TRUCK: 1947–1955

CHAPTER 14

Here we are pulling our brand-new 1950 Chevy pickup out of the garage for the first time. May 30, 2019, was the first time it saw sunlight after the full restoration. It doesn't look bad for a 69-year-old pickup.

nothing you can't do. From welding and metal working to paint and electrical, the skills necessary to do this will give you a very wide career path as well as help you think through just about any problem that comes along.

The key to the success of this project was taking everything very slow and being very methodical. Ask questions about fitment and what comes next at every step. Preplanning is everything. The forums are a great place to ask just about any question and have it answered by someone who knows. This type of work has never been easier with the advent of the internet. When I was younger, we had to travel or write actual letters or make very expensive long-distance phone calls if we wanted more information. I hope our younger generations appreciate the technological distance we have traveled over a very short period of time. I know I sure do! That being said, this written book and its contents just isn't available in one place anywhere else, so be sure to stop and appreciate the power of the written word.

About the First Drive

There is no such thing as perfection, but we do the best we can to achieve something close. In this case, the first run was almost perfect. There were little things that didn't go my way, such as the speedometer not reading correctly (fixed by regearing the transmission's speedometer drive gear), the self-canceling blinker system didn't properly self-cancel (fixed by adjusting the canceling plate under the steering wheel), and the brake pedal was hitting the top of the cab opening (which was adjusted and done).

The truck is far more powerful thanks to the 261, is far faster and capable of highway speeds thanks to the BorgWarner R10 Overdrive, has better braking thanks to the front disc brakes, is much quieter due to the sound dampening, and is an all-around pleasure to drive. Due to the other subtle improvements, such as HEI, electric fuel augmentation, PCV, and CIS, I know this truck will start right away, run perfect every time, and always be ready for action.

Some of you may be wondering about the front disc brake system. Did the decision of not using a brake booster make braking a problem? I am going with no on this one. I find that if you are used to drum brakes, the front disc brakes work better even without the booster. I made the right decision for me in not cutting up the crossmember or relocating the master cylinder to accommodate the booster. This is strictly a personal choice when going with non-stock options. If you are putting some high-horsepower performance engine in the truck, then it makes sense to put in the booster.

What Would I Do Different?

This is somewhat of a tribute truck to John Erb's original 1951, so I couldn't change the transmission on this build, but the next truck I restore will have a Tremec T5 5-speed with Overdrive. I will also concentrate on giving the driver more space by designing a seat system that allows for taller drivers. I might also go with a new set of gauges that are fully electronic to update the look a bit. Other than that, I used my knowledge of these trucks to make a specimen that uses all of the good things Chevy did throughout the Advance Design and Task Force era in a blend that I can certainly live with!

DEVE'S TECHNET RESOURCES

Be sure to bookmark devestechnet.com. I have a great deal of information concerning the Advance Design trucks and many how-to articles that could pertain to you (a partial listing follows here). It is all free! There are also several upgrades you can purchase for your restoration at devestechnet.com/Services/Index.

• Casting numbers: devestechnet.com/Home/CastingNumbers

• Keep your enclosed driveline and transmission and change the 4.11:1 rear end gears to 3.55:1: devestechnet.com/Home/DifferentialOverhaul

• Building the cab cart setup and how it is used can be found: devestechnet.com/Home/Morepix

• More info on the sandblasting system: devestechnet.com/Home/SandBlasting

• The 261 engine and all its special characteristics: devestechnet.com/Home/TheVenerable261

• Installing the PCV system process: devestechnet.com/Home/PCVInstall

• High-energy ignition upgrade: devestechnet.com/Home/HEIgnition

• Fuel system upgrade: devestechnet.com/Home/FuelSystem

• All documentation (and it's pretty extensive) that I have been able to find on the BorgWarner R10 Overdrive: devestechnet.com/Home/HowTo#driveline

• More flywheel tips: devestechnet.com/Home/Flywheel

• Seat pedestal assembly: devestechnet.com/Home/Morepics

• Outtakes of the heater valve repair process: devestechnet.com/Home/HeaterRestore

• Electric wiper install: devestechnet.com/Home/MorePix

• AutoPrime system and its safety features: devestechnet.com/Home/FuelSystem

• Alternator harness hookup: devestechnet.com/Home/WarningSystem

• 12-volt fuel gauge upgrade: devestechnet.com/Home/Native12VUpgrade

• A complete wiring diagram: devestechnet.com/Images/Projects/ADWiring System/1953%20TruckWiringDiagramlg

• Hood light kit: devestechnet.com/Services/HoodLiteKit

• "Tip of the Week" archive with lots of tips and tricks: Forums. devestechnet.com

More Resources
• Free Restoration Package from General Motors at the GM Heritage Center: gmheritagecenter.com/gm-heritage-archive/vehicle-information-kits.html

• General Motors hood alignment: Section 11-1 of chevy.oldcarmanualproject.com/shop/1948_51truck/index.htm

• Diagram for wiring your Overdrive: vintageautogarage.com/v/vspfiles/files/ODWH-Diagram-v1.00.pdf

• The Old Car Manual Project: chevy.oldcarmanualproject.com

• Dave's 235 Blog: chev235guy.blogspot.com

• Tim's Trucks: 1954advance-design.com

• Classic Parts Forums: talk.classicparts.com

• The Stovebolt Forums: stovebolt.com

SOURCE GUIDE

Bowtie Bits Antique Truck Parts
bowtiebits.com

Brothers Truck Parts
brotherstrucks.com

Chevs of the 40s
chevsofthe40s.com

Classic Industries
classicindustries.com

Classic Parts
classicparts.com

Fifth Avenue Garage
fifthaveinternetgarage.com

Jim Carters Truck Parts
oldchevytrucks.com

Juliano's Safety Belts
julianos.com

LMC Truck Parts
lmctruck.com

Mar-K Manufacturing
mar-k.com

McMaster-Carr
mcmaster.com

NewPort Engineering
newportwipers.com

RockAuto
rockauto.com

Summit Racing
summitracing.com

Wheel Smith
thewheelsmith.net

www.ingramcontent.com/pod-product-compliance
Lightning Source LLC
Chambersburg PA
CBHW081447070526
44586CB00019B/2258